A
Year
With
Jesus

Elmer Hohle

Devotions For Every Day

2nd Printing
Lutheran News, Inc.
684 Luther Lane
New Haven, MO 63068

Manufactured in the United States of America

Library of Congress Cataloging- in-Publication Data
Hohle, Elmer M., 1930 -
A year with Jesus, devotions for every day / Elmer M. Hohle.
p. cm.
ISBN 0-7586-0097-4

I. Devotional calendars. I. Title.
BV48 1158 2003
242' .2–21

Contents

Thoughts from the Translator

"Nothing is more important and vital than the forgiveness of all our sins"-so begins one of the devotions in this book. The whole of humankind stands deeply in need of this forgiveness, for we all stand exposed by God's holy Law, falling far short of His glory, and thus are doomed to eternal damnation.

What makes it possible for us to be forgiven of all our sins is God's grace as shown to us through His only Son, Jesus Christ. Through faith in our Savior and Lord, we not only have forgiveness, but also salvation and eternal life. This faith is created in our hearts by the Holy Spirit via the Word of forgiveness of the sacred Scriptures, the water of forgiveness of Holy Baptism, and the food of forgiveness of the Lord's Supper. The writers of these devotions frequently use "Word and Sacrament" as a shorthand phrase for Scripture, Baptism, and the Lord's Supper. The Holy Spirit uses Word and Sacrament as a "means of grace" to create and sustain faith in Christ. Our faith is manifested in good works motivated by the "means of grace."

One of the great joys of translating these writings was "rubbing shoulders" with fellow pastors throughout history. This translation includes devotions from several centuries containing a unified message from Scripture alone of salvation solely by God's grace through faith alone! These devotions are arranged according to the church year as observed by Christians through the centuries. Because Easter falls on various Sundays each year, these devotions may not always coincide with the current calendar. However, there should be enough extras to fill the need. Also note that these devotions are a creme de la creme collection from *Tagliche Andachten-the* German version of the well-known devotional magazine *Portals of Prayer,* which was compiled by Gerhard Bode after the German language edition was discontinued. After reading through it for two years in a row, your translator implored Concordia Publishing House to make its content available to English language readers. My heart leaps for joy that CPH has done so. I deeply appreciate the efforts of Peggy Kuethe and Jane Wilke to that end. In it's second printing, Lutheran News, Inc., New Haven, Missouri, is now helping me publish the book.

It is my prayer that God use these devotions to create Christian faith or renew that faith in you, the reader. And now, may the God of all peace, who brought back from the dead our Lord Jesus Christ, who

4

by His precious blood made an everlasting covenant with us, give you every good thing you need. Thus, you will be enabled to do what He wants you to do, as He accomplishes, through Jesus Christ, those things that please Him.

To God alone be all the glory, forever and ever.

Amen.

In Christ,

Elmer M. Hohle

Lights of the World

*Do everything without complaining or arguing,
so that you may become blameless and pure,
children of God without fault in a crooked and
depraved generation, in which you shine like stars
in the universe.* Philippians 2:14–15

Be happy! In every corner of the world, the lights are on. In businesses, houses, and churches, everything is bright with colored lights and decorations. Eyes glisten, faces laugh, and people greet one another, whether they know one another or not. It warms the heart to see such a change among people.

However, we need to look farther and deeper than decorations and moods. There exist many places where everything is not so joyful. The lonely in hospitals, nursing homes, prisons, orphanages, and even homes often find very little about which they are able to rejoice. Daily we hear about countless people who die from hunger or sickness. And how can we rejoice if we know that every day millions suffer without the knowledge of the love and atonement of Jesus Christ?

We can regard ourselves as fortunate if we have experienced the true wonder and love of God. The more we share our joy, the greater it becomes. Consequently, as children of God, we also are able to spread the love of Christ as lights in the world.

Lord Jesus, let us become lights of Your love in our dark world. Amen.

Ruth L. Krueger

7

January 2   Galatians 4:1–6

Concerning the Son of God Becoming Man

[Jesus] made Himself nothing, taking the very
nature of a servant, being made in human likeness.
Philippians 2:7

"God became Man for the benefit of you, O man.
God's Child unites Himself with our blood." Thus we sing
from a Christmas hymn by Paul Gerhardt. We sing it with
joy, but perhaps we don't fully realize the extent to which
the eternal Son of God humbled Himself.

Jesus relinquished everything from His divine
might and majesty to become our human Brother. The reason for this is simply and purely His love for us lost children of humankind. With this love and as our Substitute,
He rescues and redeems us from sin and death, and He
makes us into children of God.

"He did all this for us to show His great love for us.
For this let all Christendom rejoice and thank Him for it
into all eternity," sang Martin Luther, and we with him. We
are the beneficiaries of this self-emptying God. How can
we ever thank Him for this? In that we allow this gift to be
bestowed upon us; in that we receive this gift by faith. Yet
we are not to horde this gift for ourselves. Instead, we are
to make it known with glorifying praise to the entire
world. As Luther wrote, we can "sing joyfully, give ear,
worthy folk of Christendom!"

Let Your goodness and faithfulness be new to us
every day. God, my God, forsake me not whenever need
or death afflict me! Amen.

Manfred Roensch

8

Acts 4:1–20

Salvation through No One Else

There is no other name under heaven given to men
by which we must be saved. Acts 4:12

Our Scripture verse for today is, in the certainty of
hindsight, a harsh word. It condemns all man-made ways to
salvation. It condemns all self-righteousness, all our good
intentions to fellow humans, as well as the good works of
which we are so proud. None of the above can bring us salvation. He who wants to be saved through good works
must do it with complete perfection. This no one has ever
been able to accomplish, nor can anyone ever do it. That's
why all humankind stands condemned under the frightful
curse of the Law. The Law brings no salvation to a person.

But this verse is also comforting because it testifies
that salvation and blessedness are ours through the name
of Jesus. Day after day, let us remind ourselves that
through believing on the Lord Jesus Christ, we will be
saved. "For God was pleased to have all His fullness dwell
in Him, and through Him to reconcile to Himself all
things, whether things on earth or things in heaven, by
making peace through His blood, shed on the cross"
(Colossians 1:19–20). Hence this always means for me:
Jesus is my best Friend. Here is salvation, nowhere else! No
other person, no matter how important he may be, is able
to save you. Only Jesus can do that. He is the soul's
Salvation, your true Savior. Firmly cling to Him.

Blessed is he who says with me, "My Jesus does not
forsake me." Amen.

Herman A. Mayer

January 4   John 1:1–14

The Boundaries of the World Cannot Contain Him

The Word became flesh and made His dwelling among us. John 1:14

One can listen to the Christmas story so callously that he does not recognize what an astoundingly great wonder God accomplished through it. We Christians, however, cry out in astonishment, "Oh, the depth of the riches of the wisdom and knowledge of God!" (Romans 11:33).

The preface of John's gospel gives us a picture of a paradox. Here Jesus Christ is called the Word. This Word was God Himself, the Creator of all things. Yet this Word became the eternal Flesh—a Man like all men yet without sin. This Word that became flesh lived and walked among us in human form. Yet humankind saw His glory. Thus, Jesus Christ was at the same time the Almighty God and common man. He is our Savior.

In the first Christmas song of the Reformation, Luther gives us a portrayal of this wonder: "He whom the world could not contain lies in Mary's lap; He became a tiny Child who upholds everything. *Kyrieleis!*" ("Gelobet sei'st du, Jesu Christ"—*Kirchengesangbuch für Evangelish—Lutherische Gemeinden*, CPH)

True God and true Man, Jesus Christ, be gracious to us! Amen.

Walter W. Stuenkel

Jesus Is the Promised Messiah

"Are You the one who was to come, or should we expect someone else?" Matthew 11:3

This is a highly important question. How many people would like to hear the answer directly from Jesus' mouth! His answer is very clear: " 'Go back and report to John what you hear and see' " (Matthew 11:4). With this, Jesus points the disciples to His works, which identify Him as the Savior. They speak for Him.

What were these works? Isaiah prophesied, "He has sent me to bind up the brokenhearted, to proclaim freedom for the captives and release from darkness for the prisoners, to proclaim the year of the LORD's favor and the day of vengeance of our God, to comfort all who mourn" (Isaiah 61:1–2). Isaiah tells of the Messiah's ministry of healing for the blind, deaf, bound, and the like. But this is not to say that the work of the Messiah was solely to bring an end to all bodily suffering and misery. The misery from which the Messiah is to bring relief is spiritual misery—the sin that breaks the heart and brings one into the hand of the devil. This is what the Messiah has rescued us from. The wonders and signs Jesus performed assure us that He performed this far greater work: rescue and redemption from sin, death, devil, and hell.

Lord Jesus, never let me waver; instead, let me firmly believe that You are the promised Savior and Redeemer! Amen.

Herman A. Mayer

January 6   Matthew 2:1–12

Festival of the Epiphany

After Jesus was born in Bethlehem in Judea ...
Magi from the east came to Jerusalem.
Matthew 2:1

Today we celebrate the festival of Epiphany, one of
the oldest festivals in the church year—even older than
the celebration of Christmas. At Epiphany we celebrate
the revelation of Christ as the Son of God, the Savior of
the entire world, for Gentiles as well as Jews.

Our text speaks about the appearance of Jesus as
the King and Savior of the Gentiles. That the Wise Men
would come from the Orient—and thus from non-Jews—
was prophesied in the Old Testament. Isaiah wrote,
"Nations will come to your light, and kings to the brightness of your dawn. ... [They] will come bearing gold and
incense and proclaiming the praise of the LORD" (Isaiah
60:3, 6b).

We too have much cause to praise God and to
bring Him precious gifts, so the joyous news about Jesus'
birth, suffering, death, and resurrection may more extensively be brought to our fellowmen everywhere.

"Arise O Jesus, You who are the comfort of the heathen, the bright morning star! Let Your Word, the Word of
peace, loudly echo forth far and near so that it bring peace
to all who are held captive by the enemy; and so praise and
glory ring throughout all of heathendom!" Amen.
(*Kirchengesangbuch für Evangelish—Lutherische Gemeinden*, CPH)

Reinhold Stallman

12

Mark 10:32–34

The Announcement
of the <u>Way of Suffering</u>

*[Jesus said:] "We are going up to Jerusalem, and
the Son of Man will be betrayed to the chief priests
and the teachers of the law."* Matthew 20:18

Jerusalem was a place of joy for the circumcised
Jew. The psalmist longed for Mount Zion and the beautiful worship services there. David sang: "I rejoiced with
those who said to me, 'Let us go to the house of the LORD.'
Our feet are standing in your gates, O Jerusalem" (Psalm
122:1–2). And 12-year-old Jesus found it disturbing not to
be allowed to remain "in My Father's house" (Luke 2:49),
that is, the temple at Jerusalem.

But the adult Jesus felt compelled to lament about
this so-called City of Peace: " 'Jerusalem, you who kill the
prophets and stone those sent to you' " (Matthew 23:37).
However, He also knew that despite their rejection of Him,
the long-promised salvation was coming. The prophet Joel
said, "For on Mount Zion and in Jerusalem there will be
deliverance, as the LORD has said" (Joel 2:32b). That's why
Jesus invited His disciples to go with Him to Jerusalem and
there witness His suffering and death. He also invites us to
come along; and we know that His death saves us from "the
second death" (Revelation 20:6), from the destruction of
our soul, and from eternal calamity.

Jesus, upon my heart imprint Your image of how
You '... endured all suffering! Amen. (*Kirchengesangbuch für
Evangelish—Lutherische Gemeinden,* CPH)

Hilton C. Oswald

13

The <u>Newborn</u> King

*"Where is the one who has been born king
of the Jews? We ... have come to worship Him."*
Matthew 2:2

The Wise Men from the Orient knew of a royal birth in Judea and followed an extraordinary star to the royal city of Jerusalem. Fright filled the heart of King Herod. This newborn was a rival! Would a blood bath be instigated to sweep him out of the way? The high priests and scribes pointed to the Word, through the prophet Micah, about the little town of Bethlehem from which Israel's Lord was to come. With cunning strategy, Herod tried to destroy this child. The Wise Men, however, found the Wonder-Child in Bethlehem, worshipped Him, and generously gifted Him with their treasures of gold, incense, and myrrh.

At Epiphany, we also journey in spirit to Bethlehem to find the little Child, Jesus. We worship Him as our Savior and lay before Him the best gifts of our heart: faith, hope, and love. Thus, we with three gifts indicate that this Child of God is Man and King! Let us also spread this wondrous news so everyone sings honor and praise to our divine King!

Lord God, help us so we acknowledge You and claim You as our King! Amen.

Erwin T. Umbach

Immanuel

*The virgin will be with child and will give birth to
a son, and will call Him Immanuel.* Isaiah 7:14

With these words, the prophet Isaiah foretells the
virgin birth. Centuries later, the angel explains to Joseph
the significance of the name "Immanuel." It means "God
with us." That occasioned the apostle Paul to write,
"Beyond all question, the mystery of godliness is great"
(1 Timothy 3:16a).

What we are unable to grasp with our reason, we
receive with child-like faith. Our salvation hangs from this
mystery of the incarnation of the Son of God. We know
with certainty that He, as true man, was under the Law as
our stand-in, substitute, and advocate. We know He gave
up His life for us. We also know that, as true God, He
overpowered sin, death, and the devil and thus won for us
the victory of eternal life.

This fills our hearts with great joy and gives us a
peace that supersedes all reason. For this we are thankful to
our God from the bottom of our hearts. For we know that,
in Christ, God lives among us with His grace and richly
blesses us.

From the bottom of our hearts we thank You, Lord
Jesus Christ, that You are our Immanuel who has rescued
and redeemed us. Amen.

Gerhard C. Michael

January 10   John 1:4–12

A Star

*"I see Him, but not now; I behold Him, but not
near. A star will come out of Jacob."*
Numbers 24:17

The prophecy in which the Messiah is given the
name "Star" is spoken by a Gentile. The king of the
Moabites sent a message to a Gentile sorcerer named
Balaam, promising him all sorts of rewards if he would
curse the people of Israel, who were encamped in the
regions of Moab.

The Lord, however, saw to it that instead of cursing
the people of God, Balaam blessed Israel and uttered a glorious prophecy about the Messiah. This is a testimony to
the wondrous might of God; He can take even His enemies into His service and, through them, fulfill His Word.

In the prophecy, "a star will come out of Jacob,"
God allows Israel to look into the distant future. This star
is the Messiah, Christ the Lord. This bright Star signifies
and brings to the people of God salvation and peace from
on high. John testified about Christ: "The true Light that
gives light to every man was coming into the world" (John
1:9). In the light of this Star from the stem of Jacob, we
have salvation, life, and blessedness.

Lord Jesus, You, the true Light, enlighten us and
lead us safely and blessedly to heaven! Amen.

Walter W. Stuenkel

All Righteousness Fulfilled

Jesus replied, "Let it be so now, it is proper for us to do this to fulfill all righteousness." Matthew 3:15

John the Baptizer was called by God to prepare the way for the Messiah. He did this as he cried out, " 'Repent, for the kingdom of heaven is near' " (Matthew 3:2). The people came in huge crowds, confessed their sins, and were baptized. One day, Jesus, the Messiah Himself, came to be baptized by John. The Baptizer resisted by saying in essence, this will never do! My baptism has to do with repentance and forgiveness of sins. You, however, have nothing of which to repent, and there is nothing for which to forgive You (Matthew 3:14). Yet Jesus insisted, and John relented.

What does this indicate? Why did the sinless Son of God submit Himself to a matter that has to do with sin and forgiveness? He did so to "fulfill all righteousness." For this Jesus became human. He stepped into the midst of sinners. He became one of us. He placed Himself into our likeness. He took our obligations upon Himself. Thus Jesus, as the substitute for all people, fulfilled all righteousness, which God requires of humankind. Through Him we are saved.

Dearest Jesus, I praise You that You have fulfilled all righteousness and have granted that righteousness to me. Amen.

Herbert J. A. Bouman

January 12   Psalm 21:1–4

Divine Light

Your Word is a lamp to my feet and a light for my path. Psalm 119:105

Original light was created in the beginning when God said, "Let there be light!" (Genesis 1:3). Then it is stated, "He separated the light from the darkness" (Genesis 1:4), for the two mutually exclude each other.

Our verse for the day says, "Your Word is ... a light for my path." Our heart is darkened by sin. By nature man is spiritually blind. In this sin-fallen world, he is in darkness, unable to find his way. He stumbles and does not know where to go. Then the Word of God is proclaimed and a light goes on within him. He hears the invitation, " 'whoever comes to Me I will never drive away' " (John 6:37). Enlightened through the work of the Holy Spirit, man comes to know his Savior.

Jesus is "the true Light that gives light to every man was coming into the world" (John 1:9). Consequently, He says, " 'Whoever follows Me will never walk in darkness, but will have the Light of life' " (John 8:12). This Light guides us through this life, and finally through the dark valley of death.

We thank You, Lord God, for the brightness of Your beloved Word. Amen.

Albert T. Bostelmann

The Servant of God

"A bruised reed He will not break, and a smolder-
ing wick He will not snuff out." Isaiah 42:3

The word "servant" in our reading applies to our
Savior, the chosen of God, in whom He has great pleasure.
He has been anointed with the Holy Spirit. He is the Lord
who is worthy of all glory and honor. However, although
He is the sole Ruler, He does not come to us as ruler and
overseer who calls out from the streets and lifts up His
voice. He is meek and helps the weak.

We humans are often like a bruised reed. We cannot stand up straight nor take a straight step. Circumstances of life bring us to the breaking point, where the
light of our faith is about to be extinguished. It becomes
spiritually dark all around us, and perhaps physically dark
as well. Is there any hope? Yes, indeed, there is—for God's
Servant has come to once more straighten the bent,
bruised reed lying on the floor and to once more gently
rekindle the extinguished flame. "A broken and contrite
heart, O God, You will not despise" (Psalm 51:17b). Do
not despair! When the need is the greatest, God's help is
near. His power is mighty in the weak.

Anoint me with the oil of joy, that from henceforth
the light of faith may indeed never be extinguished in my
soul! Amen.

Herman A. Mayer

That Is the Lamb of God

*"Look, the Lamb of God, who takes away the sin
of the world!"* John 1:29

One day John the Baptizer saw Jesus coming
toward him. Immediately, he pointed to Jesus as the Lamb
of God and testified that Jesus would bear the sin of the
whole world. This is the glorious news that is so necessary
for all of us.

Martin Luther wrote, "This then is the main reason
for us to know where our sins have been laid aside. Usually
sin has only two places where it exists: Either it is with us,
in that it hangs around your neck; or it lies upon Christ, the
Lamb of God. Now if it lies upon your back, then you are
lost. If, however, it lies upon Christ, then you are blessed
and will be saved: So then, grasp the one you want."

John invites us to cast our sin upon Jesus. John
Olearius wrote a hymn that fits the picture of our text.
Paraphrased, he wrote, "Behold, He is the Lamb of God
who bears our sin. He is the One who gives Himself up as
a sacrificial offering for the whole world. Behold, He is the
Lamb of God in whom one finds forgiveness for all one's
sin, peace, rest, and complete grace!"

O Lamb of God, thanks be to You that You have
borne all my sin. Amen.

Walter W. Stuenkel

The Lamb of God

"Look, the Lamb of God, who takes away the sin of the world!" John 1:29

At the time when John the Baptizer led a mighty movement in Israel through his preaching and baptizing, the high counsel sent delegates to ask whether he was the Christ. When he denied it, they asked who he was. John answered: "I am the voice of one calling in the desert, 'Make straight the way for the Lord'" (John 1:23).

The day after this episode, John saw Jesus coming toward him and publicly testified, "Look, the Lamb of God, who takes away the sin of the world" (John 1:29).

That is true testimony about Jesus Christ: He is the Lamb of God; He is God's Son, who became man. Our belief, our comfort, our confident assurance in life and in death, is that God's Son became man and that He became the Lamb of whom all the Old Testament sacrificial lambs were prototypes. He is the true Lamb of God who bore the sin of the world and our sin as well. Our sin no longer lies upon us.

Lord Jesus, we are free from the punishment for all sin because You have carried it. Amen.

Carl Manthey-Zorn

The One and Only Messiah Promised by God

"We have found the Messiah" (that is, the Christ).
John 1:41

Andrew said to his brother, Simon, "We have found the Messiah." *Messiah* is the Hebrew word for the official Greek name *Christ*. Both mean "the Anointed One."

A woman in Samaria believed the Messiah would come. Jesus said to her, " 'I who speak to you am He' " (John 4:26). Believing, she ran to her fellow citizens and said to them, "Come, see a man... . Could this be the Christ?" (John 4:29). They believed "that this man really is the Savior of the world" (John 4:42b), the only promised Messiah and Savior from sin. Jesus reassured Martha that her brother, Lazarus, would be resurrected, and that He, Jesus, was the Resurrection and the Life through whom all believers live and in whom all who live by faith shall never die. Martha confessed, " 'Yes, Lord,' she told Him, 'I believe that You are the Christ, the Son of God, who was to come into the world' " (John 11:27).

Jesus is one whom God has anointed with the joy-oil of the Holy Spirit and power to fulfill all God's promises of salvation through His obedience and merit as our substitute.

Christ, You are Son of the living God. We laud Your fulfillment of all prophecies for our salvation. Amen.

George M. Krach

January 17   Isaiah 61

O Jesus Christ, the True Light

"Nations will come to Your light, and kings to the brightness of Your dawn." Isaiah 60:3

The Messianic prophecies and their fulfillment run like a golden thread through the entire Holy Scriptures. In the Old Testament, Isaiah wrote, " 'See, darkness covers the earth and thick darkness is over the peoples, but the LORD rises upon you and His glory appears over you' " (Isaiah 60:2). As old Simeon held the baby Jesus in his arms, he declared this baby a Light to enlighten the Gentiles and for the glory of the people of Israel. And the Lord Jesus Himself said, " 'I am the Light of the world. Whoever follows Me will never walk in darkness, but will have the Light of life' " (John 8:12).

As at the time of the prophets and the apostles, great spiritual darkness still rules over the people of the earth today. And now, as then, the whole world's comfort and only hope is in Christ, the Light of the world.

O Jesus Christ, true Light, Enlighten those who know You not, And bring them into Your flock, So that also their souls be saved. Amen.

Herbert D. Poellot

January 18   Psalm 107:1–8

Praise and Thanks

Enter His gates with thanksgiving. Psalm 100:4

Psalm 100 is a brief song, but in its few words there is much joy. With holy inspiration, the singing poet calls upon the whole world to praise God. Marvelous is the work of creation. Even more wondrous is the work of redemption. The God of Abraham has made His people into a chosen people. From the stem of Judah, the Messiah is to come in the fullness of time—as the Good Shepherd who grazes His flock upon the green meadows, who protects His flock through the deep valley of death from the "hellish wolf," who in the evening, the evening of the world, brings His flock back home.

The Good Shepherd, about whom the psalmist sings so joyfully, came long ago. He is the one who testifies, " 'I am the Good Shepherd. The Good Shepherd lays down His life for the sheep' " (John 10:11). We believe that the Good Shepherd gave up His life for His sheep—you and me.

If we ponder the love of the Lord, then our soul will also sing. Our soul will sing in God's house, sing in its own home, sing in the morning, and in the evening. The hymn of praise from the Lord's own, the hymn that rings out in thousands of languages, that breaks forth from many thousands of lips, is very pleasing to Him!

Praise the Lord, whom mighty kings glorify! That is my soul's most heartfelt longing. Amen.

Elmer Reimnitz

Matthew 11:2–15

The Savior Performs Wonders

*Then will the eyes of the blind be opened and the
ears of the deaf unstopped.* Isaiah 35:5

How gloriously were these words fulfilled by Jesus
of Nazareth! He could allow the report to come back to
John the Baptizer: "The blind receive sight, the lame walk,
those who have leprosy are cured, the deaf hear, the dead
are raised, and the good news is preached to the poor"
(Matthew 11:5). Had the Savior merely (yet gloriously)
helped those who suffered in their bodies, He would still be
the greatest miracle worker in the history of humankind.
However, what He did to bring salvation to the world surpasses all else. He opened spiritual eyes and made spiritual
ears hear so they could acknowledge Him as their Savior.

By nature, man is blind and deaf through sin. He is
incapable of opening his spiritual eyes to see or his spiritual
ears to hear. Only the Savior can free us from the power of
sin and the devil. How glorious that we are in the time of
the New Testament! We can see the prophecy fulfilled. How
thankful we can be that the Holy Spirit enlightens us to
acknowledge and know the Savior and what He has done
for us! The Savior says, " 'Blessed rather are those who hear
the Word of God and obey it' " (Luke 11:28). How thankful
we can be who possess His Word and Sacrament, through
which we are strengthened and sustained in the faith!

Sustain us, Lord, with Your Word and fight the
devil's deceit and death! Amen (from "Lord Keep us
Steadfast in Thy Word" by Martin Luther).

George J. Meyer

John 1:6–16 and Psalm 119:88–96

The True Light

[John] himself was not the Light, he came only as
a witness to the Light. The true Light that gives
light to every man was coming into the world.
John 1:8–9

Jesus Christ is the true Light. In His light, we see
the actual character of God. Without Jesus Christ, God is
a riddle, difficult to understand. We know Him only as the
Judge before whose throne of judgment we will someday
stand and give an account. Jesus Christ, however, brings us
light concerning God. He allows us to recognize that God
is the patient Father. He does not want the sinner's death,
rather the sinner's repentance and salvation. That's why He
sent His beloved Son. Through His death, the Son opens
the way to the Father for all humankind.

John directs us to Jesus Christ, the Light of the
world. With great emphasis, He tells us that without Jesus
we have God only as a Judge. Through Him, however, we
can call upon God as Father and find refuge in His patient
love. In Jesus, we have the forgiveness of all sins, the
strength to be God's children, and the joy to serve other
people. John calls upon us to receive this in faith and by it
to live with confidence and assurance.

Thanks be to You, heavenly Father, for Your great
Light, which You have allowed to shine into our lives
through Jesus Christ. Amen.

Jakob K. Heckert

Isaiah 9:1–7

God Himself Is the Savior

He is the true God and eternal life. 1 John 5:20

Our Savior, Jesus Christ, is true God, for God's Word testifies to this about Him: "In the beginning was the Word, and the Word was with God, and the Word was God. ... Through Him all things were made. ... In Him was life, and that life was the Light of men. ... The Word became flesh and made His dwelling among us. We have seen His glory" (John 1:1–14). And again, "'Let all God's angels worship Him'" (Hebrews 1:6).

Is this not a wonder? God became man. But there is more. A wonder beyond all wonders, God came to serve humankind. In the letter to the Philippians, we read, Jesus "made Himself nothing, taking the very nature of a servant ... being found in the appearance as a man, He humbled Himself and became obedient to death—even death on a cross" (Philippians 2:7–8).

He who died for us is not just a man. He is the God-Man. He did not become God, as false teachers claim. No, He was already God at all times, from eternity to eternity. He Himself said, "'I am the Alpha and the Omega,'" the beginning and the end ... "'who is, and who was, and who is to come, the Almighty'" (Revelation 1:8).

Lord Jesus, You are my complete Savior. Amen.

Roy H. Bleick

27

The Only God and Savior

"I, even I, am the LORD, and apart from Me there is no Savior." Isaiah 43:11

In opposition to all false gods, God says, "I, even I, am the LORD." Thus follows what He states in the First Commandment, "You shall have no other gods before Me" (Exodus 20:3).

In their foolishness, people make all sorts of things into gods and worshiped them. That is gross idolatry. Many also practice subtle idolatry in that they rely upon their own reason, strength, or effort or on other people's friendship. In opposition to them, the Lord says, "I, even I," He repeats and emphasizes!, "am the LORD."

What a glorious God we have, for apart from Him there is no other Savior! As Savior, He is our Redeemer. All these other gods, creatures, and things upon which people so frequently rely, deceive. They have no might. These gods are in no position to rescue people from sin and death. Our God is the only Savior. He sent Jesus as Redeemer. In Christ we find salvation, rescue, redemption, and life. How great that this true God has revealed Himself and led us to the knowledge of this salvation!

Thanks be to You, O God, for our salvation in Christ, the only Redeemer. Sustain us through faith in Him! Amen.

Otto H. Schmidt

God with Us

"And surely I am with you always, to the very end of the age." Matthew 28:20

"The best Friend is the one in heaven," a hymn writer states. However, the best Friend, who speaks to us today, assures us that He is not removed from us. He is here for us in the "twinkling of an eye." The worth of a true friend lies precisely in this: That He stands at our side and, in the most difficult hours of our life, He does not forsake us. Such a friend cannot be compensated with gold.

Children of God have a guide for life in their Savior, Jesus Christ, who surpasses the best of humans. Through Baptism, our lives are united to Him. His daily presence is sealed to us by His Word, "'I am with you always, to the very end of the age'" (Matthew 28:20). What a guarantee! Only God can promise something like this. What a comfort! God is with us in every way at all times. In all the situations of our life, He is there.

He is not prepared to help us only when we ask. He is prepared to accomplish the impossible in all situations. He Himself knows every weakness in our lives, and His forgiveness has no boundaries. His love upon the cross conquered the devil, the world, and sin so we might fully trust in Him.

We thank You, Lord Jesus, that You are our total guide in life. Amen.

Horst Hoyer

January 24   2 Peter 1:19

Let Us Walk in the Light of the Lord

When they saw the star, they were overjoyed.
Matthew 2:10

The story of the Wise Men—in hindsight, is it not also our story? Our life is one of constant wandering, often in a dark valley. Many times we think we have seen a star of hope. But, alas, it turns out to be false light. Here and there we ask for guidance, but those we ask cannot or will not bring any kind of peaceful solution.

Thus it is so important to follow the true Star! And there is one: the prophetic Word of the Holy Scriptures, a Light that shines in a dark place. There we are directed to the Morning Star that arises in our hearts (2 Peter 1:19), and it is none other than Jesus Christ, who guides us from Bethlehem to Golgotha all the way to the heavenly Jerusalem. He took our debt of sin upon Himself and swept away that over which we would have stumbled and fallen into eternal destruction. He is our guide and, above all else, He has prepared the way.

He also calls us to be lights as He says, "'I am the Light of the world. Whoever follows Me will never walk in darkness, but will have the Light of life'" (John 8:12). As His followers, we reflect the light that comes from Him.

So then let us follow the dear Lord with body and soul! Amen.

Erich Sexauer

The Light That Shines in the Dark

*And you will do well to pay attention to it, as to
a light shining in a dark place.* 2 Peter 1:19

Each of us certainly knows what it's like to stumble
around in the dark. We ultimately lose every sense of
direction. We can no longer find our way. How glad we
are, then, when a light shines and we can once more find
our way.

The apostle Peter compares the Word of God to a
light that shines in a dark place, although quite obviously
in a much more important sense than ordinary light. Peter
calls it steadfast, solid, and prophetic (2 Peter 1:19). Above
all else, it is the inspired Word from God the Holy Spirit.
As such, this steadfast and certain Word of God offers
irrevocable proof of the "power and coming of our Lord
Jesus Christ" (2 Peter 1:16). God's Word is the bright light
that shines in the darkness.

In this light, we can quite accurately see and learn
that Jesus is our only hope for salvation. This light also
serves us so we are able to say with the psalmist, "Your
Word is a lamp to my feet and a light for my path" (Psalm
119:105).

Grant, dear Lord, that we at all times may follow
Your steadfast, prophetic Word as a light! Amen.

John W. Behnken

Ephesians 5:6–10

Don't Grope About in the Dark

Then Jesus told them, "You are going to have
the Light just a little while longer. Walk while
you have the Light, before darkness overtakes you.
The man who walks in the dark does not know
where he is going." John 12:35

"It's good to whisper in the dark," is a saying that
might apply to thieves and evil activity, but can hardly be
applied to good things. It is certainly not good for anyone
to have to sit or grope about in the dark. Light is indis-
pensable for our existence. In fact, in many places clocks
are set ahead in the summer time to take full advantage of
the daylight. The night is skillfully lit to guarantee safety
and protect people from break-ins and robberies.

In contrast, it is far more difficult to overcome the
spiritual shroud of darkness that surrounds our very best
human effort to see. Only God can accomplish this.
Through the Holy Spirit, God calls believers out of the
darkness. Through His Word in Christ, He enlightens us.
The light of this Word allows us to recognize the dangers
that threaten our body and soul.

But there's still more. Just as light scatters darkness,
so this also wipes away the night of sin through the forgiveness granted to us through Christ. As long as this
Light shines on us, our life's way is assured for time and
eternity. Let us walk in the light of Christ.

Holy Spirit, continually enlighten us through faith
in Jesus Christ! Amen.

Horst Hoyer

January 27   Ephesians 5:6–10

The Lord Is My Light

*The LORD is my light and my salvation—
whom shall I fear?* Psalm 27:1

Most people are ill at ease in darkness. We feel forsaken and find ourselves defenseless against evil. This feeling especially hits home concerning spiritual darkness.

The Lord, however, is our Light and our Salvation. When our accusers and enemies try to rise against us, we need not be afraid. The Lord stands beside us and helps us in every need.

With the psalmist, we petition the Lord to sustain us in faith and worship. He helps us as we remain united with Him through Word and Sacrament.

If we languish in anxiety and need, we can call upon the Lord for help, for God Himself has invited us to do so. We can be certain that He will hear and help us at the right time and in the manner best for us.

Praise be to You for Your great grace and help in all our needs. Amen.

Jakob K. Heckert

January 28   1 Corinthians 1:18–31

The Wisdom of the Children of God

*For the message of the cross is foolishness to those
who are perishing.* 1 Corinthians 1:18

Anyone who wishes to become honorable in this
world and wants to be held in high regard by the world as
being smart and wise is seeking wisdom from the wrong
source. The apostle Paul says, "If any one of you thinks he
is wise by the standards of this age, he should become a
'fool' so that he may become wise" (1 Corinthians 3:18).
To the world, a fool and a Christian are one and the same.
But the wisdom of the world is foolishness to God.

Christ has become wisdom for us (1 Corinthians
1:30). There will come a day when the secular world will
also acknowledge the wisdom that is ours through Christ.
We have a Savior who bore our sins and paid our debt of
guilt. As our stand-in, this Savior made peace with God.
With His atoning blood, He erased our IOU of debt and
won for us righteousness, life, and salvation. To the world,
this is foolish. To the Christian, it is true wisdom.

Whoever flees to Him is God's own child.
Whoever has this Savior as a Friend is also a friend of God.
To this point, Christ says, "'I tell you the truth, whoever
hears My Word and believes Him who sent Me has eternal
life and will not be condemned; he has crossed over from
death to life'" (John 5:24).

Dear God, make us wise through faith in Christ,
Your Son and our Lord! Amen.

C. F. W. Walther

How Glorious Is God's Name!

O LORD, our Lord, how majestic is Your name in
all the earth! Psalm 8:1

Mother, father, brother, sister, grandmother, grand-
father, uncle, and aunt are words that are music to our ears.
When we think about these names, all sorts of beautiful
thoughts come to mind. We not only think about a particular person who bears such a name, we also think about
what this person has done for us or still does for us.

When we take into account, with the psalmist, that
God's name is glorious, we are also reminded of everything
God has done for us and still does for us. It is God who has
created us and sustains us. It is God who offered His only
Son for us so we, through faith in Him, are saved. It is the
very same God, who through His Spirit, ignites saving
faith and strengthens and sustains it through Word and
Sacrament. For this and other great acts of God, we glorify and praise Him as we think about His glorious name.
After this temporal life, we will glorify and praise the glorious name of our God without end, along with all the
redeemed.

Lord, grant us Your grace that we might in this life
praise Your Name! Amen.

Lester H. Gierach

January 30   John 3:1–21

Darkness and Light

*There will be no more night. They will not need
the light of a lamp or the light of the sun, for the
Lord God will give them light.* Revelation 22:5

Children especially are afraid of the night and of
darkness; and for us adults, the darkness, when we are
unable to see, is sinister. In the New Testament, especially
in the writings of the apostle John, much is said about the
opposition of light and darkness.

We humans live in the darkness of sin and in the
shadow of death. But God has allowed His eternal Light to
shine into the darkness of our world through His dear Son.
Through faith in our Lord, Jesus Christ, we no longer live
in the darkness of sin and death, but in the light of eternal
life.

Here John is speaking about this type of light. In
eternal life with God, there is no longer any night or darkness for God Himself is the Light and we shall live in His
light as He is in the light. "You will fill me with joy in Your
presence, with eternal pleasures at Your right hand" (Psalm
16:11b).

O Jesus Christ, true Light, enlighten those who do
not know You, and bring them into Your fold so their souls
also may be saved! Amen.

Manfred Roensch

January 31   2 Corinthians 5:17–21

A Gracious Visitation

They were all filled with awe and praised God.
"A great prophet has appeared among us,"
they said. "God has come to help His people."
Luke 7:16

With these words, the people of Nain expressed their amazement as they watched a youth raised from the dead. That a dead person came alive at the command of a man, apparently a man like them, was inexplicable. They had never before experienced anything like this. That fear gripped them under such circumstances is indeed no surprise.

Oh, if all had only recognized the importance of this wonder, that God had actually visited them! For this mighty Conqueror of death was the Messiah promised by God in the Old Testament, and He was the Savior of this young man as well as of every other person.

God has also visited us. He has also sent this Savior to us. "He is the atoning sacrifice for our sins, and not only for ours but also for the sins of the whole world" (1 John 2:2). He is the Savior and Redeemer of every sinner from Adam to this present time and on to the very end for all yet to be born before Judgment Day.

We thank You, faithful God, for Your gracious visitation. Amen.

F. Wahlers

Light in Darkness

You, O LORD, keep my lamp burning, my God
turns my darkness into light. Psalm 18:28

"Even though I walk through the valley of the shadow of death, I will fear no evil, for You are with me; Your rod and Your staff, they comfort me" (Psalm 23:4). For this reason, all of God's children sing and speak with sure confidence. God's children know that the God in heaven is their Refuge and Strength, even in the greatest of troubles. A favorite verse is: "Neither death nor life, neither angels nor demons, neither the present nor the future, nor any powers, neither height nor depth, nor anything else in all creation, will be able to separate us from the love of God that is in Christ Jesus our Lord" (Romans 8:38–39).

You and I can also go through life with such an assurance. We know God did not spare His only Son. The Lord God offered Him for us all. That's why He also gives us everything else that is good and wholesome for our soul's salvation. Just as a light directs our way in the darkness, so God guides and leads us through life, for His Word is "a lamp to my feet" (Psalm 119:105a).

Those who recognize this light are blessed. In the light of the divine Word, we are able to see how we can blessedly live and die. We will want to gladly hear and learn this Word and share it with others.

O Lord Jesus, You true, eternal Light, enlighten us through Your Spirit! Amen.

Lester H. Gierach

February 2   Matthew 8:14–17

Our Heavenly Physician

"I am the LORD, who heals you."
Exodus 15:26

When our first parents fell into sin, death and everything that pertains to its realm—sickness, misery, affliction, and despair—came into the world. Sin has polluted and poisoned the body and soul of humankind. "Therefore, just as sin entered the world through one man, and death through sin, and in this way death came to all men, because all sinned" (Romans 5:12). As certain it is that all men are sinners, so certainly they require a physician.

There is only one Physician who can fundamentally and forever heal the body and soul and rescue it from eternal death. That is Jesus Christ, God and Man in one person. To be the Physician for humankind, He came into the world and became human like us—only without sin. He took our sin upon Himself and bore and endured all the punishment and consequences of it. Thereby He won for us complete forgiveness of all sin, perfect righteousness before God, and eternal life with God.

Therefore, whoever believes in Jesus as his divine Physician and Savior is declared righteous by God, for the sake of Christ.

Lord, Your Word makes body and soul well. Amen.

Paul W. Hartfield

Acknowledged through Freedom

"When Israel was a child, I loved him, and out of Egypt I called my son." Hosea 11:1

At one time God told Abraham that his descendants would serve as slaves in Egypt for 400 years, but He would eventually lead them out of their tribulation. In the same way, Jesus, our Savior and the vicarious Intercessor before God, would Himself have to flee to Egypt and be led out again by God.

The slavery of God's people in Egypt represents the status of all humankind. We all have been taken captive by the devil, by the lusts of this evil world, and by the power of our own sinful flesh—and we cannot free ourselves.

God sent Moses to the Israelites; however, Moses had no power to help the people. Due to his age and his own sinfulness, he could not offer them any lasting assurance or courage. Yet it is completely different with Jesus. He is the Son of God. And, as Savior and the perfect vicarious Intercessor for humankind, He willingly became a slave so that through Him we could become totally free. Now we live in the assurance and confidence that God has rescued and saved us and has forgiven us all of our sins.

Dear God, through the redeeming work of Jesus, we are now freed from the slavery to sin. Amen.

Donald L. Pohlers

February 4   Isaiah 40:1–11

God's Word Abides Forever

*"The grass withers and the flowers fall, but the
word of our God stands forever."* Isaiah 40:8

"Lift up your voice with a shout, lift it up, do not be
afraid; say ... 'Here is your God!'" (Isaiah 40:9)

God sent this summons to Israel alongside a
prophecy about the Messiah. Since everything human is
perishable but God's Word endures, the Church of God—
with a clear voice—should, so to speak, proclaim from the
mountain tops: "Here is your God!" About the Redeemer,
the prophet says, "The glory of the LORD will be revealed"
(Isaiah 40:5a). To this, St. John responds, "We have seen
His glory, the glory of the One and Only, who came from
the Father, full of grace and truth" (John 1:14). In a glorious revelation, Isaiah catches a glimpse of the Messiah,
and admonishes the Church to proclaim Him and His
Gospel to the world.

The eternal Word of God, intended for the entire
world, is that kind of redemptive news. "For no one can lay
any foundation other than the one already laid, which is
Jesus Christ" (1 Corinthians 3:11).

Lord, praise to You for such a salvation. Let us
abide by it, And give us Your good Spirit, So that we
believe the Word, So that we receive it at all times With
humility, honor, love and joy As being God's Word, not
man's. Amen. (*Kirchengesangbuch für Evangelisch—Lutherische
Gemeinden*, CPH)

Herbert D. Poellet

41

Recognized by a Blind Person

*"Nobody has ever heard of opening the eyes of a
man born blind. If this man were not from God,
He could do nothing." John 9:32–33*

Like many people today, Jesus' disciples still had
much to learn about God's grace and His intentions—
especially how He deals with the consequences of sin.

One day the disciples saw a person who had been
born blind. According to human reason, the conclusion
drawn from his situation was that either he or his parents
had grossly sinned, so much so that God denied him the
ability to see. Although Scripture doesn't tell us, it is logical to conclude that the disciples thought they were better
than this man or his parents.

"No," said Jesus. This birth defect happened to
make known God's work and to disclose Jesus as the
Savior. The blind man actually confessed this truth in his
speech before the enemies of Jesus. No one is righteous
before God; if Jesus had been a sinner, He would not have
been able to obtain power or grace from God (John 9:33).
Jesus, however, is God's Son, and because of this He could
give the blind man his sight.

Through this miracle, the Savior reveals Himself as
God's Son. He also has given us power for spiritual vision
to confess Him before the world.

O Jesus, help me see You through faith. Amen.

Donald L. Pohlers

Recognized by the Paralytic Person

He said to the paralytic, "I tell you, get up, take your mat and go home." Mark 2:10–11

The paralytic had good friends. They spared no effort to help him; that's why they carried him to Jesus. And when they could not get through the door because of the crowd, they removed the boards from the roof and lowered their friend on a rope-fastened bed.

The Lord realized the love of these friends and understood exactly what kind of help they sought. They were solely interested in the bodily health of the paralytic. Jesus, however, knew that the man was in need of a different kind of healing—spiritual healing. Since He loved the paralyzed man, Jesus first wanted to reveal Himself as Lord and Savior by turning His attention to the man's greatest problem: sin.

Those hearing Jesus did not believe that He was the Savior. Hence they did not want to believe that He had the authority to forgive sins. But with a single word, Jesus removed their doubts. He healed the man to offer proof that He also had the power to forgive sins. He carried out this power for all of us in that He died and rose for us. That's why we rejoice. We are also forgiven.

O Jesus, Your forgiveness is my treasure. Amen.

Donald L. Pohlers

Your God Is King

*How beautiful on the mountains are the feet of
those who bring good news, who proclaim peace,
who bring good tidings, who proclaim salvation,
who say to Zion, "Your God reigns!"* Isaiah 52:7

Your God is King! This is what the messenger of
peace cried out to the people of Israel. The prophet fore-
saw a captured Jerusalem risen from the dust and a captured
daughter of Zion freed from the bonds around her neck.

Your God is King! That's what the messengers of
peace still call out today, what the preachers of freedom to
the children of God still cry out. Like those in Babylonian
captivity, we were in bondage to the devil because of sin.
However, our much greater Rescuer and Redeemer ripped
away the chains of our servitude to sin. We are free,
redeemed, saved—although it cost our Savior His life. But
God be praised! The Crucified One rose from death. And
through that resurrection, He took away death's power.

Your God is King! This cry should echo in every
land, "in the sight of all the nations, and all the ends of
the earth will see the salvation of our God" (Isaiah 52:10b).
We Christians have a great assignment before us—to take
this happy news about eternal peace with God to all the
people in the world so they too may partake of eternal
salvation.

Help me, O Lord, that I acknowledge You and that
I, along with all of Christendom, call You my King, now
and in all eternity! Amen.

Herman A. Mayer

February 8   Romans 5:1–8

The Mark of God's Love

This is how God showed His love among us: He sent His one and only Son into the world that we might live through Him. 1 John 4:9

Love cannot just be demonstrated by words; it must also be shown by action. That's what God did. He demonstrated His love for us once and for all when He sent His Son into the world, when He let Him become a man, when He let Him die for our sins upon Golgotha's cross. God did all this so we might have eternal life through Him.

If we were ever to torture ourselves over the question of whether God actually loves us, if we were ever to feel like we have been totally and completely forsaken by God, then we can continually remind ourselves: God loves me; He has given me this sign for His love; He has sent His Son for me and He let Him die for me; He awakened Him from the dead and will someday resurrect me to eternal life. After all this, would God hate me? No, God loves me, and nothing can ever make me waver about this truth. He gave me what He loves beyond all measure!

Thanks be to You, O heavenly Father, for the unending love You have shown to us through Jesus Christ, Your Son. Amen.

Manfred Roensch

February 9   John 5:1–14

Jesus, Healer of the Sick

*Then Jesus said to him, "Get up! Pick up your
mat and walk." John 5:8*

Jesus is the almighty Helper, the faithful Savior.
This Bible story demonstrates this. We yield to Him who
can help the physical needs and the greater spiritual needs
of humankind. It was for this reason above all else that
Jesus came into the world.

Just as Jesus, through His Word, healed this man
physically, so He heals. us from the sickness of sin.
Through Word and Sacrament, Jesus comes and seeks the
sinner and turns him to Himself. Jesus speaks kindly to the
sinners who feel spiritual woe. He speaks to their need,
shows them His heartfelt compassion, and offers them His
help—like He did to the paralytic: " 'Your sins are forgiv-
en' " (Matthew 9:2b).

What could be sweeter for the sinner than this
news: God is gracious to me, a sinner; I am once again reconciled to God? Believing this, one is moved with longing,
trust, and hope. With this comes the sigh from the heart,
"Lord, have mercy on me!" As we Christians hear the
Gospel, it has this effect within us. We call out to Him in
faith.

Lord, sustain us in this faith and in Your grace,
which saves us! Amen.

Walter H. Bouman

The One Who Brings Joy

*And provide for those who grieve in Zion—to bestow
on them a crown of beauty instead of ashes, the oil of
gladness instead of mourning, and a garment of praise
instead of a spirit of despair.* Isaiah 61:3

As the Savior initiated the office of the public ministry in the synagogue at Nazareth, He read from this chapter and said, " 'Today this scripture is fulfilled' " (Luke 4:21).
Jesus clearly told His listeners that He fulfilled these prophecies. " 'He has anointed Me to preach good news to the poor.
He has sent Me to proclaim freedom for the prisoners and
recovery of sight for the blind, to release the oppressed, to
proclaim the year of the Lord's favor' " (Luke 4:18–19).

When considering this prophecy, the Jews had
thought only about freedom from the Babylonian captivity. But no earthly freedom brings peace to the soul and its
longing for complete freedom from the plight and affliction of sin.

The joy of rescue and redemption is described
here. Back then, the mournfully sad smeared ashes upon
their heads, did not wash, and wore old clothes. Then
along came Jesus. Instead of ashes, He places a crown of
flowers upon their heads, anoints their faces with oil, and
replaces clothes of mourning with festival garments. The
Bride, dressed in her finery, goes forth to meet the heavenly Bridegroom. Here all sadness recedes.

I find joy in the Lord and my soul rejoices in my
God. Amen.

Herman A. Mayer

47

Words for the Weary

The Sovereign LORD has given me an instructed
tongue, to know the word that sustains the weary.
Isaiah 50:4

Here someone with an educated tongue, one who is wise, is brought to the fore. That person is no other than our Savior. In Him, of course, resides the fullness of "Godness." Upon Him rests the spirit of wisdom and understanding, the knowledge of and the fear of God. The people who heard His sermons asked in astonishment, from where does this one get such wisdom? (Luke 4:32)

What's the purpose for the educated tongue? To speak as only the Father has taught (John 8:28). Libraries are filled with books, many quite erudite. Yet despite their capacity to teach, these books do not contain words with which to invigorate the weary, comfort the downcast, bring the erring back to the true way. The Savior alone has such words.

Jesus' words are not just mere words—but actions. He not only teaches the Law, He fulfills it perfectly. He not only teaches that sin results in punishment and the punishment for sin is death, He takes sin's punishment upon Himself and enters death in the sinner's stead.

That's how Jesus speaks to the weary at the appropriate time. Just when they are worn out and overburdened, when the burden of their sin oppresses them, Jesus calls them to Himself and speaks to them with kindness and love.

I am sick; come, strengthen me, my Strength. I am worn out; refresh and renew me, sweet Jesus! Amen.

Herman A. Mayer

Luke 15:1–10

Christ Accepts the Sinners

But the Pharisees and the teachers of the law
muttered, "This man welcomes sinners and eats
with them." Luke 15:2

All sorts of tax collectors and sinners had come to
hear Jesus, and He kindly received them without exception. But Jesus' enemies cried out with an attitude of contempt and condemnation, "this man welcome sinners!"
Jesus confirmed this, and taught the truth through the
parables of the lost sheep, the lost coin, and the lost son.
He said, yes indeed, that's how it is; I take in the sinner; I
cannot do otherwise.

How many millions, caught in the depths of sin,
have been consoled and comforted by this truth, "Jesus
receives the sinner!" How many preachers of the Gospel
have used these words to heal deeply wounded con-
sciences that nothing else could heal! How many have
stood on the brink of doubt and, though there was no help
for them, were pulled back from the frightful abyss with
the comfort that grace, hope, and salvation still existed for
them!

Who of us has not already tasted this sweetness:
"Jesus, my Savior, accepts me!"

Lord Jesus, forgive us our sins! Amen.

C. F. W. Walther

John 3:16–21

The Light of the World

*"I am the Light of the world. Whoever follows Me
will never walk in darkness, but will have the light
of life." John 8:12*

When we have to endure great pain, upon a sick
bed during the night for example, how happy we are when
we once again see daylight! We should, however, rejoice
far more in the Light of the world—Jesus! He alone is the
Light that lights our way to heaven. He clearly shows how
we are to walk so we do not stumble. When we rely on the
light of Christ, we seek to serve Him in all situations. We
go blamelessly on our way. He leads us to the goal without
ever leading us into temptation or into sin.

Here on earth, we still fear that the lights may go
out during a storm. That never happens with Jesus, for He
is the certain Light at all times. Therefore, we can confidently rely upon Him as the light that leads us to salvation.
As we steadfastly cling to Him—as we follow the light He
gives us—then we desire to do His will. We remain on the
pathway that leads to heaven.

Lord Jesus, help us to faithfully follow the light
with which You lighten our way! Amen.

Gerhard C. Michael

God's Love Is from Eternity

For He chose us in Him before the creation of the
world to be holy and blameless in His sight.
Ephesians 1:4

The love that exists between married couples endures for many years. Good friends, as well, love one another for years upon years. And the love among people that has existed the longest is most certainly the love parents have for their children. Fathers and mothers love their children from birth on, yes, even before birth.

Does a love exist that is still older than parental love? Yes! It is God's love for us. God has loved us from the beginning of the world, for all eternity. The apostle Paul wrote, "He chose us in Him before the creation of the world." The time prior to the creation of the world takes us into the unending eternity of God. That's how far back God has loved us.

When our human reason "tosses in the towel" is when we hear how God calls us to Himself: " 'I have loved you with an everlasting love' " (Jeremiah 31:3). With that, all our actions and boasting are brought to naught. It is God's love alone that has chosen us through Jesus Christ.

God, You have, in Your Son, chosen me in eternity. Amen.

William Boehm

Jesus, Our Righteousness

This is the name by which He will be called:
The LORD Our Righteousness. Jeremiah 23:6

What's in a name? Among men, not very much. A man may bear the name "Gottlieb" (literally, "God lover") and yet not love God. Parents may call their son "Theodore," but they don't regard him as a "gift of God" (the literal translation of the Greek roots of Theodore).

It's not that way with Jesus Christ. His name tells us who He is and what He does for us. He is called "Jesus," and that means "The One who saves." The expression by the prophet Jeremiah in today's verse is messianic. The Savior, born of a virgin, has in addition to His human nature a divine nature: Jesus was not only man, but also Lord. As pertaining to His office, He is the Lamb of God. He was executed on a cross, and on Easter morning He rose again. Through His merit, which we seize with the hand of faith, we are righteous before God. Jesus is our righteousness.

Jesus Christ, in whom all the prophecies are fulfilled, bears many divine names. He is called "Wonderful Counselor, Mighty God, Everlasting Father, Prince of Peace" (Isaiah 9:6b). He is true man, yet also "the true God and Eternal Life" (1 John 5:20c). However, no name contains more Gospel than this one: "The LORD, Our Righteousness."

Lord Jesus, dress us with Your righteousness! Amen.

Rudolph F. Norden

Blessed News

"In fact, for this reason I was born, and for
this I came into the world, to testify to the truth."
John 18:37

Our Savior came down from heaven to bring humankind a very special message. Since this message comes from God, it is the unshakable truth. The kernel of this truth is that God is gracious and merciful, that He gave up His only Son to redeem us from sin, death, and the devil. All this, ultimately, so those who receive Him in faith will have forgiveness of sins and eternal life.

Our Savior testified to this great, glorious, blessed truth here on earth for three long years. Many who listened accepted His saving Word. And our Savior has seen to it that we still are able to hear His voice. Whenever we read the Bible, whenever we hear a pastor preach God's Word, we hear Jesus' voice. "He who listens to you listens to Me" (Luke 10:16a), He says of all faithful preachers. When the Holy Spirit opens our hearts so we rejoice and trust in our beloved Savior, we then regard it as sheer unearned grace that we today are able to hear His voice.

Sanctify us with Your truth; Your Word is truth. Amen.

Walter H. Bouman

53

John 8:41–59

Born of the Father

"For God so loved the world that He gave His one and only Son." John 3:16

This is what we confess about Jesus: "conceived by the Holy Spirit, born of the Virgin Mary." But this was not His beginning; it was His becoming man (His incarnation). Christ Himself is eternal, like His Father. St. John said of Him, "In the beginning was the Word, and the Word was with God, and Word was God" (John 1:1). The same apostle wrote, "In Him was life, and that life was the light of men" (John 1:4). "And this is the testimony: God has given us eternal life, and this life is in His Son" (1 John 5:11). "The true Light that gives light to every man was coming into the world" (John 1:9).

The Church has expressed the mystery of the wondrous person of our Savior in its confession: "begotten of His Father before all worlds." He is God's only Son. He is before the world. He is eternal. On the basis of Scripture, we dare say no more; nor dare we say anything less. That's why we confess with the entire Church of all time: "I believe ... in the Lord Jesus Christ, the only-begotten Son of God, begotten of His Father before all worlds." We agree with what Martin Luther confessed about Him: He is "my Lord."

Help me, dear God, to bravely confess Your only Son at all times to the whole world! Amen.

Fred Kramer

February 18   Mark 2:14–17

Jesus, the Physician of Our Soul

Is there no balm in Gilead? Is there no physician there? Jeremiah 8:22

Every person is by nature sinful and thus spiritually sick. As Isaiah said, " 'From the sole of your foot to the top of your head there is no soundness—only wounds and welts and open sores' " (Isaiah 1:6). Who can be his healer and helper? No fellow human can, for all men are sinners. Consequently we all find ourselves in the same situation. The psalmist said, "No man can redeem the life of another or give to God a ransom for him" (Psalm 49:7). Just as no man can be the physician of the soul, so there exists no earthly means of salvation, or salve, for the sickness of sin.

God alone can—and wants to—heal the sinner. He sent His Son "to bind up the brokenhearted" (Isaiah 61:1b). This Healer and Binding Bandage for the heart is Jesus Christ. His blood makes us clean of all sin. He, the true Physician of the soul, says to all the suffering, " 'Come to Me, all you who are weary and burdened, and I will give you rest' " (Matthew 11:28).

Jeremiah asked whether there is any balm. The answer is yes! There is a Salve—the Good News of Christ, God's Word, which makes well our body and soul. And He who proffers this means of salvation to us is Jesus Christ, our Savior.

Lord, heal us and make us holy. Sanctify us through Your Word! Amen.

Rudolph F. Norden

Genesis 3:8–24

God Is Gracious to Sinners

"He will crush your head and you will strike His heel." Genesis 3:15

"The reason the Son of God appeared was to destroy the devil's work" (1 John 3:8). And what are the works of the devil? He deceived Adam and Eve. Thus, the entire human race lost paradise and brought upon itself the wrath of God. Not only did temporal death befall the human race, it could not escape eternal death.

Nevertheless, by grace, God came to Adam and Eve in love and, with all kindness and compassion, promised them freedom from their sins and protection from eternal death.

God turned to "that ancient serpent called the devil" (Revelation 12:9) and said, " 'I will put enmity between you and the woman, and between your offspring and hers; He will crush your head and you will strike His heel' " (Genesis 3:15). This is the first promise of grace. The woman's seed, born of the Virgin Mary, suffered severely in the battle against the devil. However, He conquered the archenemy and humankind was rescued. Thus heaven was opened to us. God is gracious to us sinners.

Heartfelt thanks, dear God, for Your promise of grace and the fulfillment of it through Christ. Amen.

Arnold H. Gebhardt

False and True Anxiety

"Do not be afraid, little flock." Luke 12:32

Both of the Scripture readings suggested above announce the Savior's admonition that it is important to distinguish between false and true anxieties. Humankind, indeed, has its worries. But Christians need not worry about food or clothing, for other matters are far more important. Jesus says, " 'Do not worry about your life, what you will eat; or about your body, what you will wear. Life is more than food, and the body more than clothes' " (Luke 12:22–23).

The Savior reminds us that God allows flowers and grass to grow and He provides for animals. And He asks, " 'Are you not much more valuable than they?' " (Matthew 6:26b). Again, if God " 'clothes the grass of the field, which is here today and tomorrow is thrown into the fire, will He not much more clothe you, O you of little faith?' " (Matthew 6:30). We don't need to worry about such things.

However, we should be concerned about our soul's salvation, about our congregation, about our missionaries, etc. These are the matters Jesus means when He says, " 'Seek first His kingdom and His righteousness, and all these things will be given to you as well' " (Matthew 6:33). Given that, we can follow the words, " 'Do not be afraid, little flock' " (Luke 12:32).

Lord God, help me to seek Your kingdom first and not worry about insignificant things! Amen.

Edwin W. Leverenz

Words of Eternal Life

"Lord to whom shall we go? You have the words of eternal life." John 6:68

A person in our times finds himself amidst movement; he is constantly on the go. As such, he searches for new things that might fulfill all his physical and mental needs. But when and where can we say we have achieved the high point of our lives? Does anything like that actually exist?

From our earthly experiences, we have to answer this question with a resounding no. Only God can provide us fulfillment. Peter experienced this when he came into fellowship with Jesus. In the living Word of Jesus, Peter found fulfillment for his life and his search came to an end.

We also are invited to experience this fulfillment. The Words of Life are eternal. Because we have the same needs and requirements, they are living words for us today as well. They are written for us in the Bible, where the same Lord Jesus meets us with His Word of eternal life and offers us love and forgiveness.

Sustain us, Lord, with Your Word! Amen.

Horst Hoyer

February 22   1 Peter 1:3–9

Born for Life

*Yet to all who received Him, to those who believed
in His name, He gave the right to become children
of God—children born not of natural descent,
nor of human decision or a husband's will, but
born of God.* John 1:12–13

From the cradle to the grave—that's how the world commonly describes the time-span of our life. According to our human experience, this is correct. We are born in order to come closer to our grave with our every step.

Is that the meaning of life? Hardly. The reason for life lies in the fact that God, who is Himself Life, allows us to be born for life and not for death. And because of His love for us, God the Father offers the remedy through Jesus Christ—which is to immunize us against eternal death.

Whoever has received Jesus Christ, God's Remedy and Savior, is in essence a child of Life. That is to say, he is born from life unto Life. All of us can belong to this host of people and rejoice in His Life.

Jesus, we thank You that through Your merits we have become God's children and are born for life. Amen.

Horst Hoyer

What Do You Expect from Life?

"I have come so that they may have life, and have it to the full." John 10:10

What do you expect from life? The response to this question may evoke as many answers as there are people. Every person places his own expectations upon life: babies to swaddle, career, education, the choice of life experiences, family, etc. To what extent our expectations may be fulfilled, if we wish to spare deluding ourselves, is a mystery we can fathom only in God. Our text gives us the key for this.

If we believe on Him who is life itself, we will never be deluded. Indeed, it is for this purpose that He came—that we should have life and with it complete fulfillment. He also provides us with all we need for life in His fellowship. In today's reading, we are given a shining example of everything we may expect from the Good Shepherd, Jesus Christ, in the full assurance of our faith, which shall never be put to shame. If our true-life expectation is anchored in Him, then it is already fulfilled.

Lord Jesus, You are my Shepherd; I lack for nothing. Amen.

Horst Hoyer

February 24   John 10:1–11

The Door for the Sheep

"I tell you the truth, I am the gate for the sheep."
John 10:7

In our text, Jesus compares His kingdom of grace with a sheep stall. In the sheep stall, there was a door through which the sheep entered. Jesus tells us that He is the only door to the sheep stall. If we wish to enter into the kingdom of grace—into the holy, Christian Church—we do so only through Jesus Christ. We enter through this door only as we receive Him in faith as our sole Lord and Savior. We dare not rely upon our good works, for we can be saved only by God's grace.

Those who want to enter heaven in some other manner do not recognize Christ as the Way. Such a person is still outside of the kingdom of God. Only through the working of the Holy Spirit in our hearts does one come to the knowledge that Jesus Christ is the Way that leads into the kingdom of grace. The Spirit comes to us through the means of grace, through Word and Sacrament. God help us so we zealously cling to the means of grace!

Lord, enlighten my heart through Your Holy Spirit so I acknowledge Jesus as the only door that leads to salvation! Amen.

Gerhard C. Michael

Psalm 103:1

We Praise the Lord

Praise the LORD, O my soul, and forget not all
His benefits. Psalm 103:2

The psalmist praises the goodness of God. He has received many good things from his Creator. His heart rejoices and he breaks forth in the lovely song of praise, "Praise the LORD, O my soul; all my inmost being, praise His holy name" (Psalm 103:1). His words flow forth like a stream—words that overflow from thankfulness as he counts the wondrous things with which God has blessed him. Among all the blessings, forgiveness of sins tops the list, along with what results from it: peace with God, a peace that the world cannot give.

Like the psalmist, we, too, praise God's goodness. His peace is also our peace. What this man of God knew only from the prophecies about the Messiah, we see in the New Testament in the light of fulfillment. In spirit, we can accompany the virgin's Son from the cradle to the cross, from the open grave to the mount of ascension. Above all else, the Most High Lord ascended into heaven to prepare a place for us in His kingdom.

Who can praise the wondrous deeds of God enough? Alas, I, a poor child of man, can merely stammer and mumble; but Lord, may such stammering mumble please You. Lord, we praise You for Your benefits and blessings. Amen.

Elmer Reimnitz

February 26   Matthew 14:22–32

Jesus, Our Rescuer and Savior

"Take courage! It is I." Matthew 14:27

On this occasion, Jesus was not with His disciples
in the ship as they battled against wind and wave. During
the fourth night watch, Jesus walked upon the sea and
came to them. The disciples were frightened and said the
figure was a ghost. But Jesus spoke to them, saying, " 'Take
courage! It is I. Don't be afraid' " (Matthew 14:27). The
storm became still, and the disciples confessed, " 'Truly You
are the Son of God' " (Matthew 14:33b).

Jesus truly is the only begotten Son of the Father.
His divine eye sees His own in their need. He hastens to
help them. But when He arrives, His own frequently don't
recognize Him in His wondrous ways. Thinking perhaps
that hell is near to them, they are very much afraid. They
should, however, listen to His voice: "Be comforted, it is I;
don't be scared!" They should be of good cheer and be
comforted and fear nothing. They can rely only on Him
and His Word. But how quickly such believing trust fades
again when a new wave of misfortune threatens! All we
have left is a cry, "Lord, help me!"

The Lord will hear us. He reaches out His hand and
helps us, always, unto eternal life.

Lord, do not withdraw Your gracious hand from us!
Amen.

Carl Manthey-Zorn

1 Corinthians 3:6–13

A Precious Cornerstone

"See, I lay a stone in Zion, a tested stone,
a precious cornerstone for a sure foundation."
Isaiah 28:16

The Lord God spoke of a wise man who built his house upon the rock. In the above text, the Lord says that He has laid a cornerstone in Zion, who endures and is trustworthy. It is His Son, Jesus Christ.

He is durable. Through all the centuries, the Lord has shown Himself to be thoroughly reliable. The Church builds its work upon Him. Through faith we rely upon Him.

God the Son is a precious cornerstone—holy, without fault or flaw, worthy of all glory, and completely capable to carry out the work that the Father has entrusted to Him. And He is our only cornerstone; no other—nothing else—serves as the foundation for the hope and work of the Church.

What a blessing to have such a sure cornerstone in our confused and uncertain times, especially for the youth who so frequently appear to need directing. Alas, if only everyone might find this enduring Foundation Stone and build their lives upon Him!

Lord, I now have found the Foundation, which holds my anchor forever. Amen.

Otto H. Schmidt

1 Corinthians 1:18–23

True Wisdom: To Know Jesus

"The fear of the Lord—that is wisdom."
Job 28:28

The so-called "wisdom literature" in the Bible consists of the books of Job, Proverbs, and Ecclesiastes. The first is a dramatic composition that deals with the theme of suffering. Job is the one who suffers, and who, despite all evil, completely entrusts himself to the Lord. In Job 19:25–26, he sings the glorious hymn, "I know that my Redeemer lives, ... in my flesh I will see God." In Job 28, he asks, Where may one ... find wisdom, and where is the abode for understanding? He answers, Man cannot purchase it with gold, nor with silver. ... Wisdom weighs far more than pearls; gold and crystal are unable to compare to it. Genuine truth is repeated before the eyes of all the living.

At the end of the chapter, Job reaches this wonderful conclusion, " 'The fear of the LORD—that is wisdom;' " and the avoidance of evil is understanding. Where is wisdom? Job answered further, " 'God understands the way to it and He alone knows where it dwells' " (Job 28:23). As a result, we find genuine truth and wisdom only in God. The truth about Christ's redemption alone offers certainty and reliability. Note it well!

Dear God, help me to reach beyond everything human and grasp divine wisdom! Amen.

Edwin W. Leverenz

John 8:46–59

The Sinless One in Place of the Sinner

"Can any of you prove Me guilty of sin?"
John 8:46

Jesus was the only holy, sinless man on earth. He could step before His enemies and dare them to ascribe one single sin to Him. No ordinary person could ever do that. But Jesus was no ordinary man. Precisely, His sinlessness is a proof of His divinity. "'For You alone are holy'" (Revelation 15:4b). He was "holy, blameless, pure, set apart from sinners" (Hebrews 7:26a), "tempted in every way, just as we are—yet was without sin" (Hebrews 4:15b). The Pharisees tried in vain to hang any wrong on Him. Pilate found no fault in Him. The malefactor on the cross was forced to admit Jesus had done nothing amiss. The Scriptures testify that He committed no sin, nor was there any deceit found in His mouth. Jesus' Word was truth. He is the Truth.

It is important that we acknowledge and believe this. For if Jesus is not the holy, sinless Son of God, then He is not our Savior and He Himself stands under the curse of the Law. But thanks be to God—we are redeemed with the precious blood of Christ, as an innocent and unspotted lamb.

We thank You, Lord God, that Jesus was made a sinner for us and we, through Him, have complete righteousness. Amen.

Thomas Green

New Compassion

Because of the LORD's great love we are not con-
sumed, for His compassions never fail. They are
new every morning. Lamentations 3:22–23

In a morning hymn, we sing, "The bright sun now shines forth." Every morning since the fourth day of creation the sun rises and its light shines. And until that day arrives when, in keeping with God's will, it loses its shine (Matthew 24:29), the sun will continue to give us light.

It's like that with God's mercy and compassion. They are inexhaustible. They are new every morning. They are like a well whose water never quits flowing. The psalmist said, "For with You is the fountain of life; in Your light we see light" (Psalm 36:9).

God's mercy is like His love and grace, about which John said, from His fullness we have received grace upon grace (John 1:16). The Son of God, who was sent by the Father as our Redeemer, is full of grace and truth. Paul also testified in Romans, "Where sin increased, grace increased all the more" (Romans 5:20). Consequently, as we repent our sins and in faith come to Jesus' cross, we receive forgiveness, life, and salvation beyond all measure. All this is new for us every morning!

Heavenly Father, You give us our daily bread. Let us also experience Your grace every day! Amen.

Rudolph F. Norden

A Searching Love

*"For the Son of Man came to seek and to save
what was lost."* Luke 19:10

We stand under the protection of a very good Shepherd. He is continually concerned about protecting those who through faith have been brought into His flock, and He seeks to save those who are lost. With unending patience and love, He goes after the lost until He finds them.

Jesus demands the same understanding from His fellow-workers and under-shepherds—the same endurance and the same enduring, caring labor. A little girl asked her father, a pastor, "Father, do all those many unbelievers really get lost?" He answered, "Yes, my child." She cried out, "Why doesn't someone go after them and tell them this?" If only we would constantly remember, whenever we see people who go astray, that they are souls who have been purchased and yet are lost! Perhaps then we would labor far differently, pray far more zealously, make more generous offerings, live more carefully, and speak more often about salvation. God grant it!

O Lord God, open our understanding of the glorious confession that adorns our Church so the lost may be led to that fullness of truth that will lead them to the fullness of salvation! Amen.

N. P. Uhlig

March 3   Hosea 2:23

God's People

"The ox knows his master, the donkey his owner's manger, but Israel does not know, My people do not understand." Isaiah 1:3

At first glance this verse paints a dark, sad, joyless prospect. Israel is worse than an ox and a mule. The people do not know their Lord and do not recognize their Lord's manger.

The prophet Isaiah described an accurate picture of his time. The people had fallen far away from the Lord (Isaiah 1:2). How far? "Your whole head is injured, your whole heart afflicted. From the sole of your foot to the top of your head there is no soundness" (Isaiah 1:5b–6). Such occurrences and circumstances deserve a sharp rebuke.

We sing with John Heermann, "Whereto shall I flee, for I am loaded down with many and great sins? Where can I find rescue?" And we find the answer in God's grace. God calls us His own. He has not eternally cast us aside. In Him there is forgiveness for all who turn to Him (Deuteronomy 4:29–31).

The Lord has not nor ever shall Depart from His people. He remains their assurance, Their blessing, salvation and peace. With motherly hands He guides His own continually from here to there. Give all glory to our God! Amen. (*Kirchengesangbuch für Evangelisch—Lutherische Gemeinden,* CPH)

Luther Poellet

March 4   Luke 18:31–43

The Scriptures Testify about Christ

"They will mock Him, insult Him, spit on Him,
flog Him and kill Him. On the third day He will
rise again." Luke 18:32–33

Our Savior's suffering, bleeding, and dying on the cross for our salvation is the most important theme of the Christian faith. When Scripture briefly describes the entire Christian teaching, it simply calls it "the message of the cross" (1 Corinthians 1:18). St. Paul addressed it thus, "We preach Christ crucified" (1 Corinthians 1:23). He also said, "I resolved to know nothing while I was with you except Jesus Christ and Him crucified" (1 Corinthians 2:2).

To further describe the redemption that occurred through Christ, it is said, "For you know that it was not with perishable things such as silver or gold that you were redeemed from the empty way of life handed down to you from your forefathers, but with the precious blood of Christ, a lamb without blemish or defect" (1 Peter 1:18–19). And Christ Himself, when He indicates His purpose for coming into the world, focuses on His suffering and death and says, " 'The Son of Man did not come to be served, but to serve, and to give His life as a ransom for many' " (Mark 10:45).

Christ, You Lamb of God, who bears the sin of the world, have mercy on us! Amen.

C. F. W. Walther

March 5   Matthew 17:1–9

The Transfiguration of Christ

We were eyewitnesses of His majesty.
2 Peter 1:16

Upon the mountain of transfiguration, Christ's face shone like the bright sun. A flood of light permeated His entire body. Even His clothes were lit and shone like a light, becoming white as snow. Moses and Elijah, patriarchs from the Old Testament, also appeared in glorious splendor, confidentially conversing with the Lord. Someday all believers will see such heavenly glory revealed.

Yes, there is a life after death. Moses and Elijah are representatives of all believers in eternity. Not everything is extinguished with death. "Dear friends, now we are children of God, and what we will be has not yet been made known. But we know that when He appears, we shall be like Him, for we shall see Him as He is" (1 John 3:2). In other words, on the Last Day, Jesus will transfigure our mortal bodies so they will become like His transfigured body. Peter and the others were filled with rapturous joy and wanted to cling to this experience. And in heaven we, too, will behold with joy the Savior, who, through His blood and suffering, opened heaven to us.

Anyone who gets weary here, let him look to the goal; there is joy. Amen.

Paul F. Koenig

Isaiah 9:1–7

Christ—the Son of God

*Simon Peter answered, "You are the Christ, the
Son of the living God."* Matthew 16:16

Many in our day doubt or even deny the divinity
(literally, the "God-ness") of Christ. Some praise Him as an
extraordinary teacher, a great prophet, a glorious example
of a person with His demeanor and conduct. But they do
not admit that He is true God. The denial of Christ's divinity, however, simultaneously indicates the denial of His
miracles and the truth of the entire Bible, God's own Word.

How does Jesus Himself view Peter's response to
this question? He said, " 'Blessed are you, Simon son of
Jonah, for this was not revealed to you by man, but by My
Father in heaven' " (Matthew 16:17).

Our Christian faith does not rest upon the empty
utterances of man, but rather upon the infallible Word of
God and the witness of Christ, the Son of God. His Word
is the eternal truth. Jesus says, " 'I am the Way and the
Truth and the Life. No one comes to the Father except
through Me' " (John 14:6). Thus it is an indisputable fact:
Jesus Christ is the Son of the Living God.

I trust in You, my God and Lord! If I have You, what
more do I need? Indeed, I have You, Lord Jesus Christ, You
are my God and Redeemer. Amen.

Herbert D. Poellot

Jesus Goes to Jerusalem to Suffer

*"Everything that is written by the prophets about
the Son of Man will be fulfilled."* Luke 18:31

In the first promise of the Savior for all
humankind, it was revealed that Christ would be a suffering Savior, for it was said of Him that the serpent would
strike Him in the heel (Genesis 3:15). In the psalms and
the books of the prophets, the Redeemer of the world,
promised already in paradise, is portrayed even more
clearly. We see Him more clearly in the portrayal of a
lamb upon whom the Lord God heaves all our sins and
who shall be led to the slaughter.

In the Scripture reading suggested above, we read
the prophecy of Christ and His imminent suffering. He
tells the Twelve, " 'The Son of Man will be betrayed to the
chief priests and teachers of the law. They will condemn
Him to death and will hand Him over to the Gentiles, who
will mock Him and spit on Him, flog Him and kill Him.
Three days later He will rise' " (Mark 10:33–34). Christ
speaks very clearly and at length to His disciples about His
suffering. Whoever ponders Christ's suffering and
embraces it is led to everlasting joy. Thus, may we in spirit travel with our Savior along His road of pain and thank
Him for His suffering.

Lord Jesus, may we undertake to go with You to
Jerusalem. Amen.

C. F. W. Walther

Romans 6:1–14

Dead—Alive

"For this son of mine was dead and is alive again." Luke 15:24

The parable of the lost son demonstrates that God Himself wants to reinstate into full relationship anyone who has sunk into the deep morass of sin. The father proclaimed that he "was dead and is alive again." That is an accurate description of a lost sinner who repents. In Romans 6:23 we read, "For the wages of sin is death, but the gift of God is eternal life in Christ Jesus our Lord."

The lost son returned to his father's house in genuine repentance. He declared that he no longer was worthy to be called a son. He begged to be allowed to become only a day laborer. The father, however, was prepared to forgive him everything. He gave his son the finest clothes. He prepared him a festive banquet. He was happy.

God's unconditional love toward us is precisely the same. He desires that we come to Him contrite and repentant. He wants to forgive us. He wants to rescue us from death and make us alive. He said in Colossians 2:13, "When you were dead in your sins ... God made you alive with Christ." God forgives us for the sake of Jesus. He bestows on us the gift of the perfect garment of Christ's righteousness.

We thank You, heavenly Father, that You have made us, who were dead in sin, alive for the sake of Christ. Amen.

John W. Behnken

March 8   John 12:41–50

The Atoning Sacrifice for Sin

"See this has touched your lips; your guilt is taken away and your sin atoned for." Isaiah 6:7

"Even though there be much sin in us, with God there is much more grace" (*Kirchengesangbuch für Evangelish—Lutherische Gemeinden,* CPH). The message of these words resounds ever more clearly as we read about the prophet Isaiah. Isaiah regarded himself as lost because he was a sinner and descended from a sinful people. As he saw this vision, however, Isaiah was immediately raised up and comforted. The reason for his fear was taken from him. With a pair of tongs, the angel took a glowing coal from the altar and touched it to his tongue.

This is glorious, picturesque language. The altar in the holy sanctuary points to a sacrifice through which sin will be atoned. From the New Testament we know that Jesus Christ is offered on the cross as a sacrifice for us. The suffering of the Savior is prophesied in this passage from Isaiah. He had to allow the blazing flames of hell's fires to encompass Him so He could atone for the sin of the world. "The blood of Jesus, His Son, purifies us from all sin" (1 John 1:7b). The entire culture of sacrifice in the Old Testament directs us to Christ's atoning sacrifice upon Golgotha, just as the apostles of the New Testament gave witness. That is our comfort in life and in death.

Cleanse me with hyssop so I might become pure; wash me so I become snow white! Amen.

Herman A. Meyer

Matthew 5:17–19

Fulfilled!

Jesus took the Twelve aside and told them, "We are going up to Jerusalem, and everything that is written by the prophets about the Son of Man will be fulfilled." Luke 18:31

The suffering and death of the Savior, just like His resurrection, was a "fulfillment." The Holy Scriptures are the revelation of God. Our loving God speaks to us through His Word about His plan for our salvation in Christ. The Bible is inspired by God. No mortal could have spoken about the events that had to do with Jesus' suffering and death centuries prior to its occurrence. This prophecy could have taken place only through the inspiration of our eternal God. It is said about the Old Testament, "Men spoke from God as they were carried along by the Holy Spirit" (2 Peter 1:21).

The fruits of the Savior's passion are also taught to us in the Old Testament. According to the prophet Isaiah, "We all, like sheep, have gone astray, each of us has turned to his own way; and the LORD has laid on Him the iniquity of us all" (Isaiah 53:6).

May the Holy Spirit work mightily within us during this Lenten season!

You now sealed the Scriptures and the prophets. Man mocked, tortured, and crucified You. You were nailed upon the cross as a curse, placed into a grave. You bore my sin so I might have eternal life. I thank and praise You. Amen.

Adolph M. Bickel

Luke 6:36–42

Mercy, a Fruit of Faith

"Be merciful, just as your Father is merciful."
Luke 6:36

Many a person has asked: Do those who believe in Christ do good works so they can be justified, godly, and blessed before God? The answer, obviously, is "no."

Through faith, Christians already possess everything required to be saved. But we live among people who need the fruit of this faith. There is a time and place to show our neighbors, through good works, that we stand in faith. Just as it is a sure thing that a believer in Christ does not need good works for himself, so it is certain that the person who by faith has received everything from God will do for his neighbor out of Christian love as God has done for him.

A Christian does not need good works to have faith. However, the unending love he experiences fills his heart with such a love that he cannot help but do every good for his neighbor. St. John said, "This is how we know who the children of God are and who the children of the devil are: Anyone who does not do what is right is not a child of God; nor is anyone who does not love his brother" (1 John 3:10). And St. Paul confessed, "Though I am free and belong to no man, I make myself a slave to everyone, to win as many as possible" (1 Corinthians 9:19).

Dear Father, have mercy on us! Amen.

C. F. W. Walther

1 Peter 2:6–10

Confession of Sins

*When I kept silent, my bones wasted away
through my groaning all day long.* Psalm 32:3

After David's terrible sins of murder and adultery, nothing was more difficult for him than confessing his sin before God. His sins, of course, were already known to the all-knowing God.

Who can fool the all-knowing God? At times it appears to us as if God knows nothing about our sins. In His great long-suffering and patience, He knows the sins that continue and does not dole punishment upon the sinner. Things go well for the sinner here on earth; in outward appearance no man is able to confront Him. But the day is coming when God will bring to light what has been hidden in darkness and will expose the counsel of the heart.

Oh, let us then properly and contritely confess our sins to God! We need not be afraid before God. Upon our confession, God pronounces us free, takes us into His arms and says, "Your sins are forgiven" (Matthew 9:2). Whoever keeps silent about or denies his sins never achieves rest for his conscience or peace for his soul. Whoever confesses his sins receives mercy, for Christ, the Lamb of God, has mercy on us and gives us His peace.

God, I have sinned often and greatly. I am so sorry. For Christ's sake, forgive me my sins! Amen.

George A. Beiderwieden

There Is Salvation in None Other

"I have trodden the winepress alone." Isaiah 63:3

Thus says the Lord, and with this He testifies that He alone shall stomp on and crush the serpent's head, that He alone will accomplish the work of redemption, that He alone will win salvation for a captive and lost humankind.

It can be no other way. God is righteous. Because of this, He has to punish sin. The Lord God can crown with eternal life only someone who has done His entire will and is perfectly righteous. Consequently, anyone who wanted to rescue fallen humankind from the predicament of sin and bring salvation to the lost had to be a perfect, holy, and pure man in order to innocently suffer and die in our stead. However, He also had to be God in order to fulfill God's Law and never be guilty of violating it. He had to be God to be able to overcome sin, death, and hell. He had to be God to win for us perfect righteousness, innocence, and blessedness.

No angel, much less guilt-laden, sinful humankind, could accomplish this task. Only Jesus Christ, God and Man in one Person, could do this. And He did do it. He trod the winepress of God's wrath by Himself—for us.

Lord Jesus, my salvation comes solely through You. Amen.

C. F. W. Walther

Luke 18:9–14

God's Grace Covers Every Sin

*"But the tax collector stood at a distance. He
would not even look up to heaven, but beat
his breast and said, 'God, have mercy on me,
a sinner.' "* Luke 18:13

Many a person believes he will never be able to
find forgiveness, for his sins are so multitudinous and so
great. But this does not correspond to the power of God's
grace. We learn this from our text. Tax collectors were
known far and wide as thieves, liars, and deceivers. They
demanded more than what was due them. They were very
rich and passionately hated. The Pharisees were a sect that
claimed they could earn salvation by their works. They
despised many of their fellow humans, especially the "godless" tax collectors.

The tax collector in this passage acknowledged his
sins and humbly begged God for forgiveness and grace.
And Jesus said, " 'This man, rather than the other, went
home justified before God' " (Luke 18:14).

That's how it still is today. Whatever you have
done, no matter how great and damnable your sins may
appear, do not despair! God's grace is still far greater! Even
in the Old Testament He says, through His prophet Isaiah,
" 'Though your sins are like scarlet, they shall be as white
as snow; though they are red as crimson, they shall be like
wool' " (Isaiah 1:18).

Lord God, heavenly Father, be gracious to me for
the sake of Jesus! Amen.

Ernest H. Mueller

Prayer of Repentance

Have mercy on me, O God, according to Your
unfailing love; according to Your great compas-
sion blot out my transgressions. Psalm 51:1

The apostle Peter wrote, "He is patient with you,
not wanting anyone to perish, but everyone to come to
repentance" (2 Peter 3:9). Everyone needs to repent, for
everyone has sinned. The repentant tax collector prayed in
the temple, " 'God, have mercy on me, a sinner' " (Luke
18:13b). He was sorry that he had so grievously sinned
against God. That's why he begged for mercy. Many a person may think that his sins are so great or so manifold that
they cannot be forgiven. A person remembers the harm
caused in the past. Or one is too ashamed to confess his sin
before God.

However, would you like to prepare a joy for the
angels in heaven? Would you at the same time like to lift a
heavy burden from your conscience? Then hear what Jesus
says: " 'There is rejoicing in the presence of the angels of
God over one sinner who repents' " (Luke 15:10). We too
experience this joy as the Lord says to us, " 'Your sins are
forgiven' " (Matthew 9:2).

That's why we can confidently confess our sins to
the Lord, no matter how great or manifold they may be.

God, be gracious to me according to Your goodness, and expunge my sins according to Your great mercy!
Amen.

Albert T. Bostelmann

March 15   Psalm 51:1–13

The Prayer of a Repentant Child of God

Have mercy on me, O God, according to Your
unfailing love. Psalm 51:1

David pleaded with God after his own deep fall
into the depths of sin. Through murder and adultery, he
had grievously sinned against God and man. What should
he do? How could he ever again find rest for his soul? He
could not find it from his own self; nor through good
works. He wanted to keep the matter dead silent. Only
God could help, and indeed, only a gracious God. If God
had rewarded David according to what he deserved, he
would have been lost. Only through His great mercy could
God blot out David's sin.

We are sinful by nature and daily offend our God
by that which we do or do not do. As a result, we rightly
deserve to be eternally cast aside by God. May we constantly learn from David to humble ourselves before God
and call upon Him for grace and mercy. For Christ's sake,
He is a gracious God who forgives iniquity, transgression,
and sin. That's why we make confession in every worship
service; that's why we pray the fifth petition of the Lord's
Prayer every day; that's why we say, "Christ, thou Lamb of
God, have mercy on us!"

Have mercy, Lord—my compassionate One—on
me! Amen.

Paul F. Koenig

82

March 16   Matthew 26:47–56

The Price of Our Redemption

*"For even the Son of Man did not come to be
served, but to serve, and to give His life as
a ransom for many."* Mark 10:45

Can a person pay for eternal life with monthly installments? That's how we might formulate the question today. From the time of early Christendom, people have asked, "What can I do so I can inherit eternal life?" Although an individual may formulate the words differently, the question remains the same.

When we approach this question from the perspective of the Word of God and answer it with a categorical "no," we must never draw the deceptive conclusion to which many people fall victim—that since it can be bestowed upon one by God without our help, eternal life is cheap.

The Lenten season once more places before our eyes just how much it cost Jesus to save us. Eternal life for mortal sinners is certainly not a casual matter. It is so precious that it cost the Son of God His life. Perishable money and possessions would never have been enough to purchase salvation. That's why we confess: What priceless riches we possess through Christ! He is the ransom price for our redemption. God paid that price.

Lord Jesus, let me never forget how much it cost You so I am redeemed! Amen.

Horst Hoyer

March 17   Ephesians 2:11–18

Expensively Purchased

"I, even I, am He who blots out your transgres-
sions, for My own sake." Isaiah 43:25

An adjutant of the Russian Czar Nicholas had got-
ten into deep debt because of gambling. One evening he
was sitting before a table upon which the IOUs were lying.
He added them on a slip of paper. In despair, he stared at
the huge sum and wrote under it, "Who is able to pay this?"
With suicidal thoughts, he grabbed his pistol, laid his head
on the table, and meditated. With that he fell asleep.
When he awoke, his eyes fell upon the slip of paper.
Beneath his question, in the well-known handwriting of
the Czar, was the word "Nicholas," who during the night
had entered the officer's chamber. In the morning an emis-
sary brought the money.

In God's ledger, we were left owing a huge, unpaid
debt. During the Lenten season, we see how our debt of
sin is paid for us out of love. We see His hands stretched
out and pierced upon the cross. We also see our name
inscribed on those hands. In faith let us pray, "Hand, which
never lets go, hold me firmly!"

Lord Jesus—here, take both my hands, I can do
nothing by my own power. You know the way, You know
the goal; Lord, lead me through this pilgrimage! Amen.

N. P. Uhlig

March 18   Deuteronomy 5:28:1–10

The Fullness of His Blessing

For surely, O LORD, You bless the righteous; You
surround them with Your favor as with a shield.
Psalm 5:12

"God's little fountain is filled with water. Amen."
This little table prayer for children was indeed prayed by
many of our youth. It briefly and beautifully summarizes
God's activity. The spiritual and bodily blessings God
pours out upon us are gloriously laid before our eyes in
Martin Luther's explanation of the Apostles' Creed (*Luther's
Small Catechism*).

Paul Gerhardt (revered hymn writer who lived
from 1609 to 1678) endured much tribulation and perse-
cution in his lifetime. One would think his hymn compo-
sitions would be mostly about the trials of the cross.
However, it was not difficult for Gerhardt to sing about
God's grace and goodness. Whoever discovers his own
unworthiness constantly exalts the great blessings of God.

O Lord, let Your blessings and love Constantly be
before mine eyes! They strengthen me to promote the
good, To dedicate all my life to You; They comfort me in
times of pain, They comfort me in times of good fortune,
And they conquer within my heart The fear of my eyelids'
final closing! Amen. (P. Gerhardt)

N. P. Uhlig

Isaiah 43:22–28

Our Redeemer

"I have swept away your offenses like a cloud,
your sins like the morning mist. Return to Me, for
I have redeemed you." Isaiah 44:22

The Lord Himself is speaking to us here. He says that He is our Redeemer. As we to look to the sky, we sometimes see very dark and threatening clouds. Then the wind blows, and soon the clouds disappear. That's how the Lord tells us He makes our sins disappear. Sometimes in the morning we cannot see very far because of thick fog. As the sun ascends, the fog disappears. For the sake of Christ, the grace of God shines upon our sins and they also disappear. That's how our gracious God shows Himself to be our Redeemer.

We sinners are totally dependent upon the grace of God. Without it, we find ourselves in a hopeless situation. Without His grace, we are lost. It is a glorious comfort to us that, through His suffering and death, Jesus is our Redeemer. We cannot help but rejoice over Him! We cannot help but praise Him for His redemptive work, that He secures heaven for us!

Lord Jesus, we thank You from the bottom of our hearts for Your work of redemption. Show us how we may serve You! Amen!

Gerhard C. Michael

This Is the Lamb of God

"Look, the Lamb of God, who takes away the sin of the world!" John 1:29

During the Lenten season, we ponder the substitutionary suffering and death of the Savior of the world. Because of our sin, we are the cause of His death on the cross. Such is the price tag for our eternal rescue.

Through the death of His only Son, the Father in heaven shows His inexpressible love toward us poor, miserable sinners. Every day God shows His Creator-love toward us through all His gifts for our bodily needs. However, only through the death of His Son on the cross does He show His great Father-love to us and to all humankind. Through the cross, we catch a glimpse of the horrible price for sin. We also learn about the great worth of an immortal human soul.

O how great is God's love! Here is the Lamb of God, innocently slaughtered upon the tree of the cross. This is the Lamb who bears the guilt of the world and its children. This Lamb takes on "shame, disgrace and mockery, anguish, wounds, stripes, cross and death ... and says: I will gladly suffer this" (from "Ein Lammlein geht" by Paul Gerhardt). Again, " 'You were slain, and with Your blood You purchased men for God' " (Revelation 5:9). How shall we respond?

O Lamb of God, bearer of the sins of the entire world, have mercy on us and give us Your peace! Amen.

Paul M. Freiburger

Psalm 102:1–13

Anxiety and Temptation

Out of the depths I cry to You, O LORD.
Psalm 130:1

In the Garden of Gethsemane, the Savior called
upon His disciples to watch and pray so they would not
fall into anxious doubt and temptation.

A child of God can easily fall into temptation. One
becomes burdened with frightful thoughts over the multi-
tude and immensity of one's sins. Or a particular sin nags
us, despite the fact that we know all our sins have been forgiven. We are troubled with anxious thoughts, which often
do not let us sleep. Hence we say with David, "My tears
have been my food day and night, while men say to me all
day long, 'Where is your God?'" (Psalm 42:3). The
thoughts of our conscience make us restless.

However, we also experience with Isaiah that
temptation teaches us to take note of the Word (Isaiah
2:3b, 48:17). Dismay over sin and temptation drives us
into the Scriptures where we find comfort. David found
such comfort: "Why are you downcast, O my soul? Why
so disturbed within me? Put your hope in God, for I will
yet praise Him, my Savior and my God" (Psalm 42:11). He
has redeemed Israel, and us as well, from all sin. Such
assurance in the power of God's love through Christ
enables us to overcome temptation.

Lord, comfort me amidst temptation with the reassurance that all my sins have been forgiven! Amen.

                                              Albert T. Bostelmann

March 22   Luke 15:17–24

God's Mercy

Have mercy on me, O God, according to Your unfailing love; according to Your great compassion blot out my transgressions. Psalm 51:1

This prayer is a song of praise about God's great mercy. With this prayer, the psalmist exalts mercy as being undeserved. The Lord finds and sees nothing in us sinners that could move Him to help us. He sees and finds only that which would incite His wrath and punishment. In His undeserved mercy, however, God's heart aches because we are destined to perish under His wrath. But God's mercy is also a saving mercy. Through Christ, God has atoned for our sins. Sin and punishment have been assuaged. Our debt has been completely paid.

Indeed, God's mercy is rich. All sins, the big and severe sins, are atoned for by Christ. His blood washes away all sin so we are completely cleansed. We stand holy and righteous before our heavenly Father. All this made David eager to approach Him with the prayer, "Have mercy on me, O God." We can also rely on God for this. We can comfort ourselves and be totally certain about this.

Amidst our soul's pain, show us Your split-open heart of love; and, when we see our misery, do not let us stand still until everyone may say: God be praised, Jesus also receives me! Amen.

George A. Beiderwieden

Psalm 73:21–28

The Heart Longs for Grace

All my longings lie open before You, O LORD;
my sighing is not hidden from You. Psalm 38:9

Here David exquisitely showed what a repentant sinner can do to be freed from the anxiety of his heart and how and where he may seek help. This is actually a main factor of repentance. The repentant sinner turns to God and trusts Him for mercy. At the same time, he said, in essence, "You, my God, see how my heart longs for Your grace, how it longs for, implores, and sighs. Alas, be gracious to me; forgive me all my guilt. Let grace replace judgment! You indeed do not desire the death of the sinner; You desire that all men be helped. O Lord Jesus, You have atoned also for me upon the cross; You have also reconciled me with God."

The psalmist was quite sure about this. He prayed, "I wait for You, O LORD; You will answer, O LORD my God" (Psalm 38:15). It is also quite encouraging how David continued to pray, "O LORD, do not forsake me; be not far from me, O my God. Come quickly to help me, O LORD my Savior" (Psalm 38:21–22). This can be our prayer also so we may have a peaceful conscience and a comforted heart in midst of the agony of the misery of our sin. "I am in God's grace through Christ's blood and death."

God, do not be angry and do not enter into judgment, for Your Son, Jesus Christ, has reconciled me to You! Amen.

George A. Beiderwieden

March 24   Hebrews 7:23–28

Priests and Sacrifice

*God was reconciling the world to Himself in
Christ, not counting men's sins against them.*
2 Corinthians 5:19

In His state of humility, Christ, whom the Old and
New Testaments expressly called a "Priest," reconciled all
of humanity to God. In fact, the Bible not only announces
this reconciliation, above all else it describes the manner
and way of the reconciliation, or the means through which
this reconciliation is accomplished. Christ reconciled
humankind to God by offering Himself to God as the
atoning sacrifice.

In the New Testament, Christ is simultaneously
Priest and Sacrifice. According to Scripture, His self-sacri-
fice embraces a dual action: He gave Himself up for us
with His holy life and with His suffering and death.

In this perfect priestly work by Christ on earth,
humankind is reconciled to God once and for all. That is
to say, the grace of God is directed toward humankind, for
"He entered the Most Holy Place once for all by His own
blood, having obtained eternal redemption" (Hebrews
9:12). That's what Scripture teaches about the reconciliation of the world through Christ.

Lord Jesus, out of great love for us, You offered
Yourself up for us and have reconciled us to God. Amen.

                                              Franz Pieper

March 25   Isaiah 1:1–20

White as Snow

"Come now, let us reason together," says the
LORD. "Though your sins are like scarlet, they
shall be as white as snow; though they are red as
crimson, they shall be like wool." Isaiah 1:18

In this Bible verse, God speaks about the color of sin. According to this verse, the color of guilt is red. A murderer is publicly guilty if red blood is found on his hands. Although we may have never taken anyone's life, we still are guilty. Jesus says, " 'You have heard that it was said to the people long ago, 'Do not murder, and anyone who murders will be subject to judgment.' But I tell you that anyone who is angry with his brother will be subject to judgment' " (Matthew 5:21–22a). We all stand exposed with blood on our hands. We are all guilty.

In this verse, God also speaks about the color of purity. Our sin shall not stay blood red, instead it shall be snow-white. How is such a miracle possible? The red must be removed. Jesus took our guilt upon Himself. That which was filthy in us is "chalked up" to Him. What do we look like to God now? On account of the forgiveness Jesus has won for us, we now are white as snow.

Heavenly Father, whenever we see snow, remind us of the purity which You have bestowed upon us. Amen.

Curtis P. Giese

March 26   Psalm 13

The Hidden Failures

*Who can discern his errors? Forgive my hidden
faults.* Psalm 19:12

Hidden faults are unknown to the afflicted person;
one can call them sins of weakness. Take curse words, for
example. With many people, abusing the name of God
appears to be the norm. Without a thought, such a person
calls down God's wrath upon himself. Consider gossip.
How many people slander someone because they want to
tell something new? Some give no thought to the fact that
the reputation of the neighbor is damaged by such talk. In
addition, if a person finds himself in an embarrassing situation and stands in danger of suffering shame through the
revelation of a secret sin, that person may attempt to cover
it by lying.

It is quite possible to sin without realizing it. And,
as the psalmist pleads for forgiveness of sins that are
unknown, so we too are in need of such forgiveness. Christ
died for our hidden failures as well.

Lord, protect me from the sins I commit without
thinking. Wash me of my unknown sins! Amen.

Albert T. Bostelmann

Matthew 26:36–75

Our Pleas and Petitions

*And pray in the Spirit on all occasions with all
kinds of prayers and requests.* Ephesians 6:18

Jesus was "tempted in every way, just as we are—
yet was without sin" (Hebrews 4:15b). Because of this, we
can know with certainty that Jesus sympathizes with our
weaknesses and helps those who are tempted. For He, of
course, is the Son of God who ascended into heaven and
rules all things.

With all our weaknesses, amidst all our difficulties
and dangers, we ought to avail ourselves of Christ's love
and compassion. With heartfelt trust and without ceasing,
we can pour out our hearts to Christ and cry out to Him
for help in all of life's circumstances. We have been reconciled to the Father. He gladly hears us for the sake of His
Son. Let us seek Him. Through the Gospel, God bestows
on us the Holy Spirit and the assurance that we are His
children. We commend our way to our Father, and are
totally dependent upon Him.

Undergirded with God's promises, we continue in
prayer and pleading. Despite tears, we praise God now and
will praise Him in eternity with perfect joy along with all
the saints.

Lord Jesus, teach us to watch and pray! Amen.

A. R. Kretzmann

March 28   Luke 23:32–43

A Miraculous Exchange

*God made Him who had no sin to be sin for us, so
that in Him we might become the righteousness of
God.* 2 Corinthians 5:21

"Him" and "us," "righteousness" and "sin"—these
two pairs of words in this text catch our attention.
Actually, we are almost afraid to rely on what we see here.
Him and us, righteousness and sin do not simply stand
next to one another. Instead, they create an impression of
an amalgamation of the one into the other, even a hig-
gledy-piggledy jumbling together.

Sin and righteousness are personified and then
become interchanged. If we ask, "Who is sin and who is
righteousness?" the obvious answer is, "We are sin; Jesus is
Righteousness." And that's essentially how it is. Jesus never
ever instigated a single sin. We, on the other hand, were
conceived in sin and born corrupt through and through.
Yet the apostles say that God made Him—the sinless
Christ—to be sin. However, to this statement also belong
the eternally important words "for us." Therefore, through
Christ we, the guilt-laden people, have become righteous
before God.

That's how God reconciled us to Himself. So now
the urgent call goes out to us, "be reconciled to God!"

God, thank You for Your grace in Christ. Amen.

Herbert J. A. Bouman

Sonship instead of Servitude

God sent His Son ... to redeem those under law,
that we might receive the full rights of sons.
Galatians 4:4–5

God is rich beyond all measure, and His grace is unspeakably great. Our human reason is too limited to grasp this and our language is too weak to properly and fully express His riches. With ever-new portrayals, the prophets and apostles sought to illustrate God's love to us and explain to us how priceless our redemption actually is.

In the verse for today, the apostle Paul presented a comparison between two of life's situations: servitude and sonship. Jesus, from eternity, is the one and only unique Son of God, like no one else can ever be. We humans are under the Law of God and its demands and threats, and because we are sinners, we are subject to its punishment. We are servants. Like the prodigal son, we have forfeited all rights to sonship.

Then came the wonderful exchange. God sent His Son, the Lord of the Law, and placed Him under the Law. His Son became a servant to make us sons of God. For the sake of Christ, God accepts us with the status of children. God now is our Father!

Lord God, we heartily thank You that You, for the sake of Jesus, made us sinners into Your children. Amen.

Herbert J. A. Bouman

Matthew 26:30–35

A Loving Warning

*"This very night you will all fall away on
account of Me."* Matthew 26:31

" 'I will strike the Shepherd, and the sheep of the
flock will be scattered,' " says Jesus (Matthew 26:31). These
were serious words Christ spoke to His disciples. He is, of
course, the Shepherd who said, "I am the Good Shepherd.
The Good Shepherd lays down His life for the sheep"
(John 10:11). Here He contrasts Himself as the Good
Shepherd with the religious rulers and leaders of the Jews
whose sheep are marked for slaughter (Isaiah 11:4–17).

The 11 disciples who went with Christ to the Mt. of
Olives belonged to this scattered flock. Jesus saw beforehand
that they would shamelessly forsake Him and flee from Him.
But because He loved them, He wanted to warn them and
strengthen them in advance. That's why He also presented to
them the comforting promise of His resurrection.

That's how the Lord deals with His disciples today.
He tells us beforehand that we are to take up the cross so
we, through Christ's tribulation, might enter into the kingdom of God. He does not fail to provide us comfort. We
may confidently think about the heavenly Jerusalem and
about the blessed perfect saints who have come out of great
tribulation and are now cloaked in white garments. Thus,
He lovingly helps us and teaches us to confidently say, "I
consider that our present sufferings are not worth comparing with the glory that will be revealed in us" (Romans 8:18).

Lord, keep us close to You as our Good Shepherd!
Amen.

Paul F. Koenig

Luke 17:11–19

Thankfulness

I praise You, Father, Lord of heaven and the earth.
Matthew 11:25

Jesus' entire earthly ministry was, in one sense, permeated with thankfulness. On the night Jesus was betrayed, "Jesus ... gave thanks" (Matthew 26:26) and instituted the holy Lord's Supper. Before He went to Gethsemane, "they had sung a hymn" (verse 30). Although He carried the burden of suffering, we hear thankfulness and joy amidst His human emotions.

Our life can also be a continuous song of praise. But often we complain that there is so much tribulation and pain, a genuine vale of tears. Wouldn't it be better to follow after the Savior? Didn't He call us to do so? "Follow Me"—with thankfulness! For us there are no small manifestations of grace, only huge ones—and all undeserved. While in this world there are tears, ruination, and continual laments of death, the everlasting mountains of grace, love, and mercy are here as well. Therefore let us always give "thanks to God the Father for everything, in the name of our Lord Jesus Christ" (Ephesians 5:20).

Father, Son, and Holy Spirit, we give You heartfelt thanks for Your mercy and goodness. Amen.

Walter G. Boss

Lost

"The Son of Man came to seek and to save what was lost." Luke 19:10

Jesus was on a journey to Jerusalem, where evil hands would crucify Him. His route led Him through Jericho, on the Jordan. Here there was a man named Zacchaeus, who had climbed a tree to better see Jesus as He walked by. Zacchaeus was a publican, who in his office as tax collector often cheated others and became rich at their expense. He was despised and hated.

When Jesus saw Zacchaeus, He asked that he crawl down from the tree so Jesus could visit him in his home. When people saw this, they all complained that Jesus stayed with a sinner (Luke 19:7).

Sin, that terrible misery which burdens all mankind, manifests itself in various ways. Selfishness, personal gain, dishonor, betrayal, greed, hatred, and complaining—some of the manifestations of sin—are as common today as they were in Zacchaeus's time. Because of sin, all people are lost. But this story assures us that the Son of Man has come to seek and to save what has been lost.

Lord Jesus, keep me mindful that You have also saved me. Amen.

Herbert J. A. Boumann

John 1:5–10

The Miracle of the Cross

*"Though your sins are like scarlet, they shall be
as white as snow; though they are red as crimson,
they shall be like wool."* Isaiah 1:18

An insightful old man held up a little book that
contained a description of his entire life. Without a single
word, the first page was completely black. That was his
sin. The second page was bright red. That was Jesus. The
third page was snow-white. That was he, washed completely clean of all his sins through the blood of Christ.

By inspiration of the Holy Spirit, Isaiah prophesied, "Though your sins are like scarlet, they shall be as
white as snow." This is accomplished through the miraculous power of the cross.

That which human science, wisdom, gold, silver,
money, and all other earthly means could not accomplish
was fulfilled through the suffering and death of our Savior.
The sin of the world has been set aside through the divine,
miraculous power of the crucified Son of God. "The blood
of Jesus, His Son, purifies us from all sin" (1 John 1:7). He
washed away our transgressions so we are snow-white, like
clean wool. Upon this His blood, shed for us, we place our
hope.

Lord Jesus, You who atoned for our sins, may Your
pangs of death never be lost on us!

Paul M. Freiburger

April 3   Isaiah 42:1–9

God Cares for Us

We all, like sheep, have gone astray, ... and the
LORD has laid on Him the iniquity of us all.
Isaiah 53:6

The Lord God laid all our sin—yours, mine, the sins of the entire world—on Jesus. What a burden!

Under this burden the Innocent One was beaten, tormented, and tortured to death. We are unable to fully envision this. We can't comprehend it. How could it come to this, to murder the Innocent One? The Lord—God Himself—cast all our sin upon Him. God the Father decided it, and God the Son personally accepted this decision and took all the consequences upon Himself. Through the Gospel of Christ, God allowed this to be made known to us. His good Spirit assures us: This is the Truth!

God provided this plan of salvation for us before the beginning of the world. Jesus carried out the plan. St. Paul said, "It is written: 'No eye has seen, no ear has heard, no mind has conceived what God has prepared for those who love Him'—but God has revealed it to us by His Spirit" (1 Corinthians 2:9–10). How gloriously He has taken care of us!

O dear Jesus, I myself have perpetrated the crime for which Your hands and feet were pierced through. Thank You for the depth of Your sacrifice. Amen.

Emilio Schmidt

Revelation 21:22–27

With Jesus in Paradise

"I tell you the truth, today you will be with Me
in paradise." Luke 23:43

What would it be like to hear Jesus say, "today you
will be with Me in paradise"? It would be reason to rejoice
beyond all measure! That's how it was with the thief on the
cross. He was in severe pain and about to die, but we can
imagine that he had never felt a greater joy. What a glorious promise our dear Savior made to him! This despised
man, a convicted criminal, would soon be with Jesus in
heaven's glory.

This precious promise is also ours as we place our
hope for forgiveness in Jesus. We, too, will be in paradise
with Jesus one day. And as we keep this in mind, we can
rejoice—though we suffer and endure tribulation now as
did the thief on the cross.

During this holy Lenten season, let us ponder the
testimony of the perfect love of Jesus, our Savior. May our
desire to live with Christ for eternity ever increase!

Dear Lord Jesus, amidst the joys and tribulations of
this life, grant us the assurance that we will be with You in
paradise! Amen.

Adolph M. Bickel

April 5   Luke 19:41–48

What Christ's Tears Say to Us

As He approached Jerusalem and saw the city,
He wept over it. Luke 19:41

Does God really want eternal life for every sinner?
O how blessed we are that we can answer with a confident
"Yes." The prophet Ezekiel recorded the solemn, divine
declaration to the entire world, "'As surely as I live,
declares the Sovereign LORD, I take no pleasure in the
death of the wicked, but rather that they turn from their
ways and live'" (Ezekiel 33:11). Here God solemnly swears
by Himself that He does not wish to be the living God if
it means He would take pleasure in the death of even one
godless person.

We not only have God's own declaration that He
does not desire the death of any sinner, we also have the
tears of Christ. His tears over the misfortune of the sinners—those who persecuted and murdered Him—are a
testimony to God's compassion and mercy for even the
deeply fallen. Every human being can clearly read in the
tears of the Son of God the words that God truly does not
desire the death of any sinner! How could the Savior weep
over a death if He were pleased about it?

Lord God, You desire that all mankind be saved and
come to the knowledge of the Truth. Amen.

C. F. W. Walther

103

April 6   Mark 2:1–12

The Son of Man

"The Son of Man is going to be betrayed into the hands of men. They will kill Him." Mark 9:31

The slaughter of an animal could never fully serve as a complete sin-offering that could avail before God, for God Himself says that it is impossible to take away sin through the blood of oxen and goats (Isaiah 1:11b). Nor could the sacrifice of a friend or an only son atone for sin. God explains: "No man can redeem the life of another or give to God a ransom for him—the ransom for a life is costly, no payment is ever enough—that he should live on forever and not see decay" (Psalm 49:7–9). It is for this reason God gave up His only Son.

However, in order to completely take on the guilt of all mankind, the Son of God also had to humble Himself to become man. Jesus Christ, the God-Man, did so. In the Gospel of Mark, Jesus is called the "Son of Man" 14 times. That is, He is not just the Son of Man for one person, but also the substitute for all of humanity. Thus He states in our text for today that He will suffer and die for all of the children of Adam. He laid down His divine human life as a sacrifice for the guilt of our sin so we might have eternal life.

Spirit of Life, keep us in the faith so we may always be comforted by the death of the Son of Man in our stead. To Him be the glory! Amen.

Walter H. Koenig

Forsaken by God

My God, my God, why have You forsaken me?
Psalm 22:1

This was the anxious cry of our Savior on the cross. The words themselves are an indication of the depth of the anxiety in His soul.

People may sometimes think God has completely forsaken them. A prisoner of war in a cramped, unsanitary jail, separated from his loved ones, could easily conclude that God has forgotten him. A deeply fallen sinner, who through gluttonous eating and heavy drinking or unchaste living, has destroyed body and soul, might say with Cain, " 'my punishment is more than I can bear' " (Genesis 4:13), and think he has been forsaken by God.

But God forgets only those damned eternally in hell. As God's own, we find comfort in these words: "Where sin increased, grace increased all the more" (Romans 5:20). Jesus Christ endured being forsaken by God so we might never be forsaken by Him. And although at times it may seem to us that He has, for a tiny "wink-of-an-eye" moment forsaken us, He continuously gathers us to Himself through His body and blood with great compassion and mercy.

Lord, cast me not away from Your presence and take not away Your Holy Spirit from me. Amen.

Albert T. Bostelmann

April 8   Hebrews 4:14–5:10

Christ Our High Priest

You are a priest forever. Psalm 110:4

In the Old Testament there were many high priests and thousands upon thousands of priests. They served as mediators between God and the people and brought forward sacrifices to atone for the sin of the people. They themselves, however, were also sinful and first had to offer a sacrifice for their own sins.

Christ on the other hand is "holy, blameless, pure, set apart from sinners, exalted above the heavens" (Hebrews 7:26). The priests of the old covenant merely foreshadowed Christ. Their sacrifices pointed to the Lamb of God who would bear the sin of the world. On the great day of atonement for the world—Good Friday—Christ offered Himself as the fully atoning sacrifice. He entered the holy place of heaven to reconcile us to God.

Where would we sinful humans—who have earned wrath and damnation—be if Christ the High Priest had not lovingly accepted us and atoned for our sin? Where would we be if He hadn't interceded for us at the right hand of God? We can thank Christ Jesus that through Him we are redeemed children of God who cling in faith to Him here and will serve Him there eternally.

Lord Jesus, since You have become our reconciliation and call us Friend, the evil enemy cannot harm us. We thank You. Amen.

Paul F. Koenig

Psalm 93

Christ Our King

The LORD reigns. Psalm 97:1

Jesus Christ rules as King. Everything is subject to Him. Of Him it can be said: There shall be a King who will rule well (Psalm 103:19). In Hebrews 1:8, we read, "righteousness will be the scepter of Your kingdom." Jesus told Pilate He was indeed king. But Christ's kingdom is not of this world; it is a kingdom of power, grace, and glory. It is a kingdom in which the King Himself testifies to the truth and builds His kingdom through the preaching of the Gospel. He founded His kingdom by His suffering and death. The purpose for His work of redemption was so I may be His own, and may live and serve Him in His kingdom. Those who accept this grace by faith are citizens of His kingdom.

In His deepest suffering, the inscription on His cross read "Jesus of Nazareth, the King of the Jews." And now, after ascending into heaven, Christ sits at the right hand of God, ruling the world. On Judgment Day we shall see Him upon the throne of His glory.

We honor Christ as our great King.

Blessed is each and every heart that, by faith, accepts this King. May all come to the knowledge of this truth. Amen.

Paul F. Koenig

Redemption through His Blood

*In Him we have redemption through His blood,
the forgiveness of sins, in accordance with the
riches of God's grace.* Ephesians 1:7

Our greatest blessing is that through Christ we receive God's grace. In comparison, all our earthly treasures are worthless and perishable. In contrast, the spiritual and heavenly blessings and treasures we possess as a result of our redemption through Jesus Christ are imperishable. These are true riches, indestructible for all eternity.

Because we have a Redeemer from all sin, we owe a debt of gratitude to God for His love. God's love for us is so huge He gave up His one and only Son. Such love is so strong and mighty that it can promote the deepest sense of security and protection. St. Paul wrote of this security when he assured the Christians at Rome that nothing can separate us from the love of God which is in Christ Jesus, our Lord. And Martin Luther intoned the sense of this protection with the hymn "A Mighty Fortress Is Our God." Consider these lines: "And take they our life, Goods, fame, child, and wife, Though these all be gone, Our vict'ry has been won; the Kingdom ours remaineth."

Our redemption through Christ's blood is the most expensive and precious jewel, for where there is forgiveness of sin, there is life and salvation.

Thank You, heavenly Father, for the gift of redemption through Christ. Amen.

Herbert D. Poellot

1 Peter 1:18–18

Vicarious Atonement

For you know that it was not with perishable
things such as silver or gold that you were
redeemed ... but with the precious blood of
Christ, a Lamb without blemish or defect.
1 Peter 1:18–19

An ecclesiastical expression for Christ's works on our behalf in the state of humiliation is "vicarious atonement." This means that Christ, as our stand-in or substitute, met God's demands in our stead and completely satisfied the demands of God's justice. He satisfied God's wrath and won redemption for all.

Although the expression "vicarious atonement" is not found in the Bible, the message it conveys is simply the scriptural teaching of redemption through Christ. Like other ecclesiastical expressions not found in Scripture, it expresses a scriptural truth.

Christ most certainly was our substitute, our stand-in. "God made Him who had no sin to be sin for us, so that in Him we might become the righteousness of God" (2 Corinthians 5:21). "He is the atoning sacrifice for our sins" (1 John 2:2). Christ's words, "It is finished" (John 19:30), right before His death on the cross testify that He had completed our rescue and full redemption was now ours. Christ did for us what we could not do for ourselves.

Lord Jesus, Lamb of God, we thank You that You perfectly bore our sin on the cross. Forgive us and lead us into all eternity. Amen.

Franz Pieper

April 12   Isaiah 53:1

The <u>Vicarious</u> Lamb

*We all, like sheep, have gone astray, ... and the
LORD has laid on Him the iniquity of us all.*
Isaiah 53:6

Consider these words from the Old Testament that
led to an annual ceremony: "[Aaron] is to lay both hands
on the head of the live goat and confess over it all the
wickedness and rebellion of the Israelites—all their sins—
and put them on the goat's head. He shall send the goat
away into the desert in the care of a man appointed for the
task" (Leviticus 16:21). By God's command and through
this ceremony, the sins of the people were laid upon the
animal and carried away.

A similar yet more profound act was performed by
the vicarious Lamb of God: the sins of errant mankind
were cast upon Him. The prophet Isaiah could well proclaim, "Surely He took up our infirmities and carried our
sorrows, yet we considered Him stricken by God, smitten
by Him, and afflicted. But He was pierced for our transgressions, He was crushed for our iniquities; the punishment that brought us peace was upon Him, and by His
wounds we are healed. We all, like sheep, have gone astray,
each of us has turned to his own way; and the LORD has
laid on Him the iniquity of us all" (Isaiah 53:4–6). Christ,
the Lamb of God, became the fulfillment of Isaiah's
prophecy—the scapegoat for our sin.

O sweet Lamb, what shall I render to You in
response to the great treasure You have given me? Amen.

William Boehm

April 13   John 19:16–18

The Sacrificial Lamb

*He was oppressed and afflicted, yet He did not
open His mouth; He was led like a lamb to the
slaughter.* Isaiah 53:7

To fully atone for our sin, Christ had to be slaughtered upon the cross. It wasn't sufficient that He be driven
into the wilderness like a scapegoat. He had to be slaughtered as the Lamb of God, for "without the shedding of
blood there is no forgiveness" (Hebrews 9:22). Therefore,
Jesus died on the cross for us. In this we come face-to-face
with the horror of sin, especially since the Sin-Atoner had
to pay the price of our sin through His death. The wages
of sin can only be death. Any soul that sins has to die.

Through His sacrifice upon the cross, Christ
redeemed us from this curse of death. "Christ redeemed us
from the curse of the law by becoming a curse for us, for it
is written: 'Cursed is everyone who is hung on a tree' "
(Galatians 3:13).

When we consider the sacrifice of the Lamb of
God, we confess with the hymn-writer Paul Gerhardt, "A
Lamb goes uncomplaining forth, The guilt of all men bearing; And laden with the sins of earth, …Bears shame, and
stripes and wounds and death, Anguish and mockery, and
saith, 'Willing all this I suffer.' " In these words we see the
full impact of His sacrifice for us.

Dear Lord, our sacrificial Lamb, You were slaughtered for us. Have mercy upon us and grant us Your peace!
Amen.

William Boehm

Hebrews 7:22–27

The Selected Offering for Sin

*Aaron shall bring the goat whose lot falls to the
LORD and sacrifice it for a sin offering.*
Leviticus 16:9

God designated one day of the year—the tenth day
of the seventh month—for His Old Testament, pre-
Christian people as a great Sabbath in which He communi-
cated what He would do to grant them respite from their
sins. It was called the Day of Atonement, and it was the day
the repentant Israelites would be assured of forgiveness.

On the Day of Atonement, the people were to do
nothing. The high priest, as God's substitute, portrayed
God's judgment. Lots were be cast over two goats, and the
animal representing God was separated from the animal
representing the people. The goat representing God was
slaughtered and its blood was sprinkled in the Holy of
Holies, symbolizing atonement. The goat representing the
sins of the people was set free, symbolizing the removal of
sin and its guilt (see Leviticus 16).

As the Lamb of God, Jesus Christ carried all our
sins and was sacrificed upon the cross because of them. His
blood became the eternal atonement. Through Him we are
free. He is our respite. In the wilderness of this world, we
can now joyfully celebrate God's Sabbath, which extends
into all eternity.

Thanks be to You, Son of God, that You became
sin's sacrifice for us. Amen.

Walter H. Koenig

Palm Sunday   Isaiah 62:10–12

The King of Grace

This took place to fulfill what was spoken through the prophet. Matthew 21:4

The fulfillment of prophecy is a favorite theme of the evangelist Matthew. He used it so frequently, his book is often called "the Gospel of fulfillment." Matthew especially draws upon prophecy and fulfillment in his account of the passion history. Also, this evangelist emphasizes the kingship and kingly rule of Jesus Christ.

Christ's important and consequential journey to Jerusalem came to an end. It was the Sunday before the Passover Feast. On Friday He would die on the cross. At the beginning of this significant week, Jesus fulfilled the prophecies of Isaiah and Zechariah through His kingly entrance into Jerusalem.

But what sort of king was this? There was no pomp, no royal entourage, no crown. Instead, it is written, " 'See, your King comes to you, gentle' " (Matthew 21:5). Or in the words of Zechariah: a righteous one and a Helper, gentle and riding upon a donkey (Zechariah 9:9).

A King who entered Jerusalem on a lowly donkey, yet a wondrous King was He! He came to suffer and die upon a cross, crowned with thorns. A King as no other— our King!

Lord Jesus, help me to confess You and, with all of Christendom, call You my King, now and forever! Amen.

Herbert J. A. Bouman

April 15   2 Timothy 1:8–14

Freed from the Consequences of Sin

*[He came to] free those who all their lives were
held in slavery by their fear of death.*
Hebrews 2:15

If we have been reconciled to God through the sacrifice of Christ—if our guilt of sin has been expunged before God—then we have also been rescued from all the horrible consequences of the guilt of sin: death, the power of the devil, the rule of sin.

This cause and effect, as carried out through Christ's atonement, is the theme of all Scripture: Christ as Savior destroyed the power of death, for "it has now been revealed through the appearing of our Savior, Christ Jesus, who has destroyed death and has brought life and immortality to light through the Gospel" (2 Timothy 1:10). The devil's power over mankind was completely destroyed (Hebrews 2:14). And Christ's atoning sacrifice redeemed mankind from the rule of sin for all time (Titus 2:14).

As revealed to us through Scripture, we know with all certainty that through Christ we are redeemed from every evil. Thus our cleansing from the guilt of sin through Christ's sacrifice will always be regarded with the utmost importance. Such is the message of Lent.

Thanks be to You, Lord Jesus, that You have redeemed us from every sin, from death, and from the power of the devil. Amen.

Franz Pieper

April 16   Isaiah 53:1–12

Christ's Suffering for Us

Surely He took up our infirmities and carried our sorrows. Isaiah 53:4

Here we enter into the most holy of holies of the Christian faith. Here the suffering of Christ reaches its peak. Out of respect, we quietly stand at the foot of the cross and silently behold the "Sin-Bearer" who gave up His life into death for us.

Even after all this time, there is still nothing the believer would rather behold than this picture of the suffering Redeemer. For in this picture is the substance of his hope and the kernel of his comfort. Within this picture is the sweetest and most powerful Gospel—the Good News of God's grace. For the suffering of Christ was on our behalf. Isaiah 53 brings this so clearly to light: Jesus carried our sickness; He was wounded because of our transgressions; He took our punishment so we might have peace. He—for us; He—in our stead. The punishment, which rightly should have struck us, fell upon Him. The guilt, which had suppressed us, was laid upon Him. Christ experienced the wrath, and we are redeemed by grace.

O precious treasure! O glorious news, this clear Word about the substitionary suffering of Jesus! Here rests our salvation, peace, life, and blessedness.

O Lamb of God, You bear the sin of the world. Amen.

Otto H. Schmidt

Maundy Thursday   Luke 22:1–20

The Celebration of the Passover Lamb

*"I have eagerly desired to eat this Passover with
you before I suffer."* Luke 22:15

On Maundy Thursday we observe the institution of
the holy Lord's Supper. Before instituting this Sacrament,
Jesus celebrated the Passover meal with His disciples for
the last time. The Passover lamb was an important part of
this feast.

The Savior had a deep longing for this Passover
celebration. For Him, it was not merely a way to remember the great rescue God provided His people from the
hand of the Egyptians. It was for Jesus a preparation for the
great rescue from sin, death, and the devil that would be
won in the hours to come through the shedding of His
blood.

As He instituted His Holy Supper, the Savior took
the bread and said, "This is My body given for you" (Luke
22:19). He also took the chalice, after the supper, and said,
"This cup is the new covenant in My blood, which is
poured out for you" (Luke 22:20). With these words He
gave His body and blood through which forgiveness is
offered.

My Jesus, let Your flesh and blood be for me my
soul's greatest good! Amen.

William Boehm

Good Friday   Luke 23:44–48

The Highest Manifestation of Christ's Love

This is how we know what love is: Jesus Christ
laid down His life for us. 1 John 3:16

Good Friday demonstrates Christ's love in the clearest manner. The night before His death, the Savior said to His disciples: "Greater love has no one than this, that he lay down his life for his friends" (John 15:13). Jesus showed us this life-sacrificing love, though we were not His friends but His enemies in sin (Romans 5:8).

"Therefore, just as sin entered the world through one man, and death through sin, and in this way death came to all men, because all sinned" (Romans 5:12).

Christ died for our sin in our place, and through this death He redeemed us from sin, death, devil, and hell. He did all that and thus showed us His great love. In John 3:16, Jesus spoke these well-known words: " 'For God so loved the world that He gave His one and only Son.' " According to 1 John 3:16, the Christian responds as such: "This is how we know what love is: Jesus Christ laid down His life for us." In thanksgiving we show our love in response to His gift of love.

The One on the cross is my Love, my Love is Jesus Christ. Amen.

William Boehm

Our Life in God

For you died, and your life is now hidden with
Christ in God. Colossians 3:3

In early Christendom, the night of Silent Saturday (the eve of Easter Sunday) was when catechumens were baptized, that is, those who had come to faith in Christ and had been instructed in the Christian faith. It took place on this night to symbolize that the person was being baptized into the death of Christ. That's why the apostle Paul said to all baptized Christians, "For you died, and your life is now hidden with Christ in God." This remains a custom today in a service often referred to as the Easter Vigil.

In Baptism, we have also died with Christ, who died on the cross on Good Friday for the sin and guilt of the whole world. In so doing, He reconciled us to God. But Christ did not remain dead, and so neither will we remain dead. Indeed, from our Baptism on, we are full of life—a life that embodies within it the confidence and assurance that just as Christ went forth from the grave on Easter morning, we too shall, upon His return, come forth from our graves and inherit eternal life.

Lord Jesus, may all of us who have been baptized into Your death live in You until we through You may some day attain eternal life! Amen.

Manfred Roensch

Easter   1 Corinthians 15:51–58

Christ's Easter Victory, Our Victory

But thanks be to God! He gives us the victory
through our Lord Jesus Christ. 1 Corinthians 15:57

"It was a strange and dreadful strife When life and death contended; The victory remained with life, The reign of death was ended." These are the words of Martin Luther about Jesus' Easter victory as found in the hymn, "Christ Lay in Death's Bands."

In today's text, the apostle Paul didn't just speak in generalities about the Easter victory of our Lord. Instead, He thanked God for the indisputable fact that Christ's victory over hell, death, and the devil has become our victory as well. What does this signify, we ask. From the deepest depths of our hearts we believe that Christ rose from the dead; yet we still have to die. Does that mean that Christ's resurrection is of no significance? Oh, no! Just as Christ died for us and for our guilt upon the cross, so He also, through His resurrection, conquered death for us. Death's power has been shattered. To us who believe in Christ, death no longer holds any power over us. "The Scriptures have proclaimed that just as one death [on the cross] gobbled up the other death, death has become a laughing stock" (Luther). Although our earthly bodies die, we too will be raised to eternal life.

Lord Jesus Christ, who has risen from death, we pray that You will grant to us that which may be a blessing to us! In Your name. Amen.

Manfred Roensch

April 18   Isaiah 53:1–7

Everything Fulfilled

*"Everything must be fulfilled that is written about
Me in the Law of Moses, the Prophets and the
Psalms."* Luke 24:44

Jesus joined two of His disciples as they walked to
Emmaus on the first Easter Day. In so doing, He explained
that everything that had happened—His death and resurrection—had occurred as it had been prophesied in the
Old Testament. He began with Moses, taking one prophecy after the other, explaining how each prophecy had been
fulfilled. His suffering, His death, His resurrection were all
glorious fulfillments of these prophecies.

What a deep impression this made upon these disciples, who were still shrouded in the darkness of doubt!
How their hearts were inflamed! May our hearts also be
inflamed with joy as we—through the words of Jesus in the
Holy Scripture—recognize and acknowledge Him as our
Redeemer and receive Him with faith and love. By grace
we are saved. Thus we shall behold our dearest Friend in
heaven with our own eyes and live in His fellowship into
all eternity.

Just as the Emmaus disciples hurried back to
Jerusalem and told how they had seen Jesus, so let us zeal-
ously witness to our faith in and love for Christ, our dear
Savior.

Precious Savior, You are the promised Messiah.
Remain by our side in our journey through life! Amen.

Adoph M. Bickel

The New Grave

*At the place where Jesus was crucified, there was
a garden, and in the garden a new tomb, in which
no one had ever been laid. ... They laid Jesus
there.* John 19:41–42

The new grave in which the body of Jesus was laid
was not far from the place of the crucifixion. Since God
would not allow His Son's body to decompose (Psalm
16:10), it was proper that the body of the sinless Savior
rest in a grave in which no sinful man's bones had already
been housed.

On Easter morning, Jesus emerged from the grave
alive, and thus He opened and renewed the grave of every
Christian. Death is the wages of sin, and the grave is sin's
payment. However, the Savior stepped out of the grave as
the Victor over sin and death, devil, and hell. What this
means is that our graves are transformed. From these sleeping chambers we will go forth with transfigured bodies—
just as Jesus did.

This same song of triumph sounds forth for us:
"'Where, O death, is your victory? Where, O death, is
your sting?' ... Thanks be to God! He gives us the victory
through our Lord Jesus Christ" (1 Corinthians 15:55–57).

Jesus—my Savior, lives; I too shall behold life.
Thanks be to God for the new grave! Amen.

Rudolph F. Norden

Christ—Resurrection and Life

*Jesus said to her, "I am the resurrection and the life.
He who believes in Me will live, even though he
dies, and whoever lives and believes in Me will
never die. Do you believe this?" John 11:25–26*

"Sin entered the world through one man and death through sin, and in this way death came to all men" (Romans 5:12), for God said to Adam and Eve, "When you eat of it you will surely die" (Genesis 2:17).

Death and eternal damnation are the curse of evil deeds, of sin. But Christ abolished death's power. Truly resurrected from the dead, Christ promised His own power, "I live, and you too shall live!" Through Christ, God has given us the victory over death, coffin, and grave. We can confidently and completely trust our Good Shepherd as we say with David, "Even though I walk through the valley of the shadow of death, I will fear no evil, for You are with me; Your rod and Your staff, they comfort me" (Psalm 23:4). Christ has promised us His victory: "'I give them eternal life, and they shall never perish; no one can snatch them out of My hand'" (John 10:28).

Since we have redemption through the blood of our dear Savior, we no longer need fear temporal death. Instead we can say with all confidence, "You, death, shall lead me into the journey of eternal life." Do you believe this? It is most certainly true. Accept this truth in faith.

Christ has risen! Dear Lord, be our consolation and solace. Have mercy upon us. Lord have mercy! Amen.

Herbert D. Poellot

1 Corinthians 5:6–8

The True Passover Lamb

Christ, our Passover lamb, has been sacrificed.
1 Corinthians 5:7

"Therefore let us keep the Festival" (1 Corinthians 5:8). These are the words of Paul as he wrote to the Christians at Corinth. Why could he write this? Because Christ has been offered up for us.

If the children of Israel already had good reason to celebrate Passover, to remember their rescue from captivity and feast upon a spotless lamb, how much more do we have cause to celebrate Easter—Christ Jesus rescued us from spiritual slavery to sin! Indeed, our Easter Lamb is far better than the paschal lamb of the Old Testament. Indeed we have cause to celebrate!

What makes our Easter celebration into a true feast of joy is the focus that our Easter Lamb—who was offered up for our sin on Good Friday—was raised from the dead for us and for our righteousness. Now we believe with all certainty that God has accepted the vicarious sacrifice the Easter Lamb offered on our behalf as full payment for our sins. Through His resurrection, Christ has taken away the prickly thorns of death.

O Christ, Easter Lamb, feed us today; take away our transgressions, so we may sing "Hallelujah!" from morning until night! Amen.

William Boehm

Romans 8:31–34

For the Sake of Our Righteousness

*[Christ] was delivered over to death for our sins
and was raised to life for our justification.*
Romans 4:25

The Father laid our sins and the transgressions of
the entire world upon His Son, the Lamb who bears the sin
of the world. Jesus became our substitute and His death
became the sacrifice for the sins of the entire world. He
offered up our sin in His own body upon the tree of the
cross. His suffering and death are the payment for the punishment of our sin.

"He was pierced for our transgressions, He was
crushed for our iniquities; the punishment that brought us
peace was upon Him, and by His wounds we are healed"
(Isaiah 53:5). If Christ had remained in the grave, we
would not have been redeemed; we would still be held
captive to our sins and our faith would be worthless,
unable to save us. But Christ has risen! Through His resurrection, God testifies to the whole world that sin has been
atoned for and His wrath has been appeased. Those who
believe in Jesus Christ are righteous before God. Through
faith we are righteous for the sake of Christ. "[Christ] was
delivered over to death for our sins and was raised to life
for our justification."

As redeemed children of God. We therefore sing
with shouts of joy: Thanks be to the Conqueror! Amen.

George A. Naumann

Christ, Dead and Arisen

He was raised on the third day. 1 Corinthians 15:4

Our Lord Jesus Christ rose from the dead on the third day. With steadfast faith we firmly cling to this article of faith. It's as if we could write in large letters the words "Christ rose from the dead" so we might see, hear, remember, and know nothing else above this.

We do not speak this article of faith as if it merely occurred, much like we might tell a fairy tale or favorite story. Rather we pray that we will boldly cling to this truth in faith. We call it "faith" when we become totally and completely immersed in the belief that no other truth exists than that "Christ arose!" This faith is ours through the power of the Holy Spirit and through the Spirit's power, we can boldly exclaim what we believe.

Paul is a true master in extolling these words of faith in Romans 4:25: Christ "was delivered over to death for our sins and was raised to life for our justification." And in Ephesians 2, "As...you were dead in your transgressions and sins" (verse 1), God "made us alive with Christ" (verse 5). "And God raised us up with Christ and seated us with Him in the heavenly realms in Christ Jesus" (verse 6).

Christ has risen! He has overcome the ordeal of everyone's sin. For this we can be eternally grateful.

Christ, be our comfort and consolation. Amen.

Martin Luther

April 24   Romans 6:1–10

Buried and Raised from the Dead with Christ

Having been buried with Him in Baptism and raised
with Him through your faith in the power of God,
who raised Him from the dead. Colossians 2:12

It is exceedingly important that we persevere in the faith. It is vital that Christ remain our One and Only. In Him we have the forgiveness of sins and the certain hope of eternal life. We cling to Him. We live in Him.

So that this truth might be impressed upon our hearts, the apostle reminds us that we have been buried and resurrected with our Savior. Everything the Lord Jesus has accomplished for us—His death upon Golgotha's cross, His victorious resurrection—is viewed by God as our death, our burial, our resurrection.

How can this be possible? The answer is in our text: through Baptism. In Romans 6:3, St. Paul asked, "Don't you know that all of us who were baptized into Christ Jesus were baptized into His death?" Baptism is the means by which we enter into this vital relationship with Christ. St. Peter said that the water that carried the ark of Noah symbolizes the baptismal water "that now saves you also—not the removal of dirt from the body but the pledge of a good conscience toward God. It saves you by the resurrection of Jesus Christ" (1 Peter 3:21). What extraordinary blessings God provides for us through Baptism and His Word!

Dear heavenly Father, we thank You for the glorious blessings that are ours through Baptism. Amen.

John W. Behnken

126

Romans 3:21–31

Throne of Grace

Let us then approach the throne of grace with confidence, so that we may receive mercy and find grace to help us in our time of need. Hebrews 4:16

Through the suffering and death of Christ, our High Priest, we became reconciled to God. Through this reconciliation, Christ became the Throne of Grace that we may joyfully approach in faith. We are able to do so because of the forgiveness He won for us. God is no longer enraged with us. For the sake of Christ, He has remitted, or canceled, our sins. Thus, we no longer need be afraid before God. We have the solid assurance that we stand in grace before Him.

This is of utmost significance for us. We now belong to the people of God and can conduct ourselves as His people. By word and deed, we can confess Him as our gracious Father who stands at our side when we are weak. It is He who comforts us in our hour of need. We praise and glorify Him for the inexpressible grace He has so richly shown to us through His Son. With joy we step before His throne of Grace.

Father God, we give You heartfelt thanks for the throne of grace you have prepared through Your Son, our Lord Jesus Christ. Help us to approach this throne of grace with repentant hearts so we might receive forgiveness for our sins. In the name of Your Son, our Savior. Amen.

Gerhard C. Michael

Purchased

*For you know that it was not with perishable
things such as silver or gold that you were
redeemed ... but with the precious blood of Christ.*
1 Peter 1:18–19

Professional athletes often make a great deal of
money. However, those who are injured might be tossed
aside. Anyone who does not meet the criteria may be
immediately released from the team. We cheer loudly for
the star players. Others might get paid to bring us delight.
But in so doing, they become objects, not persons; their
personal welfare is of no concern to us.

Before God there are no such objects. The "very
least" are as important to the Lord God as the "world
famous." He created mankind like a symphony orchestra,
every person a vital and necessary instrument for harmony;
in contrast to sports teams that compete against one
another. The Lord brings freedom from such senseless
competition and offers us true value in His eyes.

We can readily turn to God for help in harmoniz-
ing with others in His beloved symphony. As He empowers us to show concern for one another and to carry the
burdens of fellow believers, the precious blood of Christ is
poured out through such love.

Dear God, without You we are poverty stricken.
You have purchased us and made us rich. Help us to give
the good gifts of Your love to others! Amen.

Thomas H. Trapp

April 27   1 Timothy 2:1–7

The Heartfelt Longing of God

He is patient with you, not wanting anyone
to perish, but everyone to come to repentance.
2 Peter 3:9

How could we ever measure God's love and heartfelt longing for us? "How great is the love the Father has
lavished on us, that we should be called children of God!
And that is what we are!" (1 John 3:1)

"This is love: not that we loved God, but that He
loved us and sent His Son as an atoning sacrifice for our
sins" (1 John 4:10). God loves us; that's why He sent His
Son to be judgment for us. "He is patient with you, not
wanting anyone to perish, but everyone to come to repentance." God is long-suffering. But if we are truly honest,
would we not have to confess, as we take note of our sinful life, that we have often rejected God's love and deserve
to be cast aside for all eternity?

But thanks be to God, that through His love and
compassion He still allows Law and Gospel to be proclaimed in this world so we may be turned from our sinful
ways and trust in Christ alone for the forgiveness of sins.

O God, grant that I thankfully acknowledge Your
love for me and relentlessly cling to You in faith! Amen.

Moritz J. Michael

April 28   Isaiah 66:10–14

The Purpose for the Resurrection

"You will flourish like grass; the hand of the LORD will be made known to His servants." Isaiah 66:14

In the book of Proverbs, Solomon wrote, "The LORD works out everything for His own ends" (Proverbs 16:4). With and through the resurrection, God demonstrated His mighty hand. Through it He demonstrated His mercy by declaring us righteous and condemning the godless. Through it He demonstrated His truth and omnipotence. Moses prayed in Psalm 90:16, "May Your deeds be shown to Your servants, Your splendor to their children." Also, above all else, "we wait for the blessed hope—the glorious appearing of our great God and Savior, Jesus Christ, who gave Himself for us to redeem us from all wickedness" (Titus 2:13–14). Through the resurrection, the Lord God demonstrated His unconditional love and showered His grace upon us.

Those who are made righteous through Christ will praise God forever; they will not only acknowledge His mercy and righteousness, they will also acknowledge, praise, and exalt Him into all eternity. They will stand before the throne and sing the highest hallelujahs to His name.

The resurrection of Jesus, of mankind, and especially of the believers is the too-good-to-be-true news of God to fallen mankind. It is worth celebrating!

Lord, our Savior, may our bones lie upon roses until our graves are conquered to the glory of Your name! Amen.

George M. Krach

Colossians 1:19–22

The Peace of God

And the peace of God, which transcends all
understanding, will guard your hearts and your
minds in Christ Jesus. Philippians 4:7

The peace that comes from God comes only through Christ. "The punishment that brought us peace was upon Him" (Isaiah 53:5). There is no longer any warfare or hatred between God and us. God Himself has established peace through Christ. We are able to live peacefully and confidently because God calls us to Him as our Friend and daily demonstrates His gracious love and care for us.

Our conscience need no longer plague us, even when we consciously become aware of our transgressions. Christ came to take all these sins upon Himself. He has taken our sins from us; they now belong to Him. He was bruised because of them. God knows how sinful and unworthy we are. But His forgiveness is ours through Christ. He desires that we have the peace of a repentant heart.

The friendship and kindness of God is ours through faith. There is nothing that can separate us from the love of God in Christ (Romans 8:38–39). If we have this friendship, we have everything. Thus we are enabled to confidently do everything through Christ and endure all things. This peace is above all understanding and preserves our hearts and minds in Christ Jesus.

I thank You, my heavenly Father, that You do not call me enemy, but call me friend. For the sake of Your Son. Amen.

Roy H. Bleick

April 30   1 Corinthians 15:51–57

Resurrection and Transfiguration

*I know that my Redeemer lives, and that in the
end He will stand upon the earth. And after my
skin has been destroyed, yet in my flesh I will see
God; I myself will see Him with my own eyes—
I, and not another. Job 19:25–27*

This text, tightly bound with the Feast of Easter, is
a fountain of hope, power, and strength for us by faith. "I
know that my Redeemer lives." With Luther we sing, "as
we are amidst our life, we are surrounded by death." In the
Old Testament we hear an unmistakable resonance of the
jubilant song of Paul, "That is why I am suffering as I am.
Yet ... I know whom I have believed, and am convinced
that He is able to guard what I have entrusted to Him for
that day" (2 Timothy 1:12).

Job 19:25–27 is widely translated, yet in every
translation, the expression, "I myself will see Him," is
retained. All can gauge their understanding with the words
of the apostle, "who, by the power that enables Him to
bring everything under His control, will transform our
lowly bodies so that they will be like His glorious body"
(Philippians 3:21).

Although we quietly rest here on earth, we patiently wait until the Last Day when our bodies will become
like that of Christ's transfigured body. Amen.

Luther Poellot

Divine Grace

The LORD is compassionate and gracious, slow to anger, abounding in love. Psalm 103:8

John wrote about the Incarnate Word in his gospel: "From the fullness of His grace we have all received one blessing after another" (John 1:16). This refers to heaps and oodles of grace. Our beloved Savior, Jesus Christ, is "full of grace and truth" (verse 14).

These words are a source of comfort as we cry out from the depths of our needy, sinful situation. The Law, given through Moses, accuses us; it always condemns. However, this grace and truth came into being through Jesus Christ (verse 17). He was fulfillment for us.

Just as we lament from our anxiety-ridden conscience, "What a wretched man I am! Who will rescue me from this body of death?" (Romans 7:24), we can also come in gratitude to our God, "In His great mercy He has given us new birth into a living hope through the resurrection of Jesus Christ from the dead" (1 Peter 1:3).

This fullness of grace comes through Christ's blood and righteousness. He saved us from eternal destruction and crowned us with His grace and mercy.

Dear Lord, thank You for the gift of Your grace. Amen.

Albert T. Bostelmann

Philippians 3:8–10

Raised from the Dead
for the Sake of Our Righteousness

[Jesus] was delivered over to death for our sins
and was raised to life for our justification.
Romans 4:25

Beyond all doubt, the words "delivered over" refer to Christ's death on our behalf. He was the world's Sin-bearer; that's what John the Baptizer called Him. And as such, Christ paid sin's debt with His life. He was our substitute and was battered, for us (Isaiah 53:5). Through His death, He redeemed us from the curse and debt of the Law.

Christ was "raised to life for our justification." With His resurrection, He not only proved that He was God's Son, but did so for the sake of our righ-teousness. Had Christ not been raised from the dead, we could not know whether God had accepted His sacrifice for our sins. The resurrection of Christ is our proof that we are declared righteous before God's judgment. We treasure the resurrection so very much, especially since it is the foundation of our justification.

Through faith in Christ, you can be certain that you are declared righteous. All who believe in Christ "are justified freely by His grace through the redemption that came by Christ Jesus" (Romans 3:24).

Lord help me so I firmly believe that You are my righteousness, today and forever! Amen.

Roy H. Bleick

Justified for the Sake of Christ

*[All] are justified freely by His grace through
the redemption that came by Christ Jesus.*
Romans 3:24

The Holy Scriptures teach with clear, concise words that God declares us righteous solely by His grace. Here the question arises: How is it possible that God is gracious to us sinners? Haven't we broken His very Law, the Commandments? Hasn't God threatened to punish sin, saying, "When you eat of it you will surely die" (Genesis 2:17)? Doesn't God *have* to keep His word? Yes, indeed, otherwise He could not be God.

How grateful we can be that God designed a way to remain righteous, punish sin, and yet be gracious! God designed this "through the redemption that came by Christ Jesus." The words of Scripture outline His plan for our salvation: God sent His only Son into the world (John 3:16). "The LORD has laid on Him the iniquity of us all" (Isaiah 53:6). "God made Him who had no sin to be sin for us" (2 Corinthians 5:21). "Christ redeemed us from the curse of the law by becoming a curse for us" (Galatians 3:13). Now God sees us as redeemed by Christ at great price. We are justified for the sake of Christ.

We thank You, dear Savior, that You have redeemed us poor sinners through Your suffering and death. Amen.

John W. Behnken

Shout with Joy to God

*Shout with joy to God, all the earth! Sing the
glory of His name, make His praise glorious!*
Psalm 66:1–2

The psalmist calls upon his companions to praise
God because His works are wondrous. He rules over all
people; no one escapes His might. Even God's enemies see
evidence of His wondrous works; He dried up the sea so
Israel could cross it on foot. God also remained faithful as
Israel lived in bitter and severe slavery. They were down-
trodden; they passed through fire and water. God led them
out of slavery and renewed them. The psalmist himself suffered much. But God heard his prayer and rescued him.
Consequently he praised God and encouraged others to
do the same.

We too experience suffering and pain in our lives.
The psalmist helps us recognize that God does not forsake
us during these times. Instead, He stands beside us and
renews us time and again. Therefore, we can join the
psalmist in glorifying and praising God every day.

We praise You, heavenly Father that You are present in every situation and that you daily renew us. Amen.

Jakob K. Heckert

May 5   2 Corinthians 5:14–21 and Psalm 144

Made Righteous

*God made Him who had no sin to be sin for us,
so that in Him we might become the righteousness
of God.* 2 Corinthians 5:21

Who is the most wicked man ever to set foot upon earth? Hitler might be considered a logical answer. What about Stalin? Judas or Genghis Kahn?

Scripture has a different answer. The most wicked man in the history of the world was Jesus Christ. How so? Jesus was God and our Savior. He was without sin. He came to take away our sin, to die for us. It is so because all our sins were charged to Him. He suffered the burden of sin for all the world—even the world's most wicked people. And God punished Him accordingly—as if He were the most wicked man in history.

All people must ultimately die because of sin. However, God's final word expressed His love for all human beings. Thus, the Righteous One was made into sin for us so we could be made righteous by means of His blood poured out upon the cross.

God now views us as righteous, eternally cloaked in His righteousness. Thus we are able to glorify and praise God and to confess His love.

God, we have been changed in our hearts by You. Help us to continuously thank You by word and deed. Amen.

Thomas H. Trapp

May 6   Psalm 18:1–13

The Agony of Death

*My heart is in anguish within me; the terrors of
death assail me.* Psalm 55:4

Death is every person's enemy. Jesus had to wrestle
with death in Gethsemane. In this battle He perspired with
bloody sweat.

The Christian also encounters the agony of death.
As the hour of his departure draws near, his conscience
accuses him of the sins he committed. Here the devil truly
seizes the opportunity and attempts to topple the
Christian into doubt, reminding him that because of his
sins he deserves eternal damnation. The Christian says,
"The anxiety in my heart is huge; Lord, lead me out of my
predicament!"

Thanks be to God, that in midst of the agony of
our death we have a sweet comfort. We know that Jesus
Christ did not only overcome the agony of His own death,
He also fully conquered death for us. Therefore, we are
empowered to say in the hour of our death, " 'Where, O
death, is your victory? Where, O death, is your sting?' ...
But thanks be to God! He gives us the victory through our
Lord Jesus Christ" (1 Corinthians 15:55–56). Christ's resurrection chases away the agony of death because He
overcame death for us.

Lord Jesus, when the hour of death draws near,
renew me with the power of Your resurrection! Amen.

Albert T. Bostlemann

Justified by Grace

For all have sinned and fall short of the glory of God, and are justified freely by His grace through the redemption that came by Christ Jesus.
Romans 3:23–24

If we all are such miserable, helpless sinners, how dare we expect a pronouncement of righteousness on God's part? How can it be possible for God—who is provoked to righteous wrath by our sins and who, consequently, should punish us—to nevertheless pronounce us righteous?

The answers to these questions become clear to us as we take note of God's Word. In no way are we able to earn the righteousness of God. That is and remains impossible. However, God's Word teaches us something quite extraordinary. Our God is not just righteous, but also gracious. He forgives us without any merit of our own. At the Council of Jerusalem, Peter directly addressed the issue of works-righteousness. He maintained that one should not lay upon the Gentiles the yoke of circumcision, and said, "We believe it is through the grace of our Lord Jesus that we are saved" (Acts 15:11). Paul very clearly wrote, "Having been justified by His grace, we might become heirs having the hope of eternal life" (Titus 3:7). Throughout the Holy Scriptures we see repeated emphasis on the grace of God. Our sin deserves God's punishment, but God's grace grants us forgiveness. What wondrous grace!

We thank You, dear heavenly Father, that You are gracious to us poor sinners. Amen.

John W. Behnken

139

Sing Praise to the Lord!

*O LORD, You brought me up from the grave; You
spared me from going down into the pit.* Psalm 30:3

With the psalmist, we sing God's glory and praise
because He continuously demonstrates His love by helping
us. However, is the Lord's help definitive? Of all the needs
and concerns that worry us now, none is more enduring
than death. While God may heal us from an illness, we still
will die someday. We say and sing that God rescues us from
every need—but will He also rescue us from death?

The psalmist makes a good case for God's rescuing
us from death. After all, how would we be able to praise
and glorify God in the grave? Yet reality serves to contra-
dict the psalmist's claims. David died and was laid in a
grave. God did not keep him alive forever.

But then came the resurrection of Jesus Christ. It is
here we see how God can—and will—lead us out from
eternal death in hell. David's Old Testament hope that he
would praise God forever is made certain in the New
Testament resurrection of Jesus. For this reason we join
David and praise our Savior.

Sing praise and thanks with liberated sound To the
Lord at all times And spread forth ever more and more His
glory through word and deed; Thus out of love and kind-
ness He shall Free us from every need, after our death,
Leading us to everlasting joy. Amen. (*Kirchengesangbuch für
Evangelish—Lutherische Gemeinden*, CPH)

Fritz Schmitt

2 Corinthians 5:14–21

An Accomplishment beyond Compare

He is the atoning sacrifice for our sins, and not
only for ours but also for the sins of the whole
world. 1 John 2:2

Jesus paid for our sins. How? He spread His obedience over our disobedience; He allowed Himself to be wounded and scourged for our transgressions; He poured out His divine blood; and ultimately offered up His life upon the altar of the cross. That's how Jesus paid our gigantic debt to God. One died for all.

God was justly angry over mankind's rebellion against Him; but Jesus stilled God's wrath through His reparation and once more reconciled mankind to the Father. He won God's favor toward mankind. God no longer sees even the tiniest spot on any one of us. In Christ, God is kindly disposed toward, and opens wide His arms of love, to us all. "God was reconciling the world to Himself in Christ, not counting men's sins against them" (2 Corinthians 5:19).

Jesus is the eternally valid Reconciler. What He has accomplished for each sin of every person is valid and binding in eternity. Is that not glorious? Yes indeed! He is the Atonement for the sin of the entire world!

Ah, so now I also am included, my Jesus; so now I am saved. Eternal thanks be to You, my God! Amen.

George J. Mueller

John 20:19–31

Christ's Atonement Has Been Sealed

Again Jesus said, "Peace be with you! ...
If you forgive anyone his sins, they are forgiven."
John 20:21–23

One of the greatest mysteries of the Christian faith is that man becomes righteous and saved before God in no way other than through faith alone. This is how Christianity is distinguished from other religions. Other religions teach that through his works man can become righteous before God and be saved. The Christian faith teaches that a man becomes righteous before God only through Christ.

Yet Christians might become anxious if consumed by the following thoughts: I do indeed believe, but am I not also a sinner like others who do not believe? Don't I sin every day in thought, desire, conduct, words, and deeds? How can my faith alone be of any help? Is it enough?

The doctrine of justification through faith is indeed a mystery, but there is a key to this mystery. The key is the resurrection of Christ. As St. Paul taught, Christ "was delivered over to death for our sins and was raised to life for our justification" (Romans 4:25).

Lord Jesus, You who forgive sins, we come to You under the burden of sin. Help us! Amen.

C. F. W. Walther

Isaiah 25:7–12

Death Has Been Gobbled Up

He will swallow up death forever. Isaiah 25:8

When Jesus came to heal Jairus's daughter, He said, "'The girl is not dead but asleep'" (Matthew 9:24). Those gathered laughed at Him. Death a "sleep"? If only!

But that is indeed the case for us, for Jesus, our Savior, "has destroyed death and brought life and immortality to light through the gospel" (2 Timothy 1:10). We say in triumph along with the apostle: "'Death has been swallowed up in victory'" (1 Corinthians 15:54).

Isaiah prophesied this even in the Old Testament when he said, "He," the Lord of Sabaoth, "will swallow up death forever." No mortal man can do that. Man has fallen into death—but now comes the Lord Sabaoth. He assumes flesh and blood, becomes our brother, takes our place, and dies, so through death He takes away the power of the devil, who had the power of death, and redeems those who had been slaves to sin and death (Hebrews 2:14–15).

Now, if death has been conquered through Christ, all the consequences of death have been conquered as well. Scripture reassures us that "He will wipe every tear from their eyes" (Revelation 21:4), the tears of bitterness and despair, of worry and anxiety, of pain and cares, of suffering and sadness.

Thanks be to God, who has given us the victory through our Lord Jesus Christ. Amen.

Herman A. Mayer

May 12   1 Peter 3:18–22 and 2 Corinthians 5:16–21

Reconciliation and Resurrection

He was delivered over to death for our sins and was
raised to life for our justification. Romans 4:25

According to Scripture, God has declared all people not guilty because of the sacrificial death of our Lord. Christ has reconciled the world to God. And this reconciliation took place prior to and apart from any action on the part of mankind. It is a fait accompli, just like the creation of the world.

This, and nothing less, is what the Scripture teaches: "For if, when we were God's enemies, we were reconciled to Him through the death of His Son, how much more, having been reconciled, shall we be saved through His life" (Romans 5:10). So then, when Christ died, our reconciliation to God was accomplished, for "God was reconciling the world to Himself in Christ" (2 Corinthians 5:19).

God reconciled humans by virtue of the fact that He no longer counted their sins against them. In other words, at the death and resurrection of Christ, God forgave the sin of the entire world. At that time He justified every sinner and absolved the entire world of sin. The saving Gospel is the message of this once-and-for-all reconciliation. The only way mankind can be absolved through this reconciliation is by faith alone. It has already been accomplished through Christ.

Christ has arisen from the bonds of death; through Him is proclaimed the forgiveness of sins. We thank You, O Lord. Amen.

Franz Pieper

May 13   Genesis 6:20–22

The Sacrifice

[Jesus] does not need to offer sacrifices day after day, first for His own sins, and then for the sins of the people. He sacrificed for their sins once for all when He offered Himself. Hebrews 7:27

Our connection to the words of this verse is this: we are in need of such a high priest. According to the Law, each high priest had to undergo a daily cleansing before he could make a sacrifice for the people. That was because these priests, as descendants of Aaron, were also sinners. After purifying themselves, they poured out the blood of the sacrificial animal for the sins of the people. This was not necessary for the High Priest to which our text refers. This High Priest, Jesus Christ, was not a sinner. He is the perfect High Priest. He is the sacrifice—the Lamb—and at the same time makes the sacrifice. That is why we say and sing, "O Christ, the Lamb of God, who takes away the sin of the world, have mercy on us. ... grant us your peace" (*Lutheran Worship*, "Angus Dei").

Yes, most certainly, through Christ we are saved. By His wounds we are healed. He has completed the cleansing of our sins for He is higher than the heavens. With heartfelt thankfulness we pray:

O sweet Lamb, what shall I render to You for the fact that You have shown me so much good? Amen.

Walter H. Bouman

Joy in the Lord

Finally, my brothers, rejoice in the Lord!
Philippians 3:1

Genuine joy is, for us as humans, like a medicine. It drives away worrisome thoughts. It allows us to view our entire life in a far more positive light.

Who can blame us if we pursue joy like the hunter pursues game? There are people who chase after all the joys and pleasures of this life and this world only to come to the conclusion that it was not all it was cracked up to be. Or consider the worthless and fleeting joys that end up leaving behind nothing more than a huge hangover and result in the opposite of true joy. Therefore, it is vital to find the true source of joy, and Paul names it for us in today's verses—our Lord, Jesus Christ. In Him we always have reason to rejoice—a joy in which we are never disappointed. Christ is the source of true joy because He has redeemed us and grants us eternal life.

Lord Jesus Christ, help us to rejoice in You. Fill us with Your joy, and set our focus on You. Amen.

Manfred Roensch

Ephesians 1:3–6

Crowned with Grace and Mercy

*[The LORD] redeems your life from the pit
and crowns you with love and compassion.*
Psalm 103:4

In this psalm, the psalmist exalts and praises God for forgiving his sins and healing his infirmities; for redeeming his life from destruction, death, and hell; and for crowning him with grace and mercy.

God sent us sinners His Son as our Substitute, Stand-in, and Mediator. In our place He fulfilled the Law—which we are unable to keep. He took upon Himself our own sins, and bore their punishment in our stead. That is how He won for us the cloak of righteousness, which avails us before God. For Christ's sake, God forgives us our sin and looks upon us as righteous.

When God forgives, we are not only spared wrath and condemnation, we are adopted as dear children of God the Father. We need no longer attempt to gain God's love. We are surrounded on every side by the merits and the mercy of God. Our heads are adorned with a golden crown; this crown is grace and mercy. One could wish for nothing more.

Lord, grant that my soul and all that is within me constantly praise You! Amen.

Roy H. Bleick

John 14:1–6

Rest for Our Souls

*"Come to Me, all you who are weary and burdened,
and I will give you rest. Take My yoke upon you
and learn from Me, for I am gentle and humble in
heart, and you will find rest for your souls."*
Matthew 11:28–29

Oh, the storms that rage over and over again within our hearts! Surrounded by a sinful world, misled by our
old Adam, and tempted by the devil, we long for rest for
our souls. Worn out and overburdened with bodily and
spiritual weakness, we wish for a peace that the world cannot give.

How precious is the invitation that Jesus, our Lord
and Savior, extends to us: "Come to Me, all you who are
weary and burdened, and I will give you rest. Take My
yoke upon you and learn from Me, for I am gentle and
humble in heart, and you will find rest for your souls."

Our Savior can extend this invitation because He
Himself won rest for our souls through His holy, precious
blood and through His innocent suffering and death.
Through our Baptism, we are united to our Savior. As we
ponder God's Word and partake of the Lord's Supper, we
are united to the Savior and find rest for our souls.

O great God, hear my need! I now desire to step
before You. Grant to me Your peace. Amen.

Adolph M. Bickel

In Our Stead

God made Him who had no sin to be sin for us,
so that in Him we might become the righteousness
of God. 2 Corinthians 5:21

How enraged we become when we learn that an innocent person has been condemned for a crime someone else committed simply because he was judged on suspicion and circumstantial evidence. Such an error in a court of justice is always covered extensively in the media, and everyone comes to complete agreement that something like it should never happen again. Yet these things do happen time and again because courts are not perfect.

As we look at our text, we see that there is no error in this court. Here Someone perfect and innocent is condemned for the guilt of others and is punished with death. The Judge who condemns Him is God Himself. We are the guilty ones who deserve death; yet He who was saddled with our guilt is the sinless Son of God. Through faith we confess with hymn writer Paul Gerhardt, "It's I, I should have to atone, be bound hand and foot in hell; the scourging and the bonds and what You endured is what my soul deserved." Yet God in His mercy laid upon His very own Son our sin and death.

Thanks be to You, Christ, that You have bestowed life upon us through Your sacrificial death. Amen.

Manfred Roensch

May 18   Isaiah 53:1–12

On Account of Our Sin

Surely He took up our infirmities and carried our
sorrows, ... and by His wounds we are healed.
Isaiah 53:4–5

"For our sake," is the main point of all evangelical preaching—that is the great mystery of the cross, the rock of our salvation, the guarantee of our salvation.

The prophet Isaiah said, "The punishment that brought us peace was upon Him" (Isaiah 53:5). Obviously we don't know to what extent this Old Testament prophet was able to fathom the full meaning of his prophecies. However, by faith we believe as we lay these prophetic words next to their New Testament fulfillment. We no longer need ask, as did the Ethiopian official, "How can I [understand this] unless someone explains it to me?" (Acts 8:31). We have been enlightened through the words of the evangelists and the apostles, and even the word of Jesus Himself, "This is My body given for you; ... this cup is the new covenant in My blood, which is poured out for you" (Luke 22:19–20). "Christ redeemed us from the curse of the Law by becoming a curse for us" (Galatians 3:13). By faith and through the power of the Spirit, we believe these blessed words, "for our sake." What Christ suffered, He suffered for us—the Innocent One for the guilty. We are free!

You bore all sin; otherwise we would have to despair. Grant us Your peace, O Jesus! Amen.

Herman A. Mayer

A Shepherd for the People

*Moses said to the LORD, "May the LORD, the God
of the spirits of all mankind, appoint a man over
this community to go out and come in before them,
one who will lead them out and bring them in, so
the LORD's people will not be like sheep without
a shepherd."* Numbers 27:15–17

The aged Moses came before God and petitioned
Him for a new leader for the people. The Lord called
Joshua as the new shepherd to protect and lead His people. For example, Joshua went ahead of the people to
explore and scout out the land (Numbers 13). He also led
the people in war against their enemies in the land of
Israel, and with the Lord, conquered it.

The name "Joshua" and the name "Jesus" both mean
"God rescues." Joshua was a forerunner of the true, future
Shepherd. Our Shepherd, Jesus, went ahead of us, into
death. He then rose from death to victory so His people
could continue on without danger. He conquered our
worst enemy, the devil. He leads us so we are not sheep
without a Shepherd (Matthew 9:36).

We are like sheep; sheep need a shepherd. We confess our sin before God, even when we think we do not
need a Shepherd. He continually comes to us through His
Word and Sacrament with His forgiveness and leads us for
His name's sake (Psalm 23:3).

Our Good Shepherd, You are always with us. We
thank You for Your leading and guidance. Amen.

Curtis P. Giese

Only One Savior

*I am the Way and the Truth and the Life. No one
comes to the Father except through Me.* John 14:6

Already through Isaiah, God had said, "I, even I, am
the LORD, and apart from Me there is no savior" (Isaiah
43:11). In today's verse, Christ repeats that He, through
His truth, is the living Way to life with the Father. Even
the godless high priest Caiphas prophesied this as he gave
advice to kill Jesus: "It would be good if one man died for
the people" (John 18:14), rather than have the entire
nation perish. Peter told the Jews, "Salvation is found in no
one else, for there is no other name under heaven given to
men by which we must be saved" (Acts 4:12). Several
dozen times in John's gospel alone, Jesus said, "I am." With
the word "I," Jesus once and for all solemnly declares that
He alone is the only Lord, Savior, and Helper. Paul wrote
that it is only through Christ that we sinners are reconciled
to God, righteous and saved. We sing, "Lord Christ, You
are the true Way to heaven" (2 Corinthians 5:19; Galatians
3:13; Ephesians 2:8–9).

Let us rejoice in our salvation! Let us constantly say
with all assurance: "I know whom I have believed, and am
convinced that He is able to guard what I have entrusted
to Him for that day" (2 Timothy 1:12).

O Savior, You are my sure and certain portion. I
desire salvation in no other. May every person say the
same! Amen.

George M. Krach

The Only Redemption

Who gave Himself as a ransom for all men.
1 Timothy 2:6

Christ reconciled us to God the Father. "For there is one God and one mediator between God and men, the man Christ Jesus, who gave Himself up as a ransom for all men" (1 Timothy 2:5–6).

If Jesus gave Himself as the ransom for all, then He is the only Redeemer and made available the only redemption. That's how it is—simple and true. A hymn composer paraphrased Psalm 49 this way: "No money or goods save me; in vain a brother attempts to free another; he has to let it stay that way eternally." But Christ "sank Himself into our need and tasted our bitter death." Thus it is true that "since One has died for all, and therefore all died." Christ, through His own blood, entered into the holy place one time and He established an eternal redemption.

Two things, then, are emphasized: "That such was preached during His time" and "He died for all, that those who live should no longer live for themselves but for Him who died for them and was raised again" (2 Corinthians 5:15).

Jesus, thanks be to You for Your redeeming death, sealed by Your resurrection. Help us to live for You! Amen.

George M. Krach

1 Thessalonians 4:12–18

Our Empty Grave

"Because I live, you also will live." John 14:19

It is written: "Up there stands the chapel, it quietly looks down upon the valley. Up there one brings to the grave those who were rejoicing in the valley. Shepherd boy, shepherd boy, someday one will also sing there of you." These words refer to death and grave, both of which confront every human.

Why is it that death and the grave are regarded as sad and frightening? Many people do not like to talk about death. Those who know nothing about life and salvation are miserable on earth. The Christian, however, need not fear the grave. For him it is nothing but a resting chamber for a short time. The glorious moment is coming when the words of Christ will be fulfilled: "I live, and you also will live." Through faith I am so tightly bound to Christ that I will not remain in the grave. The grave is only a sleeping chamber from which I will someday awake and come forth. For Christians, death and the grave are just a passing thing, and my grave will be empty someday. My dust and my ashes will once more come forth alive. "Multitudes who sleep in the dust of the earth will awake: some to everlasting life, others to shame and everlasting contempt" (Daniel 12:2).

Thanks be to You, O Christ, for Your glorious resurrection! Amen.

Moritz J. Michael

1 Peter 1:1–8

Lasting Joy

"You will rejoice, and no one will take away your joy." John 16:22

Some people cannot fully comprehend the joy the children of God feel over Christ's resurrection. This is joy that comes from God alone. In Isaiah 66:13 we read, "As a mother comforts her child, so will I comfort you." Our joy and comfort come not from ourselves, but from God.

The joy of this world is purely an outward joy, founded upon things which will soon perish. When the people of this world have no faith in Christ, they search in vain for the inward joy of the heart. The joy of Christians, on the other hand, is a genuine joy because of the assurance through God's Word that we are justified through faith, are certain of our atonement, and thus have peace with God. And we have these glorious promises: "'I will come back and take you to be with Me'" (John 14:3); "'I will see you again and you will rejoice, and no one will take away your joy'" (John 16:22).

Thus our joy shall never end; it is eternal. If Christ is risen from the dead, then He shall never again die, "death no longer has mastery over Him" (Romans 6:9). Through the power of the Holy Spirit, God's children believe in their hearts that they are eternally in a state of grace with Him and that nothing and no one can separate them from His love. That is our abiding joy!

O risen Savior, thanks be to You for the eternal joy which You have prepared for us! Amen.

Moritz J. Michael

Ephesians 1:3–6

The Purpose for Eternal Life

And the God of all grace, ... will Himself restore you
and make you strong, firm and steadfast. To Him
be the power for ever and ever. 1 Peter 5:10–11

God will one day guide us to perfection, as we live with Him in eternity. He shall grant us what we lack for the sake of Christ's merits. We have forgiveness of sins, life, and salvation—now and forever. What a joy, blessing, and glory that God will one day provide and bestow upon us!

One can say: Death provides the child of God with the greatest surprise that exists. When he closes his eyes in death and no longer knows anything about the world, he will be astonished to see God. He will see Christ and how He has loved us and offered Himself for us. That will be a surprise that will never go away; for there we will obtain the imperishable, unspotted, and never-wilting inheritance of eternal salvation and everlasting life. God sustains us for that.

Because of this and for this we want to praise God now; and for that reason and on account of this we will glorify Him and praise His grace and power forever. To God be glory, who is strong and mighty to save!

Glory be to God our Lord who has rescued us from the death of sin for eternal life with Him! Amen.

George M. Krach

Meeting up with the Resurrected One

Suddenly Jesus met them. Matthew 28:9

On the first Feast Day of Easter, as Mary Magdalene and the other Mary came early in the morning to the grave, they found it empty. Where was Jesus? The angel answered their question: "He is not here; He has risen, just as He said" (Matthew 28:6). Immediately and unexpectedly the two women met the resurrected Savior. "They came to Him, clasped His feet and worshiped Him" (Matthew 28:9). Oh, what joy! What a wonderful moment! They were the first to personally meet Jesus after the resurrection.

During the next 40 days, more than 500 people saw the resurrected Savior. And since His resurrection, many millions of poor sinners have recognized the Lord as the Holy Spirit ignited true faith in their hearts. Through Word and Sacrament, their faith has been nourished and sustained. Many of these Christians are now with Jesus in heaven—or are waiting here upon earth for the joyful journey into eternity to be and abide with the Savior.

God be praised that we have also met the Savior through faith and desire to remain eternally faithful to Him.

Most heartily beloved Jesus, sustain us in true faith until our blessed end! Amen.

Edwin W. Leverenz

Ascended into Heaven

While He was blessing them, He left them and was taken up into heaven. Luke 24:51

The Scriptures declare that 40 days after His resurrection from the dead, Christ ascended to heaven from the Mount of Olives in plain view of His disciples. His work upon earth, for which He had been commissioned by the heavenly Father, was completed. Now He was returning to His Father with the glory which He had from eternity.

But Jesus did not retire. He still sits at the right hand of the Father. That means Christ now sits in authority and reigns over everything. [God] "seated Him at His right hand in the heavenly realms, far above all rule and authority, power and dominion, and every title that can be given. ... And God placed all things under His feet and appointed Him to be head over everything for the church" (Ephesians 1:20–22). The reign of the exalted Christ redounds to the good of His Church. He who sits at the right hand of God as Lord of lords is the Head of the Church. Also, no matter how severely the Church is persecuted and besieged on earth, it will never sink or perish. Christ, who sits at God's right hand, is its Lord against whom the gates of hell are powerless.

Lord Jesus, supremely rule amidst Your enemies! Uphold Your Church that You have purchased at a great price! Amen.

Fred Kramer

1 Corinthians 15:12–28

The Knowledge of our Resurrection

I know that my Redeemer lives, and that in the
end He will stand upon the earth. Job 19:25

Christ's resurrection is inextricably intertwined with ours. If Christ did not rise from the dead, then there is no resurrection for us! We would have no hope. But thanks be to God that the apostle Paul was able to write, "But Christ has indeed been raised from the dead, the first-fruits of those who have fallen asleep" (1 Corinthians 15:20). The Savior maintained, "Because I live, you also will live" (John 14:19).

Centuries earlier Job, by divine inspiration, prophesied: "I know that my Redeemer lives, and that in the end He will stand upon the earth."

"Jesus, my redeemer lives; Likewise I to life shall waken. He will bring me where He is; Shall my courage then be shaken? Shall I fear, or could the head Rise and leave His members dead?" (*Lutheran Worship*, "Jesus Christ, My Sure Defense")

Lord, the righteousness of Your testimony is eternal. As You uphold and sustain me, I shall live! Amen.

William Boehm

May 27   Acts 2:24–32

The God of Peace

May the God of peace, who through the blood of
the eternal covenant brought back from the dead
our Lord Jesus, ... work in us what is pleasing to
Him. Hebrews 13:20–21

In this passage, God is called "the God of peace."
And why not? By the very fact that He led forth from
death our Lord Jesus, the great Shepherd of the sheep,
God indicates that He has accepted the blood Jesus shed
as our ransom. It shows that He is satisfied with Christ's
work of atonement. For that very reason, God awakened
Him from death, as the apostle testified, "He was delivered
over to death for our sins and was raised to life for our justification" (Romans 4:25).

Now we too can praise God and say, "There is now
no condemnation for those who are in Christ Jesus"
(Romans 8:1). And we can sing, "God has bestowed a
blessing upon us: Now there is unending peace, All doubt
has now been put to rest." (*Kirchengesangbuch für Evangelish—*
Lutherische Gemeinden, CPH)

God led His Son out of death through the blood of
the eternal covenant; that is to say, He raised Christ Jesus
from death after He had sealed in the New Testament an
irrevocable testament with His blood. Indeed: "He alone is
the Good Shepherd who will redeem Israel from all its sins."
(*Kirchengesangbuch für Evangelish—Lutherische Gemeinden,* CPH)

Lord Jesus, grant us Your peace! Amen.

Walter H. Bouman

Romans 6:3–5

Baptized into Christ

*For all of you who were baptized into Christ have
clothed yourselves with Christ.* Galatians 3:27

Regarding this verse in Scripture, Martin Luther
wrote, "Paul teaches us the following: Baptism is not a symbolic thing. Instead, it is a garment of Christ. Yes indeed,
Christ Himself actually is our garment. That's why Baptism
is so very powerful and efficacious." Do you treasure your
Baptism? Does it bring you comfort and joy?

Baptism is so very significant because through it we
who are baptized have put on Christ. What does it mean
to "put on Christ"?

Through our Baptism, we are "dressed" with all
that Christ accomplished for us. Through Baptism we
stand before God as sinless, righteous, and holy. As God
looks at us, He does not see our sins and death. Instead,
He sees everything that Christ is and everything Christ
has done for us. We are covered with the cloak of Christ's
own righteousness.

If you have been baptized, you have put on Christ.
Before the eyes of God, you no longer exist in your own person, but in the person of His holy Son. For comfort, remember this: you no longer stand before God in the clothing of
your sin; instead, You are clothed with Christ. Therefore,
you are now totally pure, acceptable, and pleasing to God.

Lord, grant that I constantly and thankfully live
within the comfort of faith that is mine through Baptism.
Amen.

Roy H. Bleick

Matthew 16:13–28

Shown Alive

*" 'Leave your country and your people,' God said,
'and go to the land I will show you.' "* Acts 7:3

Before His death, the Lord taught and preached
freely and publicly. Freely and publicly He gave witness to
His resurrection with personal appearances and allowed
Himself to be seen for 40 days. He did this to confirm
without doubt that He truly had risen.

He took every opportunity to speak to His disciples about the kingdom of God. He instructed, comforted,
and strengthened them so they would be well prepared for
the work He commanded when He said, *" 'Go into all the
world and preach the good news to all creation' "* (Mark
16:15).

In His Gospel, the Savior also speaks to us. With it
He instructs us about the kingdom of God. And He
encourages us to be His helpers in building His kingdom.
Oh, what blessed, enriching hours these are by which
we—just like the disciples and apostles before—are
instructed and taught by the Savior Himself!

Lord, open the door of my heart. Through Your
Word draw my heart to You. Grant that I preserve Your
Word in all its purity. Let me be Your child and heir! Amen.

Herbert D. Poellot

Ephesians 1:1–7

Forgiveness of Sins

*All the prophets testify about Him that everyone
who believes in Him receives forgiveness of sins
through His name.* Acts 10:43

Great works of art are such that we continually discover new wonders and beauty each time we view them
from various angles and vantage points.

That's precisely how it is with the great deeds of
God in Jesus Christ, His beloved Son. That's why Christ's
Easter victory over death means not only our own victory
over death, it also means that through faith in Christ and
what He did for us, our sins are forgiven. This is the same
confession which Peter once proclaimed in the home of
the Roman captain, Cornelius.

If we have forgiveness through the death of our
Lord on the cross, what then does His resurrection have to
do with the forgiveness of our sins?

St. Paul explicitly and clearly explained this in
Romans when he said that Christ was offered up on the
cross because of our sins, and He rose for the sake of our
justification and righteousness (Romans 4:25).

Christ's death and resurrection belong together.
The resurrection of Christ bestows to us the gift of forgiveness of sins won for us on the cross. And along with
this, life and salvation.

Dear God, forgive us our trespasses, and for the
sake of Christ's resurrection, grant us eternal life. Amen.

Manfred Roensch

May 31   Psalm 25:1–7

What Faith Means

*Therefore, the promise comes by faith, so that it
may be by grace and may be guaranteed to all
Abraham's offspring—not only to those who are
of the law but also to those who are of the faith
of Abraham.* Romans 4:16

God promises salvation to everyone who believes
in Jesus Christ. But what does faith mean? What happens
when we believe in God? Why and how does our faith save
us? Wherein lies its power?

Many think that to have faith means to regard
something as true. Many think that their faith is a work
that merits or earns them something. For others, faith is
nothing more than an opinion. None of these match the
biblical definition of faith.

Paul said that faith and grace belong together. The
righteousness that avails us before God is totally and completely a gift from God through His Son. That why having
faith means to totally and completely renounce ourselves
and to firmly cling to God's promise, which remains firm
and solid. The psalmist said, "I wait for the LORD, my soul
waits, and in His word I put my hope. ... for with the LORD
is unfailing love and with Him is full redemption" (Psalm
130:5–7). Faith is the solid conviction that God gives me
everything for body and soul, for time and eternity, by
grace for the sake of Christ.

I know in whom I believe: my Jesus is the foundation of faith. Amen.

Herbert J. A. Bouman

My Father Has Mercy upon Me

*As a father has compassion on his children, so the
LORD has compassion on those who fear Him.*
Psalm 103:13

It is inherently the nature of children that they,
with their mischievous and disobedient behavior, often
aggravate their father and provoke him to anger. In such
situations a father has to deal with his children not with
justice and righteousness, but with mercy. Since he recognizes the weakness and waywardness of his children, and
because he loves them, he does not want to condemn
them. Instead, he wants to keep them as his own so they
completely belong to him.

"So the LORD has compassion on those who fear
Him." If our Father in heaven were to deal with us in
accordance with what we deserve, we would be lost. As
His children, we so very often fail to meet our heavenly
Father's expectations. We, as His own children, frequently
wander away from His pathway. If we are to continue to
live, the Father of all grace has to have mercy on us and
demonstrate justice elsewhere.

My Father knows well how it stands with me. He
knows my weaknesses and sins. But He does not cast me
aside in wrath; instead, He has mercy on me. That's my
comfort. On this I rely.

Just like a father has mercy on his children, Lord
God, have mercy on us as we come to You with pure,
childlike faith. Amen.

Daniel E. Poellot

The Compassion of Jesus

*When Jesus landed and saw a large crowd, He
had compassion on them and healed their sick.*
Matthew 14:14

The above verse references glorious miracles Jesus
performed. But what help is this miracle to us? Maybe we
should really ask, of what help was this miracle to those
people?

From this miracle, they came to know one thing for
certain: "'Surely this man is the Prophet'" (John 7:40) who
was to come into the world! They surely never forgot these
miracles, and may have often thought about how Jesus so
miraculously helped them.

We can never say that Jesus no longer performs
such miracles. Rather, we take time to consider how He
still today performs great signs and wonders for us and for
all mankind. Consider the fact that still today He is merciful and patient and of great goodness and faithfulness.
Jesus Christ is also today still the Rescuer in every need.
Why? Because He is still merciful and compassionate.

His mercy and compassion drove Him down from
heaven to earth. His mercy was the reason for all His miracles and works of love. His mercy drove Him to the cross
to save us sinners and to redeem us.

Dear Savior, You are gracious and merciful and of
great goodness. For this we thank You. Amen.

Henry Blanke

Through the Name of Jesus

*All the prophets testify about Him that everyone
who believes in Him receives forgiveness of sins
through His name. Acts 10:43*

The forgiveness of sins does not mean that God
overlooks our sins. Nor does it mean that God regards sin
as if it never happened. An actual sin has happened and
remains an actuality, a done deal. So of what does forgiveness of sins consist? It consists of this: God pronounces the
sinner free of his debt of sin because through His vicarious
atonement, Christ has paid the debt of the entire world.
God forgives for the sake of and in the name of Christ!

Only a remnant of mankind avails itself of this forgiveness by faith. Only he who believes in Christ as Savior
has complete, full forgiveness. It is precisely as our text
states: Forgiveness is received by all who believe in Christ.

God desires that we daily receive forgiveness by
faith. Just as the sustaining of the world is a constant, reliable, creative act, so the justification of a sinner is a never-
ending justification. The grace in which we stand is a living stream that constantly and continuously flows from the
throne of the Lamb who was slain for us.

Lord, when I am fearful, help me to place my hope
in You. Amen.

Paul F. Wieneke

With God There Is Forgiveness

But with You there is forgiveness, therefore You are feared. Psalm 130:4

Psalm 130 is usually heard at penitential worship services. In the Scriptures, without exception, death labels all people as sinners and sin as the cause of every evil. "The wages of sin is death" (Romans 6:23). "Therefore, just as sin entered the world through one man, and death through sin, and in this way death came to all men, because all sinned" (Romans 5:12).

Such acknowledgment of sin leads to the painful question: "If You, O LORD, kept a record of sins, O LORD, who could stand?" (Psalm 130:3). The holy Judge has to regard us as guilty. All our very best deeds are unclean, like a filthy garment (Isaiah 64:6). However, the psalmist continued with this extremely comforting answer: "With You there is forgiveness ... . Put your hope in the LORD, for with the LORD is unfailing love and with Him is full redemption. He Himself will redeem Israel from all their sins" (Psalm 130:4–8).

Yes, indeed, forgiveness of all our sins is won through Christ's blood and sealed by the Holy Spirit through the Word, Baptism, and the Lord's Supper. So, where there is forgiveness of sins, there is also life and salvation. We have peace with God, and everything is to our good (Romans 5:1; 8:28).

Gracious God, thanks be to You and Your Son for guaranteed forgiveness. Help us to treasure and share it with our fellow sinners! Amen.

Otto E. Naumann

June 5   Psalm 130

Grace and Redemption

With the LORD *there is unfailing love and with*
Him is full redemption. Psalm 130:7

We can grasp the concept of grace only when we
properly recognize that our merits have been weighed and
found to fall short. This jumps out from Psalm 130:3 and
hits us square in the face: "If you, O LORD, kept a record of
sins, O LORD, who could stand?" If we were dealt with
according to our just desserts, we could not respond to any
one of a thousand accusations. We are done for.

However, with the Lord there is grace. "With the
LORD there is unfailing love and with Him is full redemption." In Christ, He has unlocked His heart of grace.
Through the Gospel, the Lord God offers us His gift of
grace. That which John describes takes place by faith:
"From the fullness of His grace we have all received one
blessing after another" (John 1:16).

In Him there is unlimited redemption. There is
redemption and eternal salvation already in this life
through the obliteration of our sins, and with them, their
curse, terror and domination, as well as ultimate and complete redemption from every evil. That's why we can sing
with Martin Luther: "Therefore I will place my hope in
God, I won't build upon my merit, My heart shall completely rely on Him And trust in His goodness."

Dear heavenly Father, thank You for the gift of
Your grace. Keep me mindful of Your Son's sacrifice on my
behalf. Amen.

Daniel E. Poellot

The Lord Is Merciful and Compassionate

Who is a God like You, who pardons sin and for-
gives the transgression of the remnant of His
inheritance? You do not stay angry forever but
delight to show mercy. Micah 7:18

The Lord is merciful and gracious, patient and
abundant with great goodness and faithfulness. That's how
the psalmist exalted God's goodness and mercy, which is as
limitless as the clouds. The prophet Micah also acknowledged that our God is a God of grace and mercy.

The mercy of God streams forth from practically
every page of the Bible. With just wrath, Adam and Eve
were driven from the Garden, yet a Savior and Redeemer
was promised to them. The entire world was destroyed
through the Great Flood, yet Noah was rescued. The children of Israel were often disobedient and ungrateful, yet
God led them into the Land of Canaan. The entire biblical
history shows us God's grace and mercy.

That's how God still considers us today: with love
and mercy. He has forgiven us our sins and does not keep
His wrath forever. God is gracious to us because His dearly beloved Son died for us and rose from the dead. Ah,
how great indeed is God's grace!

Dear Father in heaven, we laud, praise and extol
Your great grace and mercy. Amen.

Lester H. Gierach

The All-Embracing Love

"For God so loved the world that He gave His one and only Son, that whoever believes in Him shall not perish but have eternal life." John 3:16

Love is a heavenly benefit that remains for us humans even after the loss of Paradise. It increases the wealth of good times and lightens our load in difficult times. And yet earthly love is so incomplete. Motherly love is regarded as the least selfish. Nevertheless, like every other human love, a mother's love fully embraces only her own children.

Far different is the love of God. It has no restrictions. It embraces the entire world—all people, from the first to the last. It embraces the greatest saint and the greatest sinner. It embraced Paul, the most zealous apostle in the Church, who was at one time a persecutor of Christians. God's love knows no distinction between race or class. For every nation, for every generation, our text—this miniature Gospel—is appropriate and timely. God still loves our world today; He still comes to us through water and His Word, through body and blood. He also gave us His Son, so that all who believe on Him inherit eternal life. Through Christ, God receives sinners—no one is excluded.

Lord God, we thank You for Your love. Amen.

Martin Bertram

June 8   Matthew 27:24–31

Crucified for Us

God made Him who had no sin to be sin for us,
so that in Him we might become the righteousness
of God. 2 Corinthians 5:21

Christ came down from heaven and became Man
for the sake of us people and for our salvation. But how
could the marvelous incarnation of God's Son bring us salvation? We are humans—fallen, sinful humans.

The Scriptures correctly state about us: We have all
gone astray like sheep. We all have turned away and are
unworthy (Isaiah 53:6). All of us are totally unclean, and all
our righteousness is like a filthy garment (Isaiah 64:6). We
were lying under God's judgment and could not free ourselves.

But the eternal Son of God became Man for the
sake of our salvation; and, in accordance with God's will,
He was crucified for us. God laid the sin and punishment
of all mankind upon Him. "God made Him who had no sin
to be sin for us, so that in Him we might become the righteousness of God." We were not redeemed from our vain
walk of life with perishable silver or gold, but with the precious blood of Christ like an innocent and unblemished
lamb.

Thanks be to You, Lord Jesus, that You allowed
Yourself to be crucified for the guilt of our sin. Amen.

Fred Kramer

White as Snow

*"Though your sins are like scarlet, they shall be
as white as snow; though they are red as crimson,
they shall be like wool."* Isaiah 1:18

What a comforting promise from our God! When
we are concerned about our sin, when we see that it is
blood-red and that we have to stand before God in the
stain of our guilt, how comforting to know that our sins are
forgiven us. We shall be pure white; a robe of holiness will
be placed upon us in exchange for all our transgressions!

In the verses prior to our text, God had spoken
some harsh words to His ungrateful, recalcitrant, rebellious
people. He says the same to us. However, now He desires
to act in complete contradiction to what we deserve as
guilty, convicted sinners. Our sin is scarlet, as red as blood,
so we can do nothing but await His judgment. But now
comes the totally unexpected—from our viewpoint—this
glorious promise of the Lord: Your sin shall become snow-
white, like white, freshly washed wool.

God the Father lays all our guilt upon His Son. He
pronounces us righteous for the sake of Christ. How it
soothes and refreshes our heart to know this grace from
our God!

Lord, wash me thoroughly of my transgressions
and cleanse me of my sin through Christ's blood! Amen.

Otto H. Schmidt

June 10   Titus 3:4–7

God Provides Holy Baptism

*"Therefore go and make disciples of all nations,
baptizing them in the name of the Father and of the
Son and of the Holy Spirit."* Matthew 28:19

Time and again the Holy Scriptures speak about
the blessings of Baptism. "Baptism is not just plain water,
but it is the water included in God's command and combined with God's Word. It works forgiveness of sins, rescues from death and the devil, and gives eternal salvation
to all who believe. ... In Baptism the Holy Spirit works
faith and so creates in us a new spiritual life with the power
to overcome sin" (*Luther's Small Catechism*).

This is accomplished through God's grace and
commanded by Christ. The command from our Savior
actually reads: "Therefore go and make disciples of all
nations, baptizing them in the name of the Father and of
the Son and of the Holy Spirit." The command contains
this promise: through Baptism people become God's children, bear His name, live in His house, and are His heirs.
Baptism saves (1 Peter 3:21).

Do we know the day of our Baptism, and, more
important, do we know its blessings? We can live in the
grace of Baptism each day, serving the Lord who first
served us.

Lord God, You have re-birthed us through water
and Your Spirit. Continually grant this as we live as Your
baptized people! Amen.

George M. Krach

174

June 11   1 Corinthians 11:23–32

God Provides the Holy Lord's Supper

"This is My body given for you; do this in remembrance of Me. ... This cup is the new covenant in My blood, which is poured out for you." Luke 22:19–20

The Lord's Supper is "the true body and blood of our Lord Jesus Christ under the bread and wine, instituted by Christ Himself for us Christians to eat and to drink" *(Luther's Small Catechism)*. We confess this to be the true body and blood, the true, genuine, real body and the true, genuine, real blood of Christ that is essentially and actually present in the Lord's Supper. It is the body and blood of the crucified and risen Christ given and shed for the sins of the world. It is a mystery we cling to in faith. "How this can be I leave to Thee, Thy word alone sufficeth me, I trust its truth unfailing" *(The Lutheran Hymnal,* "Lord Jesus Christ, Thou Hast Prepared").

What great comfort God gives for us! In the words of Matthew, the forgiveness of our sins is sealed through Christ's body and blood poured out for us (Matthew 26:28). Our hearts are often timid and fearful; all the more reason to frequently come to the Table of the Lord. For comfort, reassurance, and full forgiveness through Christ.

Lord Jesus, Your Word is true; therefore seal to us through Your Supper the forgiveness of all our sins! Amen.

George M. Krach

My Father Thinks of Me

The LORD remembers us. Psalm 115:12

A father constantly has his children on his mind and in his heart. He often thinks about them. Even if they are already grown and self-sufficient and live far away, he never forgets them and wants the best for them.

Our Father in heaven constantly thinks about all His children here on earth. He did that already in eternity. Because God thought about us, He elected us. "In love He predestined us to be adopted as His sons through Jesus Christ, in accordance with His pleasure and will—to the praise of His glorious grace, which He has freely given us in the One He loves" (Ephesians 1:4–6). Because He thought of us, He crafted His plan of salvation to save us from the consequence of our disobedience with sinfulness. Because He thought of us, He sent His Son for our salvation. Because He thought of us, He brought us to faith through His Holy Spirit. And now our heavenly Father continually thinks about us and never neglects to keep us in His watch.

Therefore I also think about Him. I desire never to leave Him, and I cling to Him and love Him and serve Him. The fact that He thinks about me is my salvation and my hope; the fact that I think about Him is my joy and desire. He will never forget me; I don't want to forget Him.

Father, thank You for keeping me in Your watch as Your child. Help us to respond to Your love, thinking only about You. Amen.

Daniel Poellot

June 13   Psalm 32

God, Our Canopy of Grace

*Grace and peace to you from God our Father and
the Lord Jesus Christ.* Galatians 1:3

God's grace and peace extend over us like the
canopy of heaven. They encircle all of Christendom. They
bestow God's gifts to us. God's gift of grace grants us the
forgiveness of sins. God's gift of peace grants us a clear and
happy conscience. The two are constantly together.
Where there is grace, there also is peace.

The Law of God accuses the conscience. It says:
"You are a transgressor." This terrifies us. Peace flees, and
we are unable to find it again by our own searching and
any effort on our part.

No human being is himself able to do away with sin
and its thorn in the conscience. Being on guard, struggling,
achievements, pleadings, or fasting accomplish nothing.
No work of man eliminates his guilt. With such attempts a
person stresses himself out all the more. Indeed, the more
zealously he sweats and strains by the sweat of his brow to
become free from sin, the worse is his condition.

Our liberation comes only from God as an undeserved present, as a gift of grace. We are saved and receive
peace with God only by grace. God is our canopy of grace.
With Him forgiveness and peace are ours through Word
and Sacrament.

Lord, keep among us your Word of grace and the
reassurance of Your peace! Amen.

F. Samuel Janzow

Psalm 102:1–14

God's Mercy

*"Have mercy on me, O God...wash away all my
iniquity and cleanse me from my sin."* Psalm 51:1–2

Our merciful God has revealed Himself as three
distinct, yet equal Persons.

The mercy of the Father was revealed when He
sent His only Son.

The Son translated the Father's mercy into reality
by shedding His holy, precious blood to purchase the
redemption of a lost world of sinners.

The Holy Spirit has called us through the Gospel,
enlightened us with His gifts and keeps and sustains us in
the true faith.

Now, when our manifold sins, like a massive burden, become too heavy for us, we flee to the heavenly
Father who in love has mercy on us, to the Son who
allowed Himself to be laid in the grave for our sake, and to
the Holy Spirit who comforts us because He appropriates
this salvation to us.

What a comfort it is that through the three Persons
of the divine Trinity we sinners may receive this mercy!

To God the merciful Father, to God the Son who is
the only Lord, and to the Comforter Holy Spirit, be eternal glory now and into all eternity! Amen.

Albert T. Bostelmann

June 15   Psalm 147

God Knows Us

"Fear not, for I have redeemed you; I have summoned you by name; you are Mine." Isaiah 43:1

Isn't it marvelous that our dear heavenly Father constantly finds new ways to strengthen us and assure us of His love? Here is one example: God calls us by name.

The fact that God knows the number and name of all the stars shows His omniscience and power (Psalm 147:4). And the fact that God calls us by name is comforting and assuring for us. We can take comfort in the words ... fear not. The overwhelming fear of our soul's enemies—sin, death, and judgment—can recede because God the Father has redeemed us. He purchased us through the blood of His Son. We now belong to Him; and He says, "You are Mine!"

Hence, God wants to make certain we know we are indeed His own. He tells us He has called us by name. He knows us so well—is so aware of our needs and our condition—that He calls us by our very own name. That's how precious we are to the Lord! That's how precisely He watches over us! We can peacefully commend ourselves to Him for time and for eternity.

How precious it is that You have written my name into the Book of Life. May I forever exalt You, my faithful God and Lord! Amen.

Otto H. Schmidt

Ever New Mercy

His compassions never fail. They are new every morning. Lamentations 3:22–23

The thought might often cross our mind that our beloved God might indeed lose patience at hearing us beg and plead so often for this and that. If we were to offer such unending pleas and petitions to a good friend, he would soon turn his back on us. Not so with our good Friend in heaven. He is ever mindful that each is a new beginning; yet with the new day also come new assignments, new worries, new false steps and stumbling. Barely has yesterday passed with its plagues than the new day appears with similar concerns. We have barely finished laying all of yesterday's burdens before the Lord when we approach Him again with new petitions and prayers.

So it is quite comforting to hear that God never becomes weary of us and our petitions. His mercy is inexhaustible; it is new every morning. Every morning He answers our concerns with, "Don't worry, for I care for you" (see 1 Peter 5:7). Every morning He addresses our weakness, "Those who hope in the LORD will renew their strength" (Isaiah 40:31). Every morning He responds to our contrition and repentance with, "'Take heart, son; your sins are forgiven'" (Matthew 9:2).

Lord, strengthen our trust in Your unending love and mercy! Amen.

Martin H. Bertram

June 17   Jeremiah 31:1–7

Love

"Surely it is You who love the people."
Deuteronomy 33:3

From God's own mouth, Moses knew he would not enter into the Promised Land. In the context of our reading today, Moses stared death in the face, yet he stands before our eyes as a hero.

Moses had delivered a final sermon to the people of Israel and he had composed a final song (Deuteronomy 32). In this passage, with his final words, he prophesied (as did Jacob) about the future of the twelve tribes of Israel. It was a blessing inspired by God's Spirit. It actually seems as if he is seeing (as Isaiah did later) God on His throne of glory and many thousands of angels with Him. And what Moses saw did not frighten him; instead, it was something beautiful. He had often seen God's glory and described God's essence in this way: "'The LORD, the LORD, the compassionate and gracious God'" (Exodus 34:6).

Also in this final testament Moses said, "'Surely it is You who love the people.'" As a result, all the saints of God see the greatest glory in His love and grace! That is the essence of God: Love. God is love! Our human language offers no better expression to describe God's glory. His love surpasses everything that mankind calls love. So much God loved the world that He gave His Son. God loves us!

Lord Jesus, thanks be to You for Your love! Amen.

                                        Martin J. Naumann

June 18 Psalm 51:1–14

Forgiveness of Sins

Blessed is he whose transgressions are forgiven,
whose sins are covered. Psalm 32:1

The power of sin is huge. Many a person has experienced that. However, the grace of God is far greater. The Holy Bible attests to that.

Anyone who lets the devil dazzle him thinks his sin is actually quite normal and, therefore, it's not so bad. It is true that we are all sinners. But because sin is damnable, destroys peace in our hearts, and threatens our relationship with our heavenly Father, the repentant sinner flees to God with the prayer: " 'God have mercy on me, a sinner!' " (Luke 18:13). And because sin not only damns us, but also makes us filthy, we pray with David, "Wash away all my iniquity and cleanse me from my sin" (Psalm 51:2).

As we anxiously confess with the psalmist, " 'I have sinned against the LORD' " (2 Samuel 12:13a), we also shall hear the comforting words: So " 'the LORD has taken away your sin' " (2 Samuel 12:13b). Christ won this forgiveness for us. He was accused of receiving sinners (Luke 15:2). However, we can join the hymn writer by saying, therefore, that "He has also received me."

Create in me, God, a clean heart and give me a new, reassured spirit! Amen.

Albert T. Bostelmann

June 19   Matthew 6:25–32

My Father Cares for Me

*Cast all your anxiety on Him because He cares
for you.* 1 Peter 5:7

A father knows what his children need and he
exerts great effort to make it available to them. He vigor-
ously seeks to make it possible for them to have what they
may need in the future. A father cares for his children. And
children rely upon their father. If they need something,
they quickly run to him. They are confident that their
father will help if they just tell him about it.

If only we behaved in the same way toward our
heavenly Father! We so frequently forget that the Father
knows what we need, that He has nothing but good intentions toward us and has prepared every good thing for us.
We create all sorts of needless worries for ourselves in situations where the Father has long ago provided guidance
and means for us. We also forget that we can come to Him
with all our cares and concerns.

That's why the Father says to us, "Cast all your anxiety on Him because He cares for you." "Commit your way
to the Lᴏʀᴅ; trust in Him and He will do this" (Psalm
37:5). "Call upon Me in the day of trouble; I will deliver
you" (Psalm 50:15).

Heavenly Father, I trust that when my need is
greatest, You will be more than fatherly minded toward
me, Your child. Amen.

Daniel E. Poellot

Your Name—My Name

*"I have summoned you by name, you are Mine ...
everyone who is called by My name."* Isaiah 43:1, 7

The Holy Scripture places great importance upon a name. The designation of a name in these verses points to the relationship between God and His people. It also applies to individual Christians.

What does it mean that God calls you by name? His knowledge extends far beyond just your name. He knows *you*. He knows who you are. He also knows what you are and how you are. "O LORD, You have searched me and You know me. ... You perceive my thoughts from afar" (Psalm 139:1–2). It is also a loving knowledge, as God knew Moses: "'I know you by name and you have found favor with Me'" (Exodus 33:12).

What does it mean that God calls you by name? It means that you belong to Him. He is your Father, you are His child. He holds you in His hand, and nobody can take you out of His hand. You may approach Him and pray, "*Abba*, Father" (Galatians 4:6b). We say the Lord's Prayer—"Our Father"—with total confidence and certainty that He hears us. Since He has designated His name for us, we can live to His glory. "This is how we know who the children of God are and who the children of the devil are" (1 John 3:10a).

Father, blessed is the man whose name is written in Your Book of Life. Thank You for Your faithful, compassionate love. Amen.

Herman A. Mayer

Mark 1:1–11

Good News

How beautiful on the mountains are the feet of
those who bring good news, who proclaim peace,
who bring good tidings, who proclaim salvation,
who say to Zion, "Your God reigns!" Isaiah 52:7

The Gospel of Jesus Christ is known to us as the "Good News." Yet what is this Good News?

It is the knowledge the Holy Spirit works in us, through faith, that Jesus paid the price for our failures and that after death we will spend eternity in heaven with Him. Living by faith in this assurance continually fills our soul with joy.

The Good News also means that in this life we live by God's grace through faith. We were redeemed and in response to God's goodness we perform good works: proclaiming the Good News and helping the poor and the sick.

John preached the Good News concerning the "Baptism of repentance for the forgiveness of sins" (Mark 1:4). In fact, that's how the Gospel begins: The Holy Spirit, through Baptism and through the preaching of the Word, comes into our heart and works contrition (or sorrow over sin) within us. The Spirit also works faith in us whereby we are sure of the forgiveness of sins—forgiveness as a gift through the merits of Jesus Christ.

Hero from David's Branch, may Your flame of love Nurture and protect me, So that the world not disable me, Even though it yet causes me sorrow, Hero from David's Branch! Amen. (*Kirchengesangbuch für Evangelisb—Lutherische Gemeinden*, CPH)

Andrew C. Smith

June 22   Revelation 21:22–27

Our Names in the Book of Life

"However, do not rejoice that the spirits submit to you, but rejoice that your names are written in heaven." Luke 10:20

The above words are engraved into the baptismal font of one of my early parishes. When the parents and godparents brought a child for Baptism, they could read these words and know that their names, along with the name of the child about to be baptized, were really and truly recorded in heaven.

If our name is written in heaven, that means we have a legitimate claim and entitlement to a place in heaven. We ourselves have not earned or won this claim. Christ did it for us and He sealed it for us in our holy Baptism—just as Paul described it in his letter to the Galatians: "For all of you who were baptized into Christ have clothed yourselves with Christ" (Galatians 3:27). Christ's place is in heaven, and we can rejoice because our place is there too. The apostle tells us, "Since, then, you have been raised with Christ, set your hearts on things above, where Christ is seated at the right hand of God" (Colossians 3:1).

Lord, as I have been baptized with water, make me like the little child that is born anew to innocence—chosen to be Yours. Amen.

Manfred Roensch

June 23   Titus 3:3–8

I Am Baptized

You are all sons of God through faith in Christ
Jesus, for all of you who were baptized into
Christ have clothed yourselves with Christ.
Galatians 3:26–27

"Lord Doctor, are you not baptized?" That's how
Katie Luther once addressed her husband, Martin Luther,
in a short, but loaded, question when he was in despair.
Her words served as a reminder that in Baptism, God
receives us as His children and gives us a gift. They were
words of conviction and reassurance.

The fact that such a miracle is performed through a
bit of water lies in the fact that God's command and promise are in Baptism. Let unbelievers despise Baptism, it will
remain important and of great worth to us. We are not to
disregard it; instead, we through Baptism are to lay our little children into the arms of Jesus so they may become
God's children and receive Christ's blood and righteousness as a spotless, unblemished baptismal dress.

Let us consider what Paul wrote to Titus: "This is a
trustworthy saying. And I want you to stress these things,
so that those who have trusted in God may be careful to
devote themselves to doing what is good" (Titus 3:8).

Father in heaven, I am baptized! You have made me
Your own. Keep me mindful of the precious gift of Your
love. Amen.

N. P. Uhlig

Word and Sacraments

*"Teaching them to obey everything I have
commanded you."* Matthew 28:20

The Son of God came down from heaven to earth.
He became a Man, and through His life, suffering, and
death, He won forgiveness for all mankind and, along with
it, everything the soul needs for time and eternity.

However, just like a gift that is prepared but not
received does the person for whom it is intended no good,
forgiveness of sins, won for us by Christ, does us no good
if the gift is not received.

What are the means through which a person
receives the forgiveness and salvation that has been won
for him? The chief means is the Word of God. The Bible
tells an individual who repents that his or her sins are forgiven for Christ's sake. God is reconciled with them. They
shall be saved. To assure mankind of His good pleasure and
grace, God not only gives His Word, He also adds outward, visible signs. These signs in the New Testament are
the sacraments of holy Baptism and the holy Lord's Supper.
Through these, God conveys His grace to us—the grace
that comes to us through Christ.

Lord God, we thank You for Word and Sacrament,
for the sake of Christ. Amen.

C. F. W. Walther

Philippians 3:1–11

Faith and the Promise of Grace

*However, to the man who does not work but trusts
God who justifies the wicked, his faith is credited
as righteousness.* Romans 4:5

"And this is what He promised us—even eternal
life" (1 John 2:25). Thus writes John about the grace-prom-
ise of our beloved God. The grace-promises of God are all
founded upon Jesus Christ. "He is the atoning sacrifice for
our sins, and not only for ours but also for the sins of the
whole world" (1 John 2:2).

Our good works cannot earn us heaven. Indeed,
Christ purchased heaven for us with His precious blood.
What God teaches us about Christ's vicarious, substitutionary atonement, we seize by faith. "However, to the
man who does not work but trusts God who justifies the
wicked, his faith is credited as righteousness."

Our emotions can fool us. Only God's promises of
grace can still our hearts. "This then is how we know that
we belong to the truth, and how we set our hearts at rest
in His presence whenever our hearts condemn us. For
God is greater than our hearts, and He knows everything"
(1 John 3:19–20).

O Holy Spirit, grant that I may at all times rely on
Your promises of grace. In Jesus' Name! Amen.

                                        Arnold H. Gebhardt

June 26   Ezekiel 33:10–11

True Conversion

"Even now," declares the LORD, *"return to Me
with all your heart, with fasting and weeping and
mourning." Rend your heart and not your garments. Return to the* LORD *your God, for He is
gracious and compassionate.* Joel 2:12–13

People in this life are on a journey, a journey in a
foreign land. A hymn composer wrote, "I am a pilgrim
here, my home is there." The true destination is heaven. By
nature we would choose to follow the wrong path. Yet the
Lord does not want "anyone to perish, but everyone to
come to repentance" (2 Peter 3:9). With the Lord there is
forgiveness. "For He is gracious and compassionate, slow
to anger and abounding in love, and He relents from send-
ing calamity" (verse 13). He entreats us to have repentant
hearts; to be truly sorry for our sins and to believe that forgiveness is ours through Jesus Christ. He entreats us to do
so with all our hearts, demonstrating true and heartfelt
conviction.

However, Lord, I cannot know, How many faults I
have; My mind is completely shredded By sin's agony and
pain, And my heart is worn out from worry; Alas, forgive
me what is hidden, Do not count up my transgressions,
Which have angered You, Lord! Amen. (*Kirchengesangbuch
für Evangelish—Lutherische Gemeinden,* CPH)

Luther Poellot

June 27   2 Corinthians 5:17–21

What is the Meaning
of Forgiveness of Sins?

If You, O LORD, kept a record of sins, O LORD,
who could stand? Psalm 130:3

If God wanted to deal with us according to justice
and righteousness, if He were to enter into our "debt book"
every evil thought, every loveless word, every neglect of
the good, and every unjust deed ... then we would be lost
forever. But thanks be to God, that's not how He keeps
books when He deals with us. Nor does He simply say like
a lenient father: "It's okay, we'll just overlook it." For then
He would not be a just and righteous God.

How then does He deal with our sins? He does not
hesitate to chalk up the guilt—but He writes them into the
"debt book" of His Son. He chalks up the guilt to Jesus,
who took all the accusations against us upon Himself: the
guilt, the punishment, and the reparation for our sin. "God
made Him who had no sin to be sin for us" (2 Corinthians
5:21a). Now it can be said: "But with You there is forgiveness; therefore You are feared" (Psalm 130:4). We are
thankful that the wrath of God has been satisfied by our
Savior, and that the cloak of righteousness and gift of forgiveness are ours. As such we are justified through God's
grace.

Dear God, give me a repentant heart. Thank You
for the redemption that is mine through Christ. Amen.

Paul F. Koenig

191

June 28   Psalm 32

The Imputation of Sin

If You, O LORD, kept a record of sins, O LORD,
who could stand? Psalm 130:3

When reading words like this, Dr. Martin Luther
was so overcome by emotion that he would lay the Bible
down and weep. For what could be more fearsome than
the full accounting of our sin before God?

The truth is that sin is always present in us. Because
we have the old Adam in us, time and again we come in
repentance to our God. Only then do we recognize the
great grace of God in Christ that makes us snow-white. It
remains a miracle of God that our sins have been redeemed
and that we can be saved. Luther stated this beautifully in
his hymn, "For if You wanted to look at the sins and
wrongs that are done, who Lord could abide before You?
Nothing avails before You but grace and goodwill to forgive sin. Our doings of course are in vain, even in the best
of lives. ... Therefore I will hope in God; I will not build
upon my merits. My heart shall rely upon Him, and trust
in His goodness."

Dear Lord, grant us forgiveness, and let us also be
forgiving of others for Your sake. Amen.

Otto F. Stahlke

June 29   Isaiah 1:18–31

Divine Judgment

"Though your sins are like scarlet, they shall be
as white as snow; though they are red as crimson,
they shall be like wool." Isaiah 1:18b

"Come now, let us reason together, says the LORD."
Those are the words that immediately precede today's
verse. In this verse, the Lord is entering into judgment with
His people. How will that actually turn out? Anyone who
reads the verses that surround this passage might quickly
draw a conclusion. There it specifically states: "When you
spread out your hands in prayer, I will hide My eyes from
you; even if you offer many prayers, I will not listen. Your
hands are full of blood" (Isaiah 1:15). The conclusion is
that only one judgment is possible: "Take your evil deeds
out of My sight!" (Isaiah 1:16).

But, no. Instead of this frightening judgment, God
offers words of inexpressible grace. Read these passages once
more. Can this be possible? Yes, indeed, thus says the Lord,
"but where sin increased, grace increased all the more"
(Romans 5:20b). "Though sin has become manifold with us,
with God there is even much more grace" (*Kirchengesangbuch*
für Evangelisb—Lutherische Gemeinden, CPH). God, our Lord of
unending love, sent His only Son into this world to take our
sin and the punishment for our sin upon Himself. He died for
me; He has won salvation for me!

Oh, Christ, I trust You that although my sins be
blood-red, because of the power of Your blood they nevertheless turn snow-white. Amen.

Herman A. Mayer

193

The Good Shepherd

*"I am the Good Shepherd, I know My sheep and
My sheep know Me."* John 10:14

It is known that a shepherd cares for his sheep. He
leads them to fresh meadows and to quiet waters. He also
takes care that they are secure from wild animals. Thus the
sheep "have it made" with their shepherd.

That analogy also describes how things are
between Jesus and us. He is the Good Shepherd who cares
for us. We are His sheep. He sees to it that we are secure
from the wolves—the false prophets who wish to do us
great harm. He also sees to it that our souls are richly fed
and nurtured through His Word and Sacrament. Thus we
lack for nothing.

The Good Shepherd knows His sheep by name.
He has done everything for them that is necessary for their
salvation. He has sent His Holy Spirit into their hearts so
they might know Him as their Good Shepherd and follow
Him no matter where He leads. Thus, we really have it
made because we have such a Shepherd, and how gladly
can we then heed His voice as He calls us by name! In the
same manner, we can, with great longing, anticipate the
day when we will be eternally with Him in heaven!

Lord Jesus, our merciful Shepherd, lead us upon the
right path for Your name's sake! Amen.

Gerhard C. Michael

Isaiah 44:18–28

Sin and Transgression Have to Disappear

*"I have swept away your offenses like a cloud,
your sins like the morning mist. Return to Me, for
I have redeemed you."* Isaiah 44:22

The state of our human nature encourages us to detach ourselves from our sin. However, to those who truly listen to the accusation of their conscience, sin becomes an unbearable load. And it becomes quite clear that no one except God—the one against whom we have sinned—can free us from that load.

That is precisely what God has chosen to do. He takes no pleasure in the death of the godless. He would much rather forgive than condemn. Believe the Lord God's promise: "I have swept away your offenses like a cloud, your sins like the morning mist." To fulfill that promise, He sent His only Son to bear the torture of suffering and dying and even the darkness of separation from God. He did all that so Jesus might take upon Himself the punishment the sinner deserves and to shatter the power of hell. Just as the wind blows away the storm clouds and the sun's rays disperse the fog, so Christ's blood and righteousness wipe out the sins of all mankind.

To whom does this promise apply? Not to him who is smugly satisfied with himself and his own efforts; rather to him who, like the lost son, returns to the father with genuine contrition and repentance, confessing his sin and begging for forgiveness. What a compassionate gift of grace!

Downcast, I confess my sins. Grant me, my Savior, forgiveness through Your grace! Amen.

Herman A. Mayer

The Word of Reconciliation

*We are therefore Christ's ambassadors, as though
God were making His appeal through us. We
implore you on Christ's behalf: Be reconciled to God.*
2 Corinthians 5:20

These words from the apostle Paul deal with reconciliation. The concept is addressed four times in three verses.

First, let's concentrate on the opposite of reconciliation: conflict, jealousy, resentment, and animosity. Sad situations such as these exist throughout the world between couples, families, neighbors, and nations. People, who at one time were friends, oppose one another with hostility. It's terrible when a situation becomes irreconcilable. For the relationship is to return to its previous cooperative state, reconciliation must take place.

Now we concentrate on the greatest reconciliation of all. The greatest misery in the world stems from enmity between God and man. Through sin, mankind is estranged from the Lord. God's wrath is revealed because of mankind's unrighteousness. Only God can heal the breach. God was in Christ and reconciled the world to Himself. God saw to it that the reconciliation accomplished by Christ was passed on to us sinners. God established among us the word of reconciliation. Thus, God has reconciled us sinners to Himself.

God, we thank You for Your holy Gospel. Help us treasure it by faith! Amen.

Herbert J. A. Bouman

Out of Deep Need, I Cry to You

Out of the depths I cry to You, O LORD,
O LORD, hear my voice. Psalm 130:1–2

Psalm 130 may well be one of the best known and most beloved of the psalms, and the first verses are often used as memory work.

Also well known is the hymn, "From Depths of Woe I Cry to You," by Martin Luther: "From depths of woe I cry to you. O Lord, my voice is trying to reach your heart and, Lord, break through with these my cries and sighing. If you keep record of our sin and hold against us what we've been, who then can stand before you?"

Like the psalmist and Martin Luther, the children of God also cry out in their anguish—and in faith—to a merciful God for help and rescue. Our needs may be manifold, yet the basic evil and greatest need—in every case—is sin. The Christian's heart well knows where help is to be found; namely, in the wounds of Christ. In Christ, all our sins are forgiven daily. Through faith in our Savior, we are certain of this gift of love. Thus, in every need and for all eternity, God's mercy is assured to us.

To You, Lord, I cry out in my need. For the sake of Christ, You will stand beside me at all times. Amen.

Alfred C. Seltz

God's Word, a Treasure

*When Your words came, I ate them, they were my
joy and my heart's delight.* Jeremiah 15:16

That Christians have the gracious, living Word of
God is a greatness that cannot be measured by man. Nor
can this greatness be grasped by any thought or fully
described in any words.

In God's Word we find a heavenly light that lightens our way. In Scripture we have a treasure chest that
contains the forgiveness of sins. The Word of God not
only proclaims that all men's sins are wiped away by Jesus
Christ, it also reveals that it is the very hand of God that
distributes this precious goodness and blessing to mankind.

With the Word of God we have an inexhaustible,
overflowing fount and source of comfort. We also have in
it a sharp-edged sword with which we can fight all our foes
and conquer every battle.

Finally, in the Word of God we have a key to heaven.

O what great grace God bestows on all those who
are His own through Baptism—those who embrace the
truth of His Word and grace! Thus we say with the
prophet Jeremiah that God's Word is "my joy and my
heart's delight."

We ask of You, Lord God, to work through us to
share Your Word and spread the Good News of Your
Gospel to others. To You be the glory! Amen.

C. F. W. Walther

　　　　　　　　　　　　Romans 8:31–39

Our Advocate with the Father

*Who is he that condemns? Christ Jesus, who died—
more than that, who was raised to life—is at the
right hand of God and is also interceding for us.*
Romans 8:34

"Friend, how did you get in here without the right clothes?" So asked the king of a guest in one of Jesus' parables when he discovered that the guest had not put on the wedding garment that was furnished by the host of the wedding. The guest had no response for the king.

We also would find ourselves speechless before God's throne of judgment. Just like the guest in Jesus' parable, we have no excuse for our sinful state and most certainly would immediately be cast out into the darkness.

But thanks be to God! We have Someone who speaks for us before God when we cannot. He is our Spokesman—Jesus Christ. He speaks before the Father on behalf of all those whom He Himself purchased at a great price. He provides us a wedding-like garment—the cloak of righteousness which He bought for us through His suffering and death. Our holy God no longer condemns us because we are now dressed with Christ's righteousness and holiness which redeems us before God and is pleasing to Him.

Lord Jesus Christ, be my Spokesman before God so my name might be freely read from the book in which are written the names of those who are Yours! Amen.

Hilton C. Oswald

The Forgiveness of Sins

*I write to you, dear children, because your sins
have been forgiven on account of His name.*
1 John 2:12

In this verse, John wrote that our sins are forgiven
through the name of our Lord and Savior, Jesus Christ. He
has, through His perfect life, suffering, and death, won our
forgiveness. In Christ we have redemption and the forgiveness of sins.

Through His word of absolution, our Savior assures
us of the forgiveness of sin. It is indeed true that as often
as we hear the Word of the Gospel and come to the Holy
Meal our hearts are brought anew the certainty that our
sins are forgiven.

This takes place in a very special way. In confession
we repentantly admit our sin and the One to whom we
confess pronounces absolution. The Holy Scriptures speak
a great deal about this absolution, or forgiveness: we
receive it from God Himself and are not to doubt but to
firmly believe that our sins are thereby forgiven before
God in heaven.

O Jesus, Your love is so great; I come weary, naked,
and ashamed. Alas, let me find grace! Amen.

Herman A. Harms

Lifelong Love

Even to your old age and gray hairs I am He,
I am He who will sustain you. Isaiah 46:4

In marriage, the couple promises each other lifelong love. An excellent illustration of the steadfastness of such love on into old age is the common picture of hoary-headed spouses who, through the years, journey hand in hand and, with love, nurse and care for each other!

However, that picture is a mere inkling of the lifelong love of God in Christ. This love guides the uncertain steps of our childhood; it guides us through our youth. And in keeping with God's promise, it does not leave us in a lurch during old age. When our strength diminishes, He promises to carry us in hands of love. When friends and relatives are lowered into the grave before us, He assures us: "I will never forsake nor neglect you." If the years lead to woeful, nostalgic feelings and despair, He will comfort us.

We pray: Alas, abide with us, Lord Jesus Christ, since it now has become evening. Your divine Word, that bright light indeed, never may it be extinguished within us! Abide in us with Your faithfulness, my Lord and God! Grant us steadfastness and help us in every need! Amen.

Martin H. Bertram

The God of the Living

"Have you not read what God said to you, 'I am the God of Abraham, the God of Isaac, and the God of Jacob.' He is not the God of the dead but of the living." Matthew 22:31–32

We will all die someday. Death is God's judgment against us sinful, self-centered humans. Before the beginning of the world, God knew this would happen. He created mankind in His own image, conversing with Adam and Eve as a father with His children. Then the power of sin separated us from God and brought us under His judgment.

This judgment, however, is not the end—as the Sadducees who confronted Jesus had thought. God is especially the God of the living and not a god of the dead. Through Jesus Christ, He makes it possible for us to receive eternal life.

Through Word and Sacrament, the Lord God makes this new life available to all. We receive it in Baptism. Through the Word of forgiveness and through the Lord's Supper, God sustains us with His grace; new each day and given to us in love.

We thank You, Father, that You are the God of the living and that You grant us eternal life through Jesus Christ. Amen.

Jakob K. Heckert

July 9   Philippians 3:13–21

My Savior Brings Me to the Goal

*Not that I have already obtained all this, or have
already been made perfect, but I press on to take
hold of that for which Christ Jesus took hold of
me.* Philippians 3:12

Yes, my Savior, bring me to the goal line! However,
my desire is not just to enter into heaven, but to "participate in the divine nature" of God (2 Peter 1:4). In heaven,
I will be fully restored to God's image. Here on earth I am
still far from the goal; I am still far from being complete.
Sin constantly wields its power over me and hinders me
from living like a child of God. But God empowers me to
strive for the goal with all my might. Every day He
strengthens me to ever more overcome sin, to live a
changed life, and to strive for perfection in Him.

I know I cannot achieve the goal on my own.
Christ helps me. When I stumble and fall, He picks me up.
He holds me close to His heart and carries me—just like a
mother does with her child until it walks by itself.
Therefore, I do not despair when I recognize my weakness.
My Savior helps me to take one step after another, and,
ultimately, He brings me to the goal.

Jesus, our Lord and Savior, we thank You for Your
mercy. Amen.

                                        Clarence T. Schuknecht

July 10   1 Corinthians 13:1–13

Love Never Ceases

Keep on loving each other as brothers.
Hebrews 13:1

In many Christian lands, sayings that become well known often find their origins in Scripture. Sometimes a familiar saying is taken directly from the Bible. That's the case with the saying, "Love never fails" (1 Corinthians 13:8).

There hardly exists a more important truth than the enduring steadfastness and power of love. The greatest and deepest love is God's love. In love, God the Father gave His only Son to the entire sinful world to redeem and save it (John 3:16). Nothing is of more worth to us poor sinners than the love of the heavenly Father, who did not even spare His own Son but gave Him up for us (Romans 8:32). God's love never quits!

A weaker, yet miraculous, reflection of God's love is the love that resides in the heart of a Christian. Nurtured by the Holy Spirit, it is mightier than the power of mankind. Its culmination reaches all the way to heaven. May this love ever live within us!

Through the might of Your love, O God, may ever enduring love live within our hearts! Amen.

Alfred C. Seltz

The Aaronic Benediction

*"The LORD bless you and keep you; the LORD
make His face shine upon you and be gracious to
you; the LORD turn His face toward you and give
you peace."* Numbers 6:24–26

This blessing is often spoken at the conclusion of a
worship service. It points us to the holy Trinity and
reminds us of what the Lord Himself says: "'I am the Alpha
and the Omega,' says the Lord God, 'who is, and who was,
and who is to come, the Almighty'" (Revelation 1:8).

"The LORD bless you," not just in general, but "with
every spiritual blessing in Christ" (Ephesians 1:3), and keep
you. He is our guardian (Job 7:20), who protects His own
"like the apple of His eye" (Psalm 17:8). What a profound
blessing!

"The LORD make His face shine upon you and be
gracious to you," that is to say, in Martin Luther's words,
"show Himself kindly and comforting, not look at you
with a sour face ... rather joyfully and fatherly smile at you;
which is what happens as He forgives us our sin." What
undeserved favor!

"The LORD turn His face toward you and give you
peace." What a gracious gift!

Dear Lord, bless us, protect us from every evil, and
finally bring us into eternal life! Amen.

Luther Poellot

July 12   Psalm 77:1–16

Divine Comfort

*My flesh and my heart may fail, but God is the
strength of my heart and my portion forever.*
Psalm 73:26

The Lord God is a God of comfort. Christ has won
the best comfort for us in that He sacrificed His life for the
forgiveness of our sins. The Holy Spirit is called
"Comforter" because He provides the assurance of this all-
embracing comfort to us.

Despite all that, we often complain with Hezekiah,
"Surely it was for my benefit that I suffered such anguish"
(Isaiah 38:17a). We become anxious when our sins accuse
us. Yet we once more find comfort as we say by faith, "You
have put all my sins behind Your back" (verse 17c).

The Law shows us our sin and God's wrath. It
exposes our sinful desires, thoughts, words, and deeds. It
judges us and burdens us with the weight of our sin. To this
the Savior speaks this comforting invitation: "'Come to
Me, all you who are weary and burdened, and I will give
you rest'" (Matthew 11:29). We find this comfort in the
confidence that God richly and daily forgives us all our
sins for Christ's sake. "In Christ's wounds I fall asleep; they
make me pure of sin" (*Kirchengesangbuch für Evangelish—
Lutherische Gemeinden*, hymn 412, verse 1).

Father of mercy, comfort us in our tribulations so
we also may be able to comfort others! Amen.

Albert T. Bostelmann

John 10:1–11

The Good Shepherd

"I am the Good Shepherd." John 10:11

For Jesus' listeners, shepherds and herds in the fields of their homeland were a vivid image. When Jesus called Himself the Good Shepherd, He created for them a specific and meaningful word picture. A good shepherd led his sheep to green meadows and fresh water where they would be nourished. He safely guided them over dangerous ground. He pulled lambs from thorny hedges. He sought straying sheep. At risk to his own life, the shepherd protected his flock from thieves, robbers, and wolves. He watched over his herd by day and by night.

Thus Jesus, the Good Shepherd, leads us upon our life's path, sometimes upon smooth roads, sometimes over rocky ledges. Through His suffering and death, He rescued us and carries us in arms of love so we may live in His kingdom. Thus we can say with David, "The LORD is my Shepherd, I shall not be in want" (Psalm 23:1). He strengthens us. When we stray, He comes after us. He is with us even as we pass from this life into physical death. And so, in faith, we can rejoice with David, "You are with me" (Psalm 23:4).

"I am Jesus' little lamb, Ever glad at heart I am." Amen.

Martin Bertram

Do Not Be Afraid!

"I have summoned you by name." Isaiah 43:1

The nation of Israel was above all else God's possession because He created it. He had also rescued it from the slavery of Egypt and from sin. God points this out: "I have summoned you by name; you are Mine." Floods and flames of fire could not harm Israel, for the Lord was with them.

Does not this also apply to us Christians, who, through faith, are God's people? We are God's own because He created us and because Jesus Christ redeemed us with His precious blood. If God is with us, beside us, and for us, who would dare be against us? If God protects us, who can harm us? We can say with the psalmist, "God is our refuge and strength, an ever-present help in trouble" (Psalm 46:1).

Just as surely as God fulfilled the glorious promises to His people of Israel, that still happens today and will continue to happen until that Last Day when He gathers His children. Blessed are all who are called by His name and hear His voice. They need not fear.

O Jesus, true Life, You have given Yourself to me and are established in my heart; my soul and mind are delighted. Amen.

Paul F. Wieneke

Psalm 73:23–28

Comfort and Comforter

The God of all comfort. 2 Corinthians 1:3

In a world in which trouble and tribulation are experienced every day, we find an excellent description of our God in this verse. Suffering was no stranger to the apostle Paul, yet he speaks here about "the God of all comfort, who comforts us in all our troubles."

In the Scriptures we find the God of all comfort, who promises us comfort like that which a mother gives. Who does not remember from childhood the richly comforting voice of one's mother as she assuaged childish concerns? Thus God also wants to comfort us with the voice of His Word. In the Scriptures we find a God who says, "Take heart, son; your sins are forgiven" (Matthew 9:2). There we find the Holy Spirit, the One called the Comforter, whose special office is to deeply sink into our hearts the comfort of God. We are able to repeat the words of the psalmist, "My comfort in my suffering is this: Your promise preserves my life" (Psalm 119:50). And when God does not totally free us of suffering, He always gives us the assurance of His presence, and we can say, "My flesh and my heart may fail, but God is the strength of my heart and my portion forever" (Psalm 73:26).

Who shall be my comforter when I am in pain? Who upon my deathbed? Who finally on the Day of Judgment? Alas, here and there I would indeed have nothing, if I did not have Jesus.

Martin H. Bertram

209

July 16   Romans 8:35–39

My Father Is with Me

You are with me, Your rod and Your staff, they comfort me. Psalm 23:4

One of life's most bitter feelings is loneliness, especially for frightened children who feel they are totally alone. However, when God the Father says He is with us, then anxiety subsides and everything feels all right again. This is true for as long as we live. We can endure many a trouble if we know we are not alone, that Someone is with us.

Our heavenly Father has promised something special—He does not forsake those who are His. Just as He once said to Joshua: "I will never leave you nor forsake you" (Joshua 1:5c). He also testifies to all of His own through Jesus' words: "'I am with you always, to the very end of the age'" (Matthew 28:20). We can cling to this promise and be upheld by it.

What's more, this does not apply only to us, but to the entire household of God, all His people upon earth. At times, it may appear as though the Lord has forsaken His church, but "God is within her, she will not fall" (Psalm 46:5a).

The Lord is not now or ever separated from His people; He remains their confidence, their blessing, salvation and peace.

May this ever be so! Amen.

Daniel E. Poellot

July 17   Romans 8:24–27

The Support of the Comforter

"But when He, the Spirit of Truth, comes, He will guide you into all truth." John 16:13

We confess: The Holy Spirit has called me by the Gospel, enlightened me with His gifts, sanctified me in the true faith and sustains me in it; He forgives me and all believers; He will resurrect me and all the dead, and along with all believers in Christ He will give me eternal life (the explanation of the Third Article of the Apostles' Creed, the *Small Catechism*).

Jesus calls the Holy Spirit a Comforter, someone who not only dries our tears and speaks words of encouragement to us in our despair, but also places Himself at our side and provides us true support. It is His office to support us, to safely guide us, to actually give us correct advice at times when we may have strayed from the path. To us He is true strength along the way.

We confess that we often fail to treasure that which the Holy Spirit provides. If it were not for this third Person of the Godhead, we would recognize very few blessings from the work of the first two Persons. Were He to forsake us, or if we wanted to drive Him away through deliberate sinning, we would be lost. But thanks be to God that through the Holy Spirit, we can complete our journey.

Lord God, take not Your Holy Spirit from us! Amen.

Daniel E. Poellot

211

July 18   Isaiah 54:4–10

Joy after Weeping

*For His anger lasts only a moment, but His favor
lasts a lifetime; weeping may remain for a night,
but rejoicing comes in the morning.* Psalm 30:5

"After the laughter comes the crying." So goes a
saying often repeated to children. The psalmist, however,
completely reverses it. In the verse for today, he states that
laughing and joy come after the weeping. This is God's
gracious promise.

Our forefathers in the Bible understood that God
guides and directs everything in the lives of His children
with love and grace so that joy follows even times of sorrow. That's how it went in the life of Abraham, David, Job,
and other heroes of faith. That's also how it was in Jesus'
life. After the weeping in Gethsemane and upon Golgotha
came the joy of Easter Sunday.

The Lord promises: "Those who sow in tears will
reap with songs of joy" (Psalm 126:3). Through faith in our
Savior, who overcame and conquered all weeping and
mourning, eternal joy and salvation are ours as well. For
this we can glorify and exalt God, and we can offer our
praise and thanks without end.

Dear Savior, grant us the eternal joy of heaven after
the weeping of this temporal life! Amen.

Lester H. Gierach

God Stays beside Us

"Never will I leave you, never will I forsake you."
Hebrews 13:5

When through death or other separation a loved one leaves, we experience a pain that can rob us of all joy. "It is not good for the man to be alone" (Genesis 2:18) applies as much today as it did in Paradise's garden. Wise Solomon said, "pity the man who falls and has no one to help him up" (Ecclesiastes 4:10). And sadly, we could even confess that we have contributed to the loneliness of others or to our own loneliness. There is one Person, however, who never forsakes us or causes us to feel lonely.

The Savior knows from personal experience the pain of loneliness; He suffered the torture of God-forsakenness. On the cross, He was completely alone. Yet He promises us, "'I am with you always, to the very end of the age'" (Matthew 28:20). It can be said of Christians that even when we are alone, we are never alone. We find comfort in that thought, and we can comfort others with it too.

Lord Jesus, abide with us and help us also to share Your presence with others! Amen.

Daniel E. Poellot

My Father Comforts Me

I will turn their mourning into gladness; I will
give them comfort and joy instead of sorrow.
Jeremiah 31:13

Children often cry, whether for real or imaginary reasons. Their emotions are often overpowered by sadness and the tears flow. Yet when a parent comes to encourage and comfort, the crying soon stops and the child once more becomes calm and happy.

This also applies to the children of God, no matter how old they are. None are spared sadness, even if it does not plague all Christians to the same degree. Our sufferings are sometimes self-inflicted, sometimes caused by others, or sometimes unexplainable. No matter, we all know what it means to cry and be sad.

But we also know what it means to be comforted. Our Father in heaven bends down to us and takes away the reason for our sadness. He replaces our loss with a new blessing. He strengthens us so we can overcome the sadness and once more be serene and cheerful. And one day, "God will wipe away every tear from their eyes" (Revelation 7:17).

Lord God, you are and remain faithful. You comfort us after we weep. In place of the sad, dark night, You let the Star of Joy shine through! Amen.

Daniel E. Poellot

Isaiah 26:11, 21

Tribulation

LORD, *they came to You in their distress;*
when You disciplined them, they could barely
whisper a prayer. Isaiah 26:16

This verse is directed to heathens—those who do
not cling in faith to God's grace to us through Christ. They
care very little about God until some misfortune befalls
them. They forget about God until He comes with the rod
of discipline. Then they cry out to Him in their need.
Unfortunately, this is all too often the case with
Christians—those who embrace Christ in faith—as well.
That's why it is written in the sayings of Solomon: "My
son, do not despise the LORD'S discipline and do not resent
His rebuke, because the LORD disciplines those He loves,
as a father the son He delights in" (Proverbs 3:11–12).

How quickly we murmur and complain when things
go badly. We forget that with our sins we actually deserve
nothing better, indeed that we should be confronted with
much worse. We also forget that the chastening is not out of
wrath, but flows from love. "I have loved you with an everlasting love" (Jeremiah 31:3b). Obviously, "no chastening ...
we regard as joy, but is actually sadness," and yet, "Blessed is
the man whom God corrects; so do not despise the discipline of the Almighty. For He wounds, but He also binds up;
He injures, but His hands also heal" (Job 5:17–18). The
Father desires to again bring home His lost son.

Help, Helper, help in anguish and need; have
mercy on me, O faithful God! Amen.

Herman A. Mayer

July 22   Ezekiel 34:11–16

Jesus' Sheep

"My sheep listen to My voice, I know them, and they follow Me. I give them eternal life, and they shall never perish, no one can snatch them out of My hand." John 10:27–28

As children we probably sang this song: "I am Jesus' little lamb, Ever glad at heart I am; For my Shepherd gently guides me, Knows my need and well provides me, Loves me ev'ry day the same, Even calls me by my name."

This is a glorious truth for adults as well: The Lord Jesus is our Good Shepherd and we are His little lambs. He guides us to the green meadows and to fresh water. He sees to it that all our needs—bodily and spiritual—are satisfied. He protects us from all danger (Psalm 23).

Each of His sheep is precious to the Lord. He loves and knows each of us individually; He knows what each of us needs. Also, He gives each of us the glorious promise that we—redeemed from our sins through His holy life and His bitter death—will enter into eternal life. No one is able to snatch us from Him, for He constantly stands at our side and watches over us, His sheep and lambs.

Lord and Savior, Jesus Christ, You Good Shepherd, grant that we continually gladly hear Your voice and happily follow You all the way into eternity! Amen.

Reinhold Stallman

Matthew 28:16–20

The Christian's Comfort

"Surely I am with you always, to the very end of the age." Matthew 28:20

Jesus gives the repentant thief on the cross the assurance: "'I tell you the truth, today you will be with Me in paradise'" (Luke 23:43). With these words, Jesus promises the penitent sinner not only salvation in heaven, but that he will also partake of Jesus' presence and fellowship. The murderous thief will not need to be ashamed when Moses and the patriarchs see him among the blessedly saved, for Jesus is beside him.

In the above text, the gentle and humble Savior promises that He will also be with all Christians during their pilgrimage on earth. Jesus' presence at their side assures that He has forgiven them all their sins and that He stretches out His sheltering hand over them. In each life situation, on good days and bad, He is our Protector.

What a refreshing, renewing comfort for Christians! With Jesus beside us until the end of the world, we can overcome every evil—even death. Also the fear of death can evaporate. Let us think of this every day.

Lord Jesus, abide with us, for it will soon be evening in our life and in our world! Amen.

Louis J. Roehm

July 24   Psalm 91

Confident in Storms

"Take courage! It is I. Don't be afraid." Mark 6:50

These words of comfort were heard first by the disciples during a stormy night at sea. At the beginning of this Bible story, we learn that the Lord made His disciples take this journey in the boat. Perhaps they would rather have remained with the people who, after the miraculous feeding, wanted to make Jesus king by force. To keep the disciples focused on His mission, Jesus made them travel by sea.

As the storm rose, so did their anxiety. The disciples' greatest anxiety was that the Lord was not with them. Had He forgotten them? No, for He saw that they were suffering from stress (Lamentations 1:20a). They, of course, did not yet know this. They were to learn that the Lord is always with His own in every storm. As anxiety and stress were at their peak, the disciples saw a figure walking upon the sea. "A ghost!" they all cried out, and saw it as a sign that they would surely die. But then they heard His beloved voice: "Take courage! It is I. Don't be afraid." Jesus stepped into the boat, and the wind died down.

Yes indeed, with them in a storm, yet not visible! In similar fashion, the Lord is also beside His own at all times. When the need is the greatest then God's help is the closest. Be comforted! Do not be afraid!

Protect us, faithful God, in every storm! Amen.

Victor A. Bartling

Loneliness

*"Come to Me, all you who are weary and burdened,
and I will give you rest. Take My yoke upon you
and learn from Me, for I am gentle and humble in
heart, and you will find rest for your souls."*
Matthew 11:28–29

Is your life sometimes lonely? Sometimes this is so because a person has no family nearby. Or perhaps a person lives alone and is unable to leave the house. We can be lonesome when we are surrounded by many people. Perhaps we feel lonely even when members of the family are nearby. Whatever the situation, loneliness. It simply saps us of our energy.

But let us never forget that God comes to us and is ever at our side. We are assured of this in the above Bible verses. We can lay our burden of loneliness upon Him. Without cost to us, He gives us His love for the sake of Christ. He is constantly at our side with His grace because He has made us His children through Baptism. He will never forsake us.

Loneliness is a sign of a world that is not complete. That which is missing because of sin, Jesus fills in. We receive the fullness of His forgiveness, His love. In this world problems like loneliness will not disappear. However along with such problems comes the peace and joy in the Lord.

Dear Jesus, You are ever beside us. What a comfort! Amen.

Curtis P. Giese

July 26   Isaiah 40:1–8

The Comfort of Forgiveness

Comfort, comfort My people! says your God.
Speak tenderly to Jerusalem, and proclaim to
her that her hard service has been completed.
Isaiah 40:1–2

In today's text, God is speaking to His preachers. He wants them to know this so they can comfort God's people. And God's people are to know this: their preachers have an assignment to comfort them. God is very earnest about this; that's why He says it twice: "Comfort, comfort My people!"

Take note that here God speaks comfort to His own people. This comfort has, of course, been offered to everyone because Christ died for all people. However, the world seeks its comfort in other things and not from God. Consequently, the world discovers—to its horror—that none of these other things can provide true comfort.

The preachers are to comfort the children of God with this: warfare is over. The forceful lordship of sin, the tyranny of the power of darkness, which holds us in servitude, has been broken. We have received two-fold a blessing from the hand of the Lord—a two-fold, double, overflowing measure of grace. This was a marvelous exchange: two-fold for all our sins. How gladly may we listen when our preachers proclaim this comfort to us!

Lord, comfort me once more with Your help! Amen.

Otto H. Schmidt

A Comforting Word: "Don't be Afraid!"

"Do not be afraid, Abram. I am your shield."
Genesis 15:1

The words in the Bible, "do not be afraid," are especially comforting. We find this encouragement more than 70 times in the Bible, as our dear Lord seeks to comfort individuals like Abraham, Isaac, and Jacob; cities like Jerusalem; and groups of followers.

Everyone has experienced fear and anxiety. It may simply be a worry or it perhaps is something very frightening that threatens to harm us. It does not matter what it is, we can be certain about one thing: God tells us not to be afraid.

The old Abraham was in no mortal danger so he had no reason to be anxious. But he was. God had promised him many descendants, yet in his old age he was still waiting for a son. God saw this old man downcast, unhappy, miserable and sought to comfort him. "Do not be afraid," the Lord said; "I am your shield and your great reward." Then God led Abraham outside and told him that he would have as many descendants as there are stars in the sky! And that's exactly what happened.

Dear God, I thank You for the assurance in Your Word that I ought not be afraid. Amen.

Edwin W. Leverenz

Wiping Away the Tears

The Sovereign LORD will wipe away the tears from all faces. Isaiah 25:8

Tears can be a sign of sorrow, despair, pain, or doubt. In this life we often have occasion for tears. The world is a vale of tears. It became that through sin.

The Lord God knows and sees our tears. He knows too well our suffering. In love for us, He promises that He will wipe away all tears from our face. He removes the thorny sticker that has caused our tears. Like a mother comforts an anxious child and wipes away its tears, the Lord deals with us. He comforts us with His Word, forgives our sins, and promises us eternal life. In an especially glorious way, He will wake us from death and as we enter into heaven, He will graciously bend down and, with inexpressible divine kindness, will wipe the tears from our faces for all eternity. In a funeral hymn we are reminded that "Christ shall wipe away all of the departed one's tears; He already possesses that for which we still long; into His ears shall be sung that which no ear has ever heard." What great love from our great Lord!

Dear God, dry our tears through the hope of eternal life! Amen.

Otto H. Schmidt

John 16:20–23

The Comforted Ones

"Blessed are those who mourn, for they will be comforted." Matthew 5:4

When a child is in pain, he or she immediately seeks a parent for comfort.

That's how it is with us and our heavenly Father. In this world we suffer much pain. There exist illness, grief, worry, sorrow, and tribulation of all sorts. However, we are not like orphans who have no loving parent to turn to. We have a Father in heaven who is filled with love for us. In all our grief and pain, He gives us divine comfort. His Holy Spirit keeps us mindful of Jesus and His work of redemption. He assures us that our sins are forgiven, and we are comforted.

As God's comforted children, it is also our great privilege to comfort others. There is much opportunity to do that. One can speak a cheering word to the sick and troubled. One can help through acts of service, especially on behalf of the poor and needy and victims of war.

Ultimately we will also partake of the eternal comfort in heaven. There we will—along with others who believe in Jesus as their Savior—enjoy and savor the complete, perfect comfort of heaven. We comfort one another today with God's promise of eternal comfort.

We thank You, dear Father, for Your lovely comfort. Grant that we always embrace it! Amen.

Reinhold Stallman

July 30   Matthew 11:25–30

Come to the Wedding!

"'Tell those who have been invited that I have pre-pared my dinner.'" Matthew 22:4

The Savior continuously issues this invitation to us, *"'Come to Me, all you who are weary and burdened, and I will give you rest'"* (Matthew 11:28). He wants to give eternal rest for our souls. After death and Judgment Day, it will be too late to be saved. The invitation to the wedding in heaven comes to us in this life. Everything is ready. Through God's Word and Sacrament, the Savior brings us forgiveness and peace now—today. Here is complete salvation from sin and its horrible consequence—sadness, deception, death. That's why Jesus' precious invitation comes to us. Here is comfort for every heartache. The Savior gives us the eternal joy of heaven. Everything has been won for us and guaranteed to us through His suffering and death for us.

Oh, if only every father, every mother, every son, every daughter would only hear this invitation and, through the mighty working of the Holy Spirit, would receive this blessing by faith! No one shall ever regret being a guest at this heavenly banquet of the Lamb.

Dear Savior, help us to take to heart Your kind, gracious, blessed invitation! Amen.

Paul M. Freiburger

The Burdensome Weight of Sins

Surely I was sinful at birth, sinful from the time
my mother conceived me. Psalm 51:5

What David confesses here about the burden of his sins is the confession of each repentant Christian. For when the Christian sees how his life-long burden of guilt was laid upon Jesus Christ, and how our Savior so gladly and willingly bore the entire load, then the thankful song breaks forth.

With deep feeling, Pastor Paul Gerhardt knelt at the foot of the cross, thought about his sins, and said: "I, I and my sins—which like little seeds are found like grains of sand upon the seashore—they have stirred up the misery and the sad, agonizing torment which smites You."

We humans and our sins caused Jesus' suffering. These sins are so multitudinous that we are unable to grasp all the Savior had to endure to free us from the burden. However, He perfectly accomplished this and more as He was offered up for our sake and, for the sake of our righteousness, was raised from the dead. Thus we are reassured in Scripture, "'Though your sins are like scarlet, they shall be as white as snow'" (Isaiah 1:18).

Dearest Lord Jesus, let Your death and suffering in my stead rest within my heart! Amen.

Walter W. Stuenkel

Romans 15:4–13

The Comfort of the Scriptures

For everything that was written in the past was
written to teach us, so that through endurance and
the encouragement of the Scriptures we might have
hope. Romans 15:4

The true comfort of the Scriptures lies in Christ.
He says: "'these are the Scriptures that testify about Me'"
(John 5:39).

The true comfort of the Scripture lies in the Savior
of the world, about whom Isaiah prophesied: "In that day
the Root of Jesse will stand as a banner for the peoples; the
nations will rally to Him" (Isaiah 11:10).

God the Holy Spirit accomplishes a spiritual gar-
dening project in the heart of man that changes its waste-
land into a garden of Eden. The seed is the Word of God.
The sower is Christ, as well as everyone who helps to
spread God's Word in the world: pastors, teachers, missionaries, parents, all Christians big and small. A true, well
cared-for garden of God in the heart of man, through faith
in Christ Jesus, is a glorious blessing.

Lord, steadfastly teach us to use Holy Scripture to
better know Christ and His Comfort, and that we place all
our trust and hope in Him alone for our soul's salvation!
Amen.

Herbert D. Poellot

Isaiah 42:1–9

God Sustains the Weak Faith

A bruised reed He will not break, and a smolder-
ing wick He will not snuff out. Isaiah 42:3

If there is one thing that can frighten a believer, it
is thinking he is not praying properly or that he has too
little faith. But even in this the anguished soul can take
comfort.

It should serve as a comfort to such an anguished
soul that any prayer spoken in Jesus' name, based upon His
blood and merit, is a true prayer. There is nothing more
proper than this. And a faith plagued by doubt is just as
genuine and beatific as a strong faith. The true desire to
come to God in prayer is a demonstration of true faith
because such a longing is the work of the Holy Spirit.

Every weak faith can seize Jesus and His holy merits and wounds. Satan cannot extinguish the light of faith
in the heart, since darkness indeed cannot extinguish the
light. Reading the Bible, waiting upon the Lord ... all these
strengthen faith.

Faith is God's gift, and God will not require more of
you than what He has given you. Christ also died for the
weak in faith. He prays for them, that their faith, although
weak, may ever more strengthen and never cease.

Strengthen my faith when weak and break the
work of the devil so I nevermore despair, instead that I may
constantly carry Christ in my heart! Amen.

Martin Luther

The Comfort of the Gospel

*Comfort, comfort My people! ... proclaim to her ...
that her sin has been paid for.* Isaiah 40:1–2

The Old Testament prophets did not only know
the Law, they knew the Gospel. The prophet Isaiah in particular, from chapter 40 on, dispenses and bestows the
comforting words of the Gospel. The slavery to sin has
been ended, now there is forgiveness for iniquity.

The Gospel of forgiveness is the comfort for all
ages. It offers freedom from sin's rule of captivity. Sin is the
cause for all misery upon earth. It has made mankind into
slaves. It rules them and drives them to every evil. "What I
do is not the good I want to do; no, the evil I do not want
to do—this I keep on doing. ... What a wretched man I am!
Who will rescue me from this body of death?" (Romans
7:19–24).

And when a person succumbs to sin, the Law accuses him. It threatens him with the everlasting punishment of
hell. Such is the warfare, the tyranny Isaiah says has ended
because our sin has been forgiven. O sweet word of comfort! "Speak tenderly to Jerusalem," says our text. This
comfort of forgiveness is the only thing that can restore
and give new life to broken, crushed hearts. And it is ours
through faith in Christ.

Do not despair, You have help at the door. He who
soothes and comforts your heart is standing there. Amen.

Herman A. Mayer

Micah 7:18–19

Comfort

Surely it was for my benefit that I suffered such anguish. In Your love You kept me from the pit of destruction; You have put all my sins behind Your back. Isaiah 38:17

These are the words from Hezekiah, a godly king in Judah, who had been sick and had been healed from that sickness (verse 9). Within the context of this verse, however, is something far more spiritual than physical healing alone. Hezekiah was fearful about his sins, believing that because of his sin he deserved to be ill. He was in pain and agony of the soul, and did not know how to help himself.

The Lord, however, saw Hezekiah's anguish and heard his prayer (Isaiah 38:30). Out of compassion and love, God rescued Hezekiah from death, adding 15 years to his life. He accomplished an even greater rescue for Hezekiah's soul. God hurled all his sins behind Him. Psalm 79:8 tells us that God forgives all sins and no longer holds them against us. Martin Luther said it this way: "Where there is forgiveness of sins, there is also life and salvation." Where there is physical healing, there is prolonged life. Where there is the spiritual healing of forgiveness, there is eternal life.

"Jesus sinners will receive. Even me He has forgiven; And when I this earth must leave, I shall find an open heaven. Dying, still to Him I cleave—Jesus sinners will receive." Amen. (*Lutheran Worship*, hymn 229)

Luther Poellot

August 6   Hebrews 7:21–25

Jesus, our Priest

*"You are a priest forever, in the order of
Melchizedek."* Hebrews 7:17

Christ is a High Priest, but not according to the
Order of Aaron or from the house and descent of Levi. For
if that were the case, we would not have benefited at all
and He could not have prepared an everlasting salvation
for us.

No, Christ is a High Priest according to the Order
of Melchizedek. The Bible tells us nothing further about
the origin and descent of Melchizedek, this mysterious
person. But as Christ is without beginning or end. His
priesthood is eternal, established by the heavenly Father.
That's why we can say Jesus has an imperishable priesthood and that through His sacrifice, He saves those who
come to God through Him for all eternity. And He continues to come before God, praying on our behalf.

So very blessed are we to have an advocate before
the throne of the holy God whose intercession is new
every morning. Our High Priest takes our side and intercedes for us. And His priestly office brings us comfort in
every situation of life—in sickness and tribulation, in life
and in death.

Jesus, our High Priest, we thank You that You sacrificed Yourself for us and still pray for us. Amen.

Walter H. Boumann

Hebrews 13:1–6

Jesus' Presence

*"And surely I am with you always, to the very
end of the age."* Matthew 28:20

What a glorious promise! The Savior promises His
disciples collectively and individually His almighty presence until the end of days. They are His sent ones whom
He will never let out of His sight. They can at all times
count on His gracious presence—both in work in spread-
ing the Gospel and in their private lives. His grace and
almighty power will guide them in all their ways.

This glorious comfort applies to us as well, every
day and every hour. Have we encountered difficulties in
life? He will never lay more upon us than we can bear. Are
we sick? God tells us, "I am your Lord, your Physician"
(see Matthew 9:12). Have we lived to a ripe old age yet
experienced all sorts of heavy burdens? "Even to your old
age ... I will sustain you" (Isaiah 46:4). Have we lost a
loved one? "The girl is not dead but asleep" (Matthew
9:24). Is the angel of death knocking on your door? "Fear
not, for I have redeemed you; ... you are Mine" (Isaiah
43:1b). Are current events chasing terror into every corner of your mind? "And we know that in all things God
works for the good of those who love Him" (Romans
8:28). He holds everything in His hand. Nothing can
happen but what He has foreseen and what blesses us.
Blessed is he who trusts in Him.

We believe, Lord; help our unbelief! Amen.

Otto E. Sohn

The New Jerusalem

*I saw the Holy City, the new Jerusalem, coming
down out of heaven from God.* Revelation 21:2

What Christian has not wished for a clear picture
of heaven, of the new Jerusalem? The Bible tells us what
will not be there—hunger, thirst, tears of sorrow, death,
crying out, and pain. Instead, God promises joy, full sufficient satisfaction, eternal life. We read: "Our present sufferings are not worth comparing with the glory that will be
revealed in us" (Romans 8:18). What supreme, ecstatic
happiness!

In Revelation, John uses many symbolic portrayals
of earthly treasures to explain to us, who have not yet been
glorified, the glories of heaven. In the new Jerusalem, he
saw golden streets, gates of pearl, mountains of jasper,
foundations decorated with all sorts of jewels, a city of
pure gold like unto pure glass. In heaven, we will also see
our loved ones who died holding to their faith in Christ.
The most glorious part is that we shall see God face to
face. The exalted Redeemer shall graze us and lead us to
the fountains of living water.

My exalted Redeemer, I long for the new Jerusalem,
where I shall praise You forever. Amen.

Gottfried H. Naumann

August 9   Psalm 25

Our Heavenly Home

Our citizenship is in heaven. Philippians 3:20

He who at all times keeps his eyes fixed on the fact that our actual home and citizenship is in heaven will find a constant source of great comfort in this life. He is a foreigner on this earth; heaven is his home; he is a citizen of heaven. While he still is in this world and is diligent in his earthly calling, he nevertheless longs for what is to come. At all times he remembers that his dwelling here is temporary, and as a result he intensely seeks the future one. And what abiding assurance to know that this heavenly home is already now his. He is already a citizen with the saints and God's invited. He is able to sing: "Who shall rob me of the heaven which God already has reserved for me by faith?"

What a glorious comfort to know this in our earthly vale of tears! What a comfort for the hour of death! The apostle says: "We wait for the blessed hope—the glorious appearing of our great God and Savior, Jesus Christ" (Titus 2:13). In our death, the Savior, Jesus Christ, appears to us to take us to Himself into eternal life. And there we will be at home with Him. "Blessed are the dead who die in the Lord from now on" (Revelation 14:13). Jesus says, "'where I am, My servant also will be'" (John 12:26).

Lord Jesus, because You died for me, I receive a treasure: eternal life in my Father's house. Amen.

Herman A. Harms

233

August 10   Isaiah 43:1–3

"I Will Be with You"

"I will not leave you as orphans; I will come to you." John 14:18

Among the greatest sorrows of life is to be forsaken. If we are without family or relatives, if we have no close friends, if no one accepts us and we end up being all alone, then all other sorrows weigh even more heavily upon us. Such loneliness is a frequent experience for very old people, but it can happen to anyone—like with the disciples of the Lord Jesus, as they carried Jesus to the grave and their earthly fellowship with Him ended abruptly. Is loneliness our cross? Do we say with the sick man at the pool of Bethesda, "I have no one"?

The Savior says, "I will come for you." And that is not just for a convenient visit but for lasting support at our side, every day until the end of the world. Christ knows what forsakenness means more than any other man, and He says to us: "I will not leave you as orphans." Clinging to this promise strengthens us and takes the sting out of loneliness. With Christ beside us, we are not alone.

I know You will not forsake me; Your truth remains eternally steadfast for me. You are my true, faithful Shepherd, who will protect me forever. Amen.

Daniel E. Poellot

Psalm 118:1–14

Trusting God

*How priceless is Your unfailing love! Both high
and low among men find refuge in the shadow of
Your wings.* Psalm 36:7

"Trust in the LORD with all your heart and lean not
on your own understanding," says the wise Solomon
(Proverbs 3:5). Despite that admonition, we frequently
rely upon our own intelligence, upon our own righteousness—like the Pharisee in the Temple. Or, we rely upon
the promises of another, forgetting that they cannot make
good on their promises in all circumstances.

But we can in every circumstance place our trust in
the Lord. "For the Word of the LORD is right and true; He
is faithful in all He does" (Psalm 33:4). God the Father testifies that He loves us, that He *is* love. He promised to
send His only Son—and He did. He says to repentant sinners, "Your sins are forgiven you," and they *are* forgiven. He
promises, "I will never leave you nor forsake you" (Joshua
1:5). Jesus reinforced that when He said, "'and surely I am
with you always, to the very end of the age'" (Matthew
28:20). In the hour of our death, we may confidently say
that the Lord will protect our departure and our entry.
That He has promised.

Lord, I trust in You. Let me nevermore be put to
shame! Amen.

Albert T. Bostelmann

Isaiah 40:1–11

The Voice of the Good Shepherd

"My sheep listen to My voice, I know them, and they follow Me." John 10:27

The picture of a shepherd is a beloved motif in Christian art. Jesus as the Good Shepherd among the sheep of His flock, with a little lamb that had strayed tucked safely in His arm, is a picture that has given joy to Christians for centuries. This is quite understandable, for the picture of the Good Shepherd is not a fantasy of some Christian artist. Rather, it goes back to the words of our Lord and Savior Himself, in which he portrays Himself as the Good Shepherd.

"My sheep listen to My voice," Jesus says. "I know them and they follow Me." With this He shows us that He, the Good Shepherd, gathers and keeps together His flock with His own voice through His Word. "Praise God," says Luther in the Smalcald Articles, "a seven year old child, knows what the Church is, namely ... the little lambs who hear the shepherd's voice." The Church of Jesus Christ is there where the voice of the Good Shepherd sounds forth, there where the Gospel about Jesus Christ, the Savior of sinners, is proclaimed.

Lord Jesus, Shepherd of Your sheep, continually call us to You through Your Gospel! Amen.

Manfred Roensch

August 13   Isaiah 43:1–7

We are the Lord's!

Whether we live or die, we belong to the Lord.
Romans 14:8

What comforting words: we are the Lord's! Whoever believes this is happy and comforted, is afraid of no one and of no evil, not even in sickness or before a major surgery. He places all his cares upon the Lord. He feels secure and hidden under the wings of the Most High. Indeed, in life and in death we are the Lord's.

Yet, by nature, we stand under the Law. The Law condemns us because of our sin and our conscience supports this judgment. But then comes the Gospel and brings us the glad tidings of our reconciliation to God through Christ's blood and death. His blood cleanses us from all sin. Because Christ has redeemed and won us, we now are the Lord's. That's why we steadfastly cling to this truth: "Whether we live or die, we belong to the Lord." Yes, and even in death, for our death is regarded as precious to Him. What a glorious comfort! In Romans 8, Paul said, "I am convinced that neither death nor life, neither angels nor demons, neither the present nor the future, nor any powers, neither height nor depth, nor anything else in all creation, will be able to separate us from the love of God that is in Christ Jesus our Lord" (Romans 8:38–39).

Lord Jesus, I live for You; Lord Jesus, I die in You; Lord Jesus, I am yours; whether dead or alive, save me! Amen.

Walter H. Bouman

My Father Watches over Me

He who dwells in the shelter of the Most High
will rest in the shadow of the Almighty.
Psalm 91:1–2

Children are exposed to many dangers against which they are defenseless. Therefore, their parents must vigilantly watch over them and protect them from danger. Their power and wisdom often protects children when they otherwise might suffer harm.

Our Father in heaven is a master at this, not just when we are children, but throughout our lives and into old age. God the Father is our shelter and umbrella. He has promised this: "When you pass through the rivers, they will not sweep over you. When you walk through the fire, you will not be burned; the flames will not set you ablaze" (Isaiah 43:2).

That's why we can confess that our Father in heaven shelters us from all danger and protects and preserves us from every evil, all because of His sheer fatherly, divine goodness and mercy, without any of merit or worthiness on our part.

I lie down and sleep in total peace, for You alone, Lord, help me so I may live safely. Amen.

Daniel E. Poellot

Psalm 46

Faithful Waiting

Be still before the LORD and wait patiently for
Him. Psalm 37:7

Sitting quietly is difficult for a little child. And to remain quiet is often difficult for grown children, especially if sickness and need have the upper hand or when we are tortured by worries about food or money. That's often when we become impatient, bad tempered, and despairing.

In today's verse, the psalmist says, "be still before the LORD." Confess God as your Father in Christ, and rely totally on Him. Our gracious God and Father guides and directs all things, not some blind fate. "If the sin in this world sends me a cross to bear, if anguish and pain press upon me, should I despair because of that? No, for God will direct it!" That's what being still before the Lord means. Stop, pause, and place your cross into the hands of the Father whose Son bore the ultimate cross.

"Wait patiently," reads our text. God is already underway with His help. Did He not promise, "While they are still speaking I will hear" (Isaiah 65:24)? His help may not come in the manner or time we prescribe, but He knows what is best and for our good. He offers help in His own way and in His own time.

Wait my soul, wait upon the Lord; Commend everything to Him, He so gladly helps! If everything breaks, God does not forsake us; The need obviously is not greater than the Helper. Amen.

Paul F. Koenig

239

The Flowers

"See how the lilies of the field grow." Matthew 6:28

How lovely and beautifully the lilies grow, without humans or the lilies themselves bearing any concern over it. "They do not labor or spin" (Matthew 6:28). Although they do not make or purchase their own clothing, they are not without dress or covering. Instead, they have a most beautiful garment, a garment so beautiful that the Savior said, "'I tell you that not even Solomon in all his splendor was dressed like one of these'" (Matthew 6:29).

Why ought we to consider the lilies and the other flowers? The Savior gives the answer, "'If that is how God clothes the grass of the field, which is here today and tomorrow is thrown into the fire, will He not much more clothe you, O you of little faith'" (Matthew 6:30). Furthermore, our Lord has prepared for us a most glorious cloak, the perfect righteousness of Christ, whereby we too stand before God. Therefore, don't worry; instead, first and foremost, strive after the kingdom of God!

He who never forgets the flowers is also my kind Father. My soul, praise Him! Amen.

William Boehm

The Lord Is Near and Helps

A righteous man may have many troubles, but the
LORD delivers him from them all. Psalm 34:19

The Lord is near. The Lord helps. These are two truths that time and again are evident in the lives of the children of God. That's how it has always been. Think about the life's journey of the patriarchs, about the history of the children of Israel, about the prophets of the old covenant and about the apostles and evangelists of the New Testament. The Lord stood beside all of them with His love and grace and mercy. He helped them in their need. He did not forsake nor neglect His own.

Also today the gracious, loving, benevolent God is near us. His promise stands solid: "'I am with you always, to the very end of the age'" (Matthew 28:20). In His eternal love, He especially helps those whose heart is broken. These are those of us who acknowledge our sinful state and rely upon the Savior. We know that the Savior has paid our debt of sin and has borne our punishment. Since the Savior, Jesus Christ, has done all this, the Lord is near with His help, here in this time and there in eternity.

We thank You, dear Lord, that You are near us and help us every day. Amen.

Lester H. Gierach

Ephesians 2:11–22

True Hope

Perseverance, character; and character, hope.
And hope does not disappoint us, because God has
poured out His love into our hearts by the Holy
Spirit, whom He has given us. Romans 5:4–5

"Don't give up hope!" "Hope for the best!" These admonitions, or others like them, are typical of what we often hear. Life without hope is most certainly unbearable. And thus mankind hopes for the sick to become well, the unemployed to obtain a job, the couple to have a blessed marriage, a nice home, a prosperous life, and so forth. However, hope is often mingled with anxiety: if things don't turn out as hoped, then what? If our hope rests upon our own effort, upon the friendship of others, upon favorable circumstances, then we can only hope with worry.

However, the Bible encourages us to be "joyful with hope." This is possible only if we place our hope in God. This is a hope that looks beyond death and the grave. The apostle Peter calls this "living hope," which is rooted in the redemption wrought by Christ and which has been revealed to us through His resurrection. Our hope rests upon this!

My heart exquisitely rejoices in the fact that I am of good courage and wait upon You. I completely rely upon Your name. Help, help, help! To this I say: Amen. (*Kirchengesangbuch für Evangelish—Lutherische Gemeinden*)

Paul T. Kreiss

August 19   Matthew 7:7–11

God Wants to Save You

"Call upon Me in the day of trouble, I will deliver
you, and you will honor Me." Psalm 50:15

The Christian life is not a vacation resort; it is a
battlefield. Christians encounter fearsome enemies and
powerful temptations to conquer. The devil, the evil
world, and our own sinful flesh are not friends or allies
when it comes to Christian living and eternal salvation.
Such inevitabilities cause difficulties, misery, anxiety, and
stress in the lives of the children of God.

That's why God's Word and promise are so comforting. The Lord's gracious invitation is, "Call upon Me in
the day of trouble." And He follows this invitation with
the promise, "I will deliver you!" God is able to do this
because He is the almighty God. With Him nothing is
impossible. In fact, He has already rescued us from the
greatest trouble: the problem of sin. The Lord Jesus has
saved us from sin through His holy life and innocent suffering and death.

Dear God, guide and lead us so we may call on you
in every need, and glorify, praise, and thank You! Amen.

Lester H. Gierach

August 20   Exodus 40:34–38

My Father Guides Me

You guide me with Your counsel. Psalm 73:24

Children often stumble and fall as they take their first steps. It is necessary for a father to take his child's hand and lead him or her with care so he or she may safely go. Childish stubbornness and a desire for independence causes the little one to want to shake off the father's hand but, nevertheless, with the father's hand things go much smoother.

As children of God, we would do well to remember that. At times, as we gain experience and take on greater responsibility, we want to deal with various matters independently. Yet it remains true that we can hold onto the Father that He might hold and guide us so we may proceed with greater confidence.

That's why this is my life's plan: "In all matters I let the Most High counsel," for "He leads me with fatherly hands, His gracious eye guides me" (*Kirchengesangbuch für Evangelisch—Lutherische Gemeinden*). Then everything goes well. In His hand no missteps occur, no detour, no wrong way. "He who gives directions, routes and roads to the clouds, sky and winds shall also find ways upon which your feet may trod" (*Kirchengesangbuch für Evangelisch—Lutherische Gemeinden*).

The reason we gladly allow ourselves to be led by God's gracious hand is because from His Word we learn that He has the best in mind for us. As miraculous as it appears, so blessedly it is nevertheless intended.

Dear Lord, lead me and guide me. Amen.

Daniel E. Poellot

August 21   Isaiah 41:1–14

A Triple Clanging of the Bell

So do not fear, for I am with you; do not be dismayed, for I am your God. I will strengthen you and help you; I will uphold you with My righteous right hand. Isaiah 41:10

A godly Christian once called this verse a threefold clang of the bell, which plants wonderful renewal in the heart. The first clang tells us, "do not fear, for I am with you." Just as a child is afraid of the dark of the night, sometimes we become anxious and afraid in the darkness of the future and we don't know our way in or out. "I am with you," says the Lord. We are not alone. "There is nothing that can happen to me but that which He has foreseen and what is a blessing for me" (*Kirchengesangbuch für Evangelisch—Lutherische Gemeinden*).

With the second clang of the bell, we are told, "do not be dismayed, for I am your God." Never run away! To come to God; to remain with God, is important. Our heavenly Father reassures us by saying, "hold on to Me, I am your God."

The third is a three-part clang: "I will strengthen you and help you; I will uphold you." Come what may, everything has been provided for. And although the world is filled with devils that actually want to destroy us, in our weakness He is our strength, in our helplessness He helps us. And when we are completely desperate, He raises us up. Grab hold! Hold on tight! No evil will befall you.

So then take my hands, Lord, and lead me until my blessed end and into all eternity! Amen.

Herman A. Mayer

1 Corinthians 12:18–27

Prince, Captain, Hero

He is the head of the body, the church; He is the
beginning and the firstborn from among the dead.
Colossians 1:18

Christ is the head of His Church. This expression
does not seem all that unusual to us. We have heard it
often in sermons and during Bible class, and in our minds
this seems self-evident and correct. But do we really understand just what the apostle Paul wishes to communicate
with this picture, that Christ is the Head of the body (the
Church)? Do we see that with this, Paul precisely describes
the inextricable unity between our Lord Jesus Christ and
us, who belong to His Church?

The body cannot live without the head, nor the
head without the body. Together they are an inextricable living fellowship. The pious Landgrave Zinzendorf
sang, "He the Head, we His members; He the Lamp and
we the light; He the Master, we the brothers; He is ours,
we are His." Our Lord Christ is the beginning and the
firstborn from the dead. He will not allow the members
of His body to remain dead but shall lead them into eternal life.

Lord Jesus, Head of Your Church, grant that we living members remain in Your body! Amen.

Manfred Roensch

The Blessing of Trusting God

The blessing of the LORD brings wealth, and He adds no trouble to it. Proverbs 10:22

How often have we heard the saying, "All that is good comes from the blessings of God." Yet how difficult it is for us to hold onto this truth in our lives, especially in times of trouble. When illness, infirmity, pain, and doubt burden us, we frequently lose the fortitude of our faith and trust in God.

Solomon said, by inspiration of the Spirit, "The blessing of the LORD brings wealth, and He adds no trouble to it." When we trust in God rather than relying on our own efforts, we can sing with an 18th century composer, "Everything depends on God's blessing and on His grace, beyond all money and goods. Whoever places his hope in God shall, safe and sound, totally obtain the freedom of a hero's courage."

The blessing of trusting God rests in the sure confidence that God's grace is our portion—not because we have earned or deserved it, but solely because Jesus Christ has reconciled us to God. Then everything we, by faith, think, say, or do increases to our blessing. Thus may it be with us all, today and always!

As God wills, it has to be; if God wills, I am prepared. Lord, strengthen my faith! Amen.

Walter W. Stuenkel

The Hand of Faith

"Take heart, daughter, ... your faith has healed you." Matthew 9:22

Only faith connects us to Jesus and imparts His gifts and blessings to us. This is demonstrated in the story about the healing of the bleeding woman to whom Jesus said, "take heart, ... your faith has healed you." She had suffered for 12 years. She had heard about Jesus and thought, "If only I could see Him, then I would merely have to touch the hem of His cloak to obtain His healing power." She pushed herself through the crowd so she could touch His garment, and she was healed. Jesus turned around and asked, "Who touched Me?" Jesus well knew who it was. Power had gone out from Him to her through her strong faith.

Through this story, everyone can know what faith does. Jesus told this woman to take comfort because her faith in His mercy and goodness allowed her to receive His healing power. When we are heavy-laden, we too can approach Him, trustingly, to "touch" the hem of His cloak. The Lord feels our contact and says, "take heart, ... your faith has healed you."

O Jesus, strengthen our faith and help us! Amen.

Victor A. Bartling

A God-fearing Challenge

"You come against me with sword and spear and javelin, but I come against you in the name of the LORD *Almighty."* 1 Samuel 17:45

This familiar story in the Old Testament describes a decisive battle between the giant, Goliath, and youth, David, a mere shepherd. If Goliath were to win, Israel would lose the important battle. However, should David overcome the giant, Israel would be victorious. While the Philistine Goliath bragged about his great power and weapons, David called upon the Lord, who led David to defeat his proud opponent with a slingshot. David even took off the giant's head with Goliath's own sword.

David is the picture of an unpretentious, straightforward believer who places His trust in God and His Word. With that he decisively overcomes that which the world offers with its haughty arrogance. At the same time, the picture of David points to our Redeemer, whose victory over the devil has freed us from all our enemies so we obtain victory and are able to serve God in peace.

So often people assume a foolhardy self-reliance in their own abilities to defeat the giants in this world. May God bestow on us a victorious faith in Christ!

Forgive us, O Father, our haughtiness and grant us the humility of true faith in Christ! Amen.

Gerhard T. Naumann

Psalm 121

My Father Wakefully Watches

He who watches over you will not slumber. Psalm 121:3

A faithful father watches over his child, and stands ready to help and protect. In so doing, he indicates that his child's welfare is of great importance to him. Anyone who is a parent well knows how many sleepless hours this requires. Yet it is done gladly and out of love.

That's how our Father in heaven watches over us— every day and hour of our lives. He does not turn His eye away from us for a single moment. He knows everything that happens to us. Hence no enemy is able to pounce on us without His knowledge; no misfortune is able to overcome us.

With the watchfulness of our heavenly Father, our salvation is also certain. Since He is watching over us, then He will sustain us in our faith, protect us against the workings of the devil, and support us in the hour of death. "Nothing can happen to me but what He has foreseen and is a blessing to me." (*Kirchengesangbuch für Evangelish— Lutherische Gemeinden*)

At the same time, we acknowledge that all our ways are known to Him, even those steeped in sin. Through Jesus, we can come to Him for forgiveness and for guidance and power to walk according to His will. Protection and forgiveness are ours, at all times, for the sake of Christ.

Heavenly Father, watch over those who hope in You, both late at night and early in the morning, that You will protect and save them. Amen.

Daniel E. Poellot

One God and One Mediator

For there is one God and one mediator between
God and men, the man Christ Jesus.
1 Timothy 2:5

Because of sin, man was eternally banished from Paradise by God and ultimately cast from the source of all joy and salvation. Then along came a Mediator, "the man Christ Jesus."

Jesus Christ is true God and true Man. Therefore, He is an acceptable mediator between God and men. He has appeased the wrath of the Father and paid the price to full satisfaction for us. He is our Prince of Peace who made reconciliation between God and mankind. Through Jesus' blood, we are once more brought near to God. "In Him we have redemption through His blood, the forgiveness of sins, in accordance with the riches of God's grace" (Ephesians 1:7).

Now we have peace with God. We stand in God's grace through Christ's blood and death. What can ultimately harm us? How do I view all trouble? If He is at my side, as He most certainly is, then all of hell's deceit can assail me. In Christ, God's grace rests upon me. By trusting in my Mediator, I am certain of God's blessings. Through Him, God will give me all things. (*Kirchengesangbuch für Evangelish—Lutherische Gemeinden*)

May all my doings and endeavors take place in the name of Jesus Christ, for He is my Mediator. Amen.

Herman A. Harms

Under God's Protection into Old Age

Even to your old age and gray hairs ... I will
carry you; I will sustain you and I will rescue
you. Isaiah 46:4

The comparison between the true, living God and the ineffective, dead idols becomes especially clear in this chapter. In Isaiah 44, the prophet denounced the worthlessness of idol worship. Those who make idols might search in the forest for a beautiful beech-tree, oak-tree, or cedar-tree. He uses half of it as firewood and with the remainder He carves an idol that is not living and cannot hear him as he bows down to pray.

How totally different it is when the everlasting, living God says to His children, "I will carry you." He carries us from our mother's womb, from infancy, on into life. "'For in Him we live and move and have our being'"(Acts 17:28). He not only has created us, He also sustains us. He richly and daily cares for us with all we need to sustain body and life. He protects and guards us from every evil.

Even in old age, when sight and hearing fail, when body and mind fail, He still comes to our aid. He reassures us anew: "I will do it; I will pick you up and carry you and save you." How many a person has been sustained by this word of comfort!

I trust in You, my God and Lord. If I have You, what more do I want or need? Amen.

Herman A. Mayer

A Prayer for God's Protection

Keep me as the apple of Your eye; hide me in the
shadow of Your wings. Psalm 17:8

David speaks poetically: "Keep me as the apple of Your eye; hide me in the shadow of Your wings." He also speaks about the godless who deign to "destroy" us. He compares the godless with lions that desire the prey; that's why he prays for God's protection. With confidence he trusts that God wants to guard him like a person protects the apple of one's eye.

David experienced much danger as a young shepherd and in the battle with Goliath. As he grew older, King Saul persecuted him. But David was constantly under God's protection. As a result, he was filled with thanksgiving, and he lauded, glorified, and praised God with many psalms.

In our daily life, we also encounter many dangers. It matters not where we are—at work, on the road, at home—God's protection is always there. Satan's darts and arrows do not always fly past us. Sometimes they hit their mark. Let us not only pray for protection, but let us with David daily exalt, praise, glorify, and thank God for the care He shows us, especially for the salvation He has provided for us through Christ Jesus.

Dear heavenly Father, protect me like the apple of Your eye. Amen.

Otto F. Stahlke

Titus 3:3^7

Trusting Him Who Has Washed Us

And that is what some of you were. But you were washed, you were sanctified, you were justified in the name of the Lord Jesus Christ and by the Spirit of our God. 1 Corinthians 6:11

At Corinth there was sin, disgrace and all sorts of major offenses. But Jesus died for people like that. God sent the apostle Paul to instruct them. And He assembled the Christian church from among them.

By nature we are no better. Even when we appear outwardly good, God's Law shows us the sin that still resides in our hearts. For people like that, for people like us, Christ died. God has given us His Word. From among us God has assembled a Christian congregation.

There were true Christians in Corinth that we may not want as neighbors. However, for the sake of Christ, God washed them, cleansed them, forgave them, and accepted them. We still sin every day. Through Baptism God has washed, cleansed, forgiven, and accepted us. From eternity we have been His accepted children and heirs of salvation.

Dear Lord and Savior, we thank You for the bath of rebirth and renewal. Amen.

John M. Drickamer

Our God of Hope

*May the God of hope fill you with all joy and
peace.* Romans 15:13

God provides a living hope for us in Christ, our
Savior. It is the hope of eternal life. This hope is necessary
amidst the trials and misery of this present time. This hope
fills us "with all joy and peace" by faith. The concerned
heart of the sinner experiences joy through faith in the certainty that we receive full and free forgiveness in Christ
through the waters of Baptism and His body and blood at
the Lord's Altar.

With this joy, the restless heart also receives peace,
the peace of God which sustains in us trust that God is our
beloved Father and Jesus is our Savior and Brother. He is
beside us every day until the end of the world (Matthew
28:20). If our heart is filled with this peace by faith, then
the hope of everlasting life will be inspired in us to the
same degree so our entire life will be ruled by it.

The God of hope gives us these glorious blessings
through the power of His Holy Spirit, who works in our
hearts through the Gospel. "Our train is heaven bound"
shall now be our motto.

Gracious Father, God of Hope, grant us faith, and
along with it, joy and peace in Christ! Amen.

Herman A. Harms

Up to Here, and No Farther

[God said,] "This far you may come and no farther." Job 38:11

We hear the loud voice of God in nature: when there is thunder and lightning, when the waves of the sea roar, when an earthquake threatens destruction. God is the Creator and Sustainer of all things. We cry to Him for help for every need. In this sinful world, there are also gruesome tyrants who rear their head and oppress, torture, and even destroy. Governments and nations justly defend themselves against such evil.

At times it appears as if God no longer is God, and as if totally godless powers have won the battle. However, the almighty God has set boundaries for all powers of nature and for every tyranny. He commands every power as to just how close they may come. The Lord God says, "This far you may come and no farther." God's children can take great comfort in these words. God loves us. He will not allow us to be defeated. He redeems us through Christ's blood, forgives us all our sins, stands beside us in every need, and helps us in every situation.

Into Your hands we commend ourselves, dear God, for time and for eternity, through Jesus Christ. Amen.

Alfred C. Seltz

Christian Hope

But I trust in Your unfailing love, my heart rejoices in Your salvation. Psalm 13:5

If we speak about hope in human terms, it is always with uncertainty, for amidst "hope" there constantly hovers doubt. That is, what we hope for may not turn out the way we want.

It is completely different with our beloved God. In Him there is no wavering. He is forever the same kind, merciful God, benevolent Father in heaven. He is and remains unchangeably faithful to us. His grace shall never depart from us. In His Son, our Savior, His grace manifested itself, and for the sake of His Son, He has accepted us. We are His dear children and He is our beloved Father. We rely on Him. He is our hope.

There is no doubt in our Christian hope for it is solidly grounded upon Him and upon His promises. Therefore, our hope is combined with joy for we know the Lord so gladly and willingly offers it to us—no matter the circumstances. That's why worry or doubt never need disturb our heart. We hope solely in Him; He works all things to our good out of fatherly love for us.

I rejoice in You, Lord, and am not denied. Amen.

Eugene Seltz

In Good Hands

Even to your old age and gray hairs ... I will
carry you; I will sustain you and I will rescue
you. Isaiah 46:4

We travel from one year to the next. One year follows another, until finally we reached a mature age. How have we come so far? Because God has faithfully kept His promise to us: "Even to your old age ... I will carry you."

With advancing age also comes frailties of the body. The joints become stiff, the movement becomes ever slower. No wonder one frequently hears older people sigh, "forsake me not in my old age." Then comes God's comforting reply: "I will do it; I will lift up and carry you." So it goes with us at times, but He watches over us, even when our lives near an end.

When our life's journey ends, the Lord God stands beside us and says, "I will rescue you." Thus we are in good hands and are safely lifted into eternity. We can thank Him in all eternity that He has saved us, and we are healed of all our earthly frailties. Then our mouth will be filled with laughter and our tongue will be full of praise.

Lord, graciously sustain us at all times, especially difficult days, and bring us to a blessed end! Amen.

Walter H. Bouman

Psalm 91

Never Forsaken

*I was young and now I am old, yet I have never
seen the righteous forsaken or their children begging bread.* Psalm 37:25

St. Paul advised his young coworker, Timothy,
"godliness has value for all things, holding promise for
both the present life and the life to come" (1 Timothy 4:8).
God has demonstrated this to His children from day one,
for God's Word does not lie. When our need is the greatest, God is nearest.

The psalmist also experienced the depth of God's
love. For with his own eyes, he never saw any righteous
person ever forsaken nor a godly person in need of bread.
This Word of God remains true for us. Of course, children
of God sometimes fall into need, some even suffer much
tribulation, before they enter the kingdom of God. But
God never forsakes His own.

God's Son, Jesus Christ, was forsaken by God so we
would never be. Our Savior cried out from the cross, "My
God, My God, why have You forsaken Me?" (Matthew
27:46), as He atoned for us the punishment of death and
hell. Through faith in Him, we will someday live eternally
in joy. "Whoever believes in Him shall not perish but have
eternal life" Jesus promises (John 3:16).

Dear Savior, strengthen within me the trust that
You will never forsake me! Amen.

Lester H. Gierach

A Strong Citadel

God is our refuge and strength, an ever-present
help in trouble. Psalm 46:1

The powerful, comforting hymn, "A Mighty Fortress," serves as a reminder of Psalm 46. In the words of this hymn, Martin Luther gave a powerful witness to his trust in God for certain victory, describing our Lord as an impenetrable citadel.

This hymn retains a particular theme Luther often used—strong trust and a joyful attitude of faith in difficult times. Throughout our lives we can triumphantly sing with our fellow believers: "A mighty fortress is our God, A sword and shield victorious; He breaks the cruel oppressor's rod And wins salvation glorious. The old satanic foe has sworn to work us woe. With craft and dreadful might He arms Himself to fight. On earth He has no equal."

Luther knew without a doubt that the devil prowls about like a growling lion. However, his resistance was strong and sturdy through faith in Jesus, his Savior. May the same ever be true for us!

Lord, we are weak sinners, but through You we are able to overcome. Amen.

Walter W. Stuenkel

God Our Refuge

Lord God, You have been our dwelling place
throughout all generations. Psalm 90:1

God is eternal. "Before the mountains were born or You brought forth the earth and the world, from everlasting to everlasting You are God" (Psalm 90:2). Without beginning and without end, He is the unchangeable, almighty, gracious God.

As far as we are concerned, "The length of our days is seventy years—or eighty, if we have the strength; yet their span is but trouble and sorrow, for they quickly pass, and we fly away" (Psalm 90:10). Zacharias Hermann describes our brief life-span this way: "We step out of the cradle into the grave."

We have frightening times. The devil, the world, and our sinful flesh cause us to doubt. We fall into temptation. When we finally go through the dark valley of death, we might be led to lament, "the anxiety in my heart is huge," were it not for the absolute certainty that we can say, "Lord God, You are our Refuge forever and ever." Because of Jesus, we have access to His grace. Because of Jesus, the Lord God will receive us. In this comfort, we live and will someday die a blessed death.

Lord Jesus, grant that at my life's end I take my refuge in Your wounds. There I find forgiveness! Amen.

Albert T. Bostelmann

Job's Confession

I know that my Redeemer lives, and that in the
end He will stand upon the earth. Job 19:25

Job was a remarkable man, a rich landowner
through whom God teaches His people. Although he was
God-fearing, Job still lost everything. Deathly ill, his faith
in God was so heavily besieged that he actually slandered
God. Yet Job remained faithful and he confessed, "May
the name of the LORD be praised" (Job 1:21).

Where did Job find this hope? His wife and children could not help. Only God could. "I know," Job sang,
"that my Redeemer lives, and that in the end He will
stand upon the earth ... . I myself will see Him with my
own eyes" (Job 19:25–27). Job had an Advocate, a Savior.
Through Him, Job would once more be raised, able to
stand righteous before God. His belief was so staunch that
these words could well have been engraved in lead and
stone.

What a confession of faith! As New Testament
believers, we clearly see Jesus after His death and resurrection as our righteousness, and can—despite whatever our
miseries may be—also happily confess that our Savior
will make all things whole again. And that we, too, will
rise from the dead and joyfully see God with our own eyes.

Dear God, let what Job proclaimed remain
engraved upon our hearts, for the sake of Jesus! Amen.

Walter H. Koenig

Matthew 14:22–32

My Father Holds Me Firmly

*Yet I am always with You; You hold me by my
right hand.* Psalm 73:23

Without a tight grip on the father's hand, a tod-
dling child is often unable to stand upright. And when a
father sees his child in need and danger, he grasps the
child's hand in protection so the child is not harmed.

In like manner, God loves and protects His children. It can be said that, "if you think you are standing
firm, be careful that you don't fall!" (1 Corinthians 10:12)
The fact that we do not fall cannot be attributed to us,
but to God, who holds us firmly. Also the fact that the
children of God remain upon the pathway to salvation is
not due to our own strength; instead we "are shielded
by God's power until the coming of the salvation that is
ready to be revealed in the last time" (1 Peter 1:5). Even
when Peter was in danger of drowning, the Lord Jesus
grabbed him by the hand and rescued him.

I do not want to resist the hand of God, for He
firmly and securely holds me. It's when I start to believe
that I no longer need God to hold my hand that, by grace,
He steadies me once more, firmly guiding me. And
I thankfully say to Him, "You hold me by my right hand."

Dear Father, may You never remove Your hand
from us! Amen.

Daniel E. Poellot

Trusting in God

It is better to take refuge in the LORD than to trust in man. Psalm 118:8

In the first commandment, God tells us, "you shall have no other gods." God desires that we, above all else, place our trust in Him. Without fail, as we hold to the true knowledge of God and fear and love Him with our whole heart, we will also trust the Lord completely and fully place our hope in Him. Thus the psalm reads, "We wait in hope for the LORD; He is our help and our shield" (Psalm 33:20). In brief, through such a heartfelt trust in God, we truly confess Him as our God.

Not to a certain degree or at specific times, but at all times and under all circumstances we can place our trust in the Lord. Because of His love to us, it becomes our desire to honor the one true God and have Him as our God. As Christians, we confess that we often fail to keep this commandment more than any other. This confession leads us to repentance and we petition God for grace and forgiveness. As a result, we are guided to the true faith in God and in Jesus Christ, our Savior. And whoever believes has eternal life (John 3:16).

Lord, we place our hope in the belief that You are gracious to us. Our heart rejoices that You so eagerly rescue us. Amen.

Paul F. Wieneke

The Lord Listens

The LORD is close to the brokenhearted and saves those who are crushed in spirit. Psalm 34:18

The verse for today offers a wonderfully comforting divine promise. Let us note that this word of comfort does not come from men, but from God. God hears when the righteous cry out, and it is God who rescues them from every need.

This is the Lord who made heaven and earth and gave us the gift of our body and soul. And He has sustained them all to this very hour. This is the Lord who has all power in heaven and in earth. With God nothing is impossible. He does far more than what we ask for or can understand. This is the God who invites us to pray to Him. We can come before Him with the cries of our hearts, always secure in the knowledge that He will help us.

And how could it be otherwise? Why, He did not even spare His only Son; instead He gave Him up for us all. He gave us the ultimate Gift, and He gives the smaller gifts as well. How can we doubt that He will grant all we need according to His will?

Help us, dear Father in heaven, to be steadfast in our trust that we can call upon You in every need! Amen.

Lester H. Gierach

We Are the Lord's

Whether we live or die, we belong to the Lord.
Romans 14:8

As Martin Luther's beloved daughter lay dying, he prayed, "I love her very much, but dear God, if it is Your will, I will gladly let her be acquainted with You." Then he said to his child, "My little daughter, you would like to remain here with your father, yet are you gladly willing to go to the other Father?"

"Yes, dear daddy, as God wills," said the child. "You beloved little daughter," Luther replied, "the spirit is willing but the flesh is weak." Then the father turned away from the bed and said, "I love her so very much; but whether we live or die, we are the Lord's." She died as he held her in his arms. Then, as she was about to be laid in the coffin, Luther said, "You dear sweet child, how well off you are. I am happy in spirit, but very sad in the flesh. It is a marvelous miracle to know that you are at peace, and that everything is well with you." As the people came to her burial, he said to them, "Do not be sorrowful, I just sent a saint to heaven." Later Luther said to Melanchthon, "She has happily gone away with well-being. Blessed are the dead who die in the Lord."

We are, indeed, the Lord's in life and in death!

We thank You, Lord Jesus Christ, that You have taken away death's power. Amen.

Henry Blanke

I Place My Hope in You

"LORD, what do I look for? My hope is in You."
Psalm 39:7

We humans so often allow ourselves to be misled by the issues of this earthly life that we tend to forget how fleeting everything is. Obviously the future is the only tangible life we have. Obviously we must accept the responsibilities that are placed upon us. Obviously we feel the trials and tribulations that press upon us. Despite all this, the fact is undeniable: everything will come to an end—my life, my work, all the affairs of this world.

What then? The subject of Psalm 39 addresses this question: "Where shall I place my trust? I place my hope in You." We rely upon God's grace, for it shall never allow us to sink into the bitter anxiety of death. We trust in His love, for not even death itself can separate us from His love. We build upon His omnipotence, which pulls us across death and the grave. We have this comfort because the Prince of life has opened wide the gate of heaven and promised us eternal life.

Everything, everything we see has to fall away and disappear; Whoever has God remains standing forever. Grant this to us, dear Father in heaven! Amen.
(Kirchengesangbuch für Evangelisb—Lutherische Gemeinden)

Daniel E. Poellot

Our Lord Knows Our Weakness

*For we do not have a high priest who is unable to
sympathize with our weaknesses, but we have one
who has been tempted in every way, just as we are—
yet was without sin. Let us then approach the throne
of grace with confidence, so that we may receive
mercy and find grace to help us in our time of need.*
Hebrews 4:15–16

There once was a king who loved his people and
wanted to help them. He wanted to get to know his people
better, so he often came out of his castle and dressed so no
one could recognize him. He talked with many people—
children, old people, bankers, and farmers. In this way, he
could better know them and learn about their needs.

In the letter to the Hebrews, we read about our
Lord, who actually knows us, although He is the Lord of
the entire world. He came to earth, suffered with us, and
learned about our weaknesses—yet He was without sin.
He knows the depths of our sorrows and the heights of our
joy because He Himself experienced it all. Above all else,
He knows that we need His grace. To give us that, He died
upon the cross for our sin. He gives us this most beautiful
gift through His Word and Sacrament. He constantly
abides with us. He is a King who really loves His people.

Lord Jesus, You are a king filled with love. All praise
to You, our Lord! Amen.

Curtis P. Giese

God Our Father

*But You are our Father, though Abraham does not
know us or Israel acknowledge us; You, O LORD,
are our Father, our Redeemer from of old is Your
name.* Isaiah 63:16

The designation of God as "Father" is seldom used in
the Old Testament. In the New Testament, the name of
"Father" became the prevailing tone. This is a great mystery
that our Savior reveals to us. This is the fruit of His suffering,
death, and resurrection. Therein lay our salvation and our
blessedness. In other words, the God in heaven is my Father
and I am His child. He who carries the entire world in His
almighty hand also holds me in His fatherly hand. What He
does for me, He does out of sheer fatherly, divine goodness
and mercy, without any of all my merits and worthiness.

God, my Father! I can rely upon Him. He sees further than I, His child. I am permitted to complain to Him
about my needs, be they great or small. "If He does not
help with every whim, He still helps when it is necessary"
(*Kirchengesangbuch für Evangelish—Lutherische Gemeinden*). I can
also confess my sins to Him, for He is my Father and
Redeemer. He will grant me strength to battle against sin
and to live to His glory. And finally, when it comes to
dying, the Father will send forth His servants to bring me,
His child, home into the His house.

Provide care, Father; take care of my worries. You
Yourself provide care for my tranquility today as well as
tomorrow! Amen.

Herman A. Mayer

September 15   Deuteronomy 28:1–6

Benediction

The LORD will keep you from all harm—He will watch over your life. Psalm 121:7–8

May the Lord watch over you—that's what the psalmist said—"the sun will not harm you by day, nor the moon by night" (Psalm 121:6). From God's guiding hand and watchful eye, the psalmist changes the subject to protecting wings that stretch out over us from heaven. Just as a hen gathers her chicks under her wings, so the faithful Protector of mankind envelopes His children with His omnipotence and faithfulness. As we journey through our earthly life, we can go on our way, confident of the Lord's protection and assured by the blessing given us through Psalm 121. This blessing preserves and protects our entry into and exit from His house and our home.

God blesses us and watches over us in our earthly calling and daily work! God also watches over and preserves our exit from this world so we will have a peaceful departure. He protects our exit so it is an entry into His heavenly kingdom, our eternal home.

Lord, bless us with a peaceful death and make us heirs of heaven! Amen.

Walter H. Bouman

September 16   Isaiah 51:1–11

The Strong Arm of the Lord

Awake, awake! Clothe yourself with strength,
O arm of the LORD; awake, as in days gone by.
Isaiah 51:9

The thrice-repeated wake-up call could be translated with the command "wake up." It seemed to the people as if God was asleep. He didn't seem to hear them; it appeared as if He was doing nothing. How often in our lives do we pray out of need, and, if the Lord doesn't respond the way we want Him to, we think we have to wake up God with our pleading. This is what the disciples did when Jesus slept through a storm that was threatening their boat and their lives. "Lord, help us, we are dying!" The Savior was with them in the ship, although He was asleep. They thought He was not aware or didn't care (Luke 8:22–25).

Who were the disciples to question Christ, and who are we to question God? Perhaps He feels it necessary to awaken us, for He never sleeps—we do. We so easily forget about God during good times, turning to Him only when sin results in difficulties in our lives. But tribulation awakens us and makes us aware again of God's power and presence. Let us place both the good and the bad into His hands, for He can work good from even the most difficult of times.

Dearest Lord God, if it appears to us that You do not help at every interval, we rest in the assurance that You work all things to our good in Your time. Amen.

Herman A. Mayer

271

The Fulfillment

Not one of all the LORD's good promises to the house of Israel failed; every one was fulfilled. Joshua 21:45

"It all happened," is the theme of the book of Joshua. Everything that God had promised was fulfilled. The Israelites obtained the Promised Land. They lived in houses they had not built, harvested where they had not sown, received the fruits of vineyards they had not planted. They conquered their enemies. Each tribe became what God intended. Truly, it all happened! How could it be otherwise? The Word of the Lord is true and He most certainly keeps His promises. His Name is "I AM WHO I AM!" (Exodus 3:14). "I AM" the faithful God, the true God, who makes all His words come true.

Indeed, we have one God; before Him all doubts, anxiety, and heartache disappear. God has also promised a land to us—the kingdom of heaven, where there is fullness of joy, where we will find the place our Lord and Savior prepared for us after His resurrection. Someday He will bring it to pass. There we will be able to say with great joy, "Everything has been fulfilled; He has retained for us everything that He has promised—but only far more gloriously than we ever could have imagined" (*Kirchengesangbuch für Evangelish—Lutherische Gemeinden*). And just as God, by grace, gave the people of the covenant that which He had promised, so He gives to us salvation for the sake of Christ.

Lord, You have done all things perfectly; Your Word is true. Praise and thanks be to You! Amen.

Martin J. Naumann

September 18   Jeremiah 10:14–16

Let Your House Be Built by God

Unless the LORD builds the house, its builders
labor in vain. Psalm 127:1

In light of today's high construction costs, whoever is in a position to build a home is well advised to find an experienced architect and a reputable construction firm. Quality work is of great significance for the durability of a home. In the case of those who are not so diligent, the test of time and weather confronts them with the bitter, stark reality that the labor was in vain.

In this verse, the psalmist warns us about such fraudulent activity and admonishes us to hold on to the Creator to build our house and life. God has proven that He never works in vain. Just like plaques are placed on many historical or otherwise significant buildings, by God's grace, may we joyfully and publicly inscribe upon our lives "Built by God"!

With such conviction, we can be assured that the construction of our life has an eternal foundation and is guaranteed by Jesus Christ and His work of salvation. Be built up through His Word and Sacrament as God, by the Spirit, takes up residence in your heart. There exists no better foundation!

Lord God, heavenly Father, we thank You that we may commend the building of our life to You through Jesus Christ, our Lord. Amen.

Horst Hoyer

An Eternal Home

Our citizenship is in heaven. And we eagerly await a Savior from there, the Lord Jesus Christ.
Philippians 3:20

The Bible refers to us as children of God, the redeemed, believers, and many other names. We might also be called "pilgrims."

What does this mean? It means that we are here on earth away from our real home, which is elsewhere. At the end of all time, the Lord Jesus will come again in glory to take us to our true and correct home. Since we are merely here for a short while, we might not allow ourselves to be too deeply rooted and entrenched here. We refrain from embracing the world or acting as if we will live here forever. Instead, we want to lead our lives in such a way that we do not endanger our "homeward journey."

A diplomat in a foreign country never forgets where his home is and whom he represents. Likewise, we "foreigners" will want to properly retain our ties with our eternal home by staying connected to God through Word and Sacrament, being renewed daily in forgiveness through Christ. Through Jesus, God has by grace bestowed upon us this home for free. Therefore, may our heavenly citizenship be deeply imprinted upon our heart—today and every day.

Pour Your Spirit upon me, Father, so I never ever relinquish my heavenly citizenship. Amen.

Robert Bugbee

In God's Hands

My times are in Your hands. Psalm 31:15

When David chose the words "my times," he was referring to his entire life—his sufferings and joys, his good fortune and misfortune, his good and evil days. What a comfort for us Christians! If, like David, our time is in God's hands, then it is in good hands, in the hands of a loving, heavenly Father who for Christ's sake is gracious to us. How essential this comfort is for us who sin daily and well deserve the punishment that is rightly ours! If God wanted to respond to us with justice and righteousness, we could never ever stand before Him. But to God we say, "But with You there is forgiveness; therefore You are feared" (Psalm 130:4).

In our heavenly Father's hands we are in capable hands, the hands of an all-knowing, almighty, ever-present God. He knows all there is to know about us; He sees our tears and knows our sorrows. No hair falls from our head without His knowing it. And He provides help and counsel in every need. "He has a way for every way, He does not lack for means; His acts are sheer blessing, His pathway is pure light" (*Kirchengesangbuch für Evangelish— Lutherische Gemeinden*). The Lord God is constant, an eternally beloved and benevolent Father.

In how many needs have You not, O gracious God, spread your wings over us? You are ever faithful and merciful to us. To You be the glory! Amen.

Paul F. Koenig

My Father Takes Me Home

*Giving thanks to the Father, who has qualified
you to share in the inheritance of the saints in the
kingdom of light.* Colossians 1:12

Even a child can be called an heir. According to the decree of the father, the time ultimately comes when the child receives his inheritance, when perhaps the child becomes the owner of and takes over his father's property as his own.

"Now if we are children, then we are heirs—heirs of God and co-heirs with Christ" (Romans 8:17a). Our sonship with God guarantees that we are chosen to inherit His kingdom. He takes us home. The Father's house becomes ours.

It most certainly is ours already. But we still live in a time of waiting and do not yet enjoy the Father's house. "Now we know ... we have a building from God, an eternal house in heaven, not built by human hands" (2 Corinthians 5:1).

However, the concept of inheritance itself would indicate that our eternal Father's house is not ours because we have deserved it or earned it on our own. The Father, who has provided the inheritance for us through His Son, through His Holy Spirit, makes us qualified to obtain this inheritance. To Him be praise and thanks for His grace in all eternity!

See what sort of love the Father has shown to us in that we are called His children! Amen.

Daniel E. Poellot

Isaiah 40:6–8

Everything Earthly Passes Away

*"All men are like grass, and all their glory is like the flowers
of the field. The grass withers and the flowers fall, because
the breath of the LORD blows on them."* Isaiah 40:6–7

After the glorious, comforting sermon at the beginning
of Isaiah 40, there immediately follows a stern call to repentance, for the glory of the Lord shall be revealed. But who is
able to stand before the Lord? The prophet hears a voice:
"Preach!" He responds: "What should I preach?" The answer:
"All flesh is hay." Here, the word "flesh" refers to mankind,
which has been corrupted by sin. Along with everything that it
is and has, mankind is merely grass that will soon dry up.

This verse describes the vanity and failure of
mankind. Even the best of mankind—his wisdom and knowledge, all his discoveries and inventions—is like a flower
which soon withers. Why does that happen? "Because the
breath of the LORD blows on them," or as Moses says, "We
are consumed by Your anger and terrified by Your indigna-
tion" (Psalm 90:7). Because of sin, we are subject to God's
wrath. Left on our own, we would surely wither. But thanks
be to God that through Christ we have life!

Man passes away like grass, "But the word of the
Lord stands forever" (1 Peter 1:25). Those are glorious
words of grace! They are the very words that still ring forth
from the Gospel today.

Your divine Word, that bright Light, may we,
indeed never turn from it! Amen.

Herman A. Mayer

Colossians 1:12–23

My Eternal Savior

Jesus Christ is the same yesterday and today and forever. Hebrews 13:8

Jesus Christ, in whom everything was fulfilled that God had spoken through the prophets, shall continue to be the same loving, faithful Savior into eternity. We can, with steadfast confidence, rely upon His Word and never doubt His participation in our cares and concerns. Amidst the ever-changing affairs of this life on earth, we seek a solid grip with which to be led and a solid foundation upon which we may rest. We have each in the Lord Jesus.

Should everything earthly be ripped away, Jesus and His salvation will still stand firm for us. If human friends are unfaithful, Jesus will never forsake us. If we languish and pine away under the burden of a cross, Jesus shall always stand beside us to comfort and strengthen us. If the devil holds our sins up to us, if our conscience accuses us, Jesus who died and rose again is here. In His Word, the Savior has once and for all opened up His heart to us. He is the foundation that holds and keeps us anchored forever. As He was from the beginning, so also He shall remain forever.

Lord Jesus, how blessed to us is the assurance that Your Savior-heart stands open for us at all times! Amen.

Clarence T. Schuknecht

I Believe ... in God the Father

"This, then, is how you should pray: 'Our Father in heaven.'" Matthew 6:9

We confess with all of Christendom: "I believe in the one, true God—Father, Son and Holy Spirit." This Triune God, so highly exalted above us, who are dust and ashes, is not far from us. In the Lord's Prayer, Christ teaches us to call upon God as "Father." This means He wants us to know that God is our true Father and we are His true children, so we, with confidence and with all reassurance, may petition Him like little children do their earthly fathers.

But how dare I, a poor sinner, so confidently approach the great God and call Him "Father"? I cannot do that by virtue of my own merit nor by virtue of my own worthiness, but only for the sake of Christ, my Savior. In the fullness of time, God sent His Son into the world, born of a woman and placed under the Law, so He could redeem those who were under the Law, that we might obtain the right of sonship. Since we are God's children, God has sent the Spirit of His Son, who cries out, *"Abba,* Father," into our hearts. That's why we can confidently say, "Our Father in heaven!"

I thank You, my God, that I may call You Father. May I be and remain Your child! Amen.

Fred Kramer

In Christ

Remain in Me and I will remain in you.
John 15:4

The portrayal of Christ as the genuine Vine, of God the Father as the vineyard Gardener, and of us Christians as the branches on the Vine, has much to say to us about Christian faith and life. No Christian can stand alone by his own power. Of ourselves we have no spiritual life, but are spiritually dead. The true life of the Christian is rooted in Christ. It receives its nurture and strength from Him. Christ is the Vine; we are the branches. Just as a branch cannot live and bear fruit if it is cut off from the vine, so the Christian, if he is separated from Christ, cannot live. Without fail, he will wither and fail to produce fruit. That's why Jesus admonishes His disciples, "Remain in Me and I will remain in you."

This happens only as we, by faith, stand with Him. This faith is nurtured and strengthened through eager, zealous hearing of the Word of God and our participation in the holy Sacraments. Thus we abide in Christ, and—miracle of grace!—He also abides in us and nurtures us with His power so we might be equipped to produce true fruit to the glory of God and for the benefit of our neighbor.

Lord, abide in me so I also may abide in You and bear fruit to Your glory! Amen.

Fred Kramer

The Gift of the Holy Spirit

Do not cast me from Your presence or take Your
Holy Spirit from me. Psalm 51:11

To pray for the fullness of the Holy Spirit is a most urgent and blessed prayer; for in this life we have need for a leader, teacher, and comforter. And that's the Holy Spirit. He leads us into all truth. He teaches us to know Christ; He clarifies things for us. He comforts us in all kinds of sufferings and tribulations, even in the hour of our death. Those who may pray this prayer are the old and the young, the great and the small, the parents on behalf of themselves and their children, for the Holy Spirit is a security deposit of our inheritance. Anyone in whom the Holy Spirit does not dwell here will not be saved there. For it is only with the Spirit that we can live a godly life here on earth and inherit eternal life.

Through the means of grace, the Holy Spirit sustains us in saving faith. By faith the Holy Spirit works a renewal of our whole lives—in spirit, will, attitude, and desires—so we might strive to live according to God's will. May it ever be so!

Create in me, O God, a pure heart and give me a new, reassured spirit! Amen.

J. F. Starck

The Spirit Comes through the Gospel

*Did you receive the Spirit by observing the Law,
or by believing what you heard?* Galatians 3:2

In his letter to the Galatians, the apostle Paul speaks of the freedom of the children of God through the working of the Holy Spirit. He wrote, "But if you are led by the Spirit, you are not under law" (Galatians 5:18). Anyone who has received the Holy Spirit is free from the curse of the Law and can be certain that, through Christ, all his sins are forgiven.

Paul asks the Galatians whether they received the Holy Spirit through the works of the Law or through the preaching of the Gospel. Did your works of the Law bring you peace? Did the Law renew your hearts and make you willing to listen to God? Or did the Gospel work this faith in you?

The answer to this question is that it is not through our keeping of the Law, but through the proclamation of the sin-forgiving grace of God in Christ that we receive all the blessings of faith. Nor did the Law make us willing to obey God. Instead, as we came to know the Gospel, our obedience became a response to the love of God in Christ.

Lord, let me hear the Gospel of Christ, and through it make me free to serve You! Amen.

Clarence T. Schuknecht

Deuteronomy 6:4–15

The One Almighty God

*"I am the LORD your God, who brought you out
of Egypt, out of the land of slavery. You shall
have no other gods before Me."* Exodus 20:2–3

When I as a Christian confess that I believe in only
one almighty God, I then confess that this one almighty
God is my God, the only one whom I honor, whom I love
above all else, whom alone I trust, from whom alone I
await all good things in this life and the next.

Apart from this only almighty God there exists no
other god. That's why I dare not have any other gods. I
dare not fear and honor anyone or anything else in this
world above Him. I dare not love anyone or anything in
this world as much as I love Him. I dare not place my trust
upon anything in this world except upon Him alone. I can
trust Him, for He is the almighty God, with whom nothing is impossible. No tribulation I may encounter in this
life is so huge that He cannot lift it, no misfortune so
severe that He cannot change it. That why He alone shall
be my God. I will fear, love, and trust in God above all
things, for He first loved me in Christ.

Dear God, give me Your Spirit so I fear and love
and trust in You above all else! Amen.

Fred Kramer

God, Everything in All Things

From Him and through Him and to Him are all things. Romans 11:36

Everything comes from God. He is the Creator of everything. "In Him we live, move and have our being" (Acts 17:28). The apostle Paul further says to the Athenians: "'The God who made the world and everything in it is the Lord of heaven and earth and does not live in temples built by hands. And He is not served by human hands, as if He needed anything, because He Himself gives all men life and breath and everything else'" (Acts 17:24–25).

When mankind fell away from God and rebelled against Him, God sent His Son as Redeemer and Savior. Through Him, the Son of God, our heavenly Father reconciled mankind to Himself. "God was reconciling the world to Himself in Christ, not counting men's sins against them. And He has committed to us the message of reconciliation" (2 Corinthians 5:19).

And to Him all things. Through His Holy Spirit, our Lord God calls, gathers, enlightens, and sanctifies the host of believers, and sustains them in the one true faith. "No one can say, 'Jesus is Lord,' except by the Holy Spirit" (1 Corinthians 12:3b).

In the morning, God, we praise You, and in the evening we pray to You. Through Jesus, we can at any and all times come to You. Amen.

Herman A. Harms

Trusting Him Who Comes

Now there is in store for me the crown of righteousness, which the Lord, the righteous Judge, will reward to me on that day—and not only to me, but also to all who have longed for His appearing. 2 Timothy 4:8

Jesus lives in our hearts. He has not forsaken us. However, in a certain sense He is away from us. Since His ascension into heaven, He no longer walks with His disciples upon earth like He did before.

So we cannot see Him with our physical eyes. Would we like to see Him? Why yes, of course! O how a bride longs for her bridegroom! That's how the Church of Jesus longs for its heavenly Bridegroom.

He has promised His visible return. He will come. He will take us home with Him. How much longer will we have to wait? We don't know when He will come. We, however, know that He *is* coming.

Will that be a day of jubilation for us? Most assuredly! But why? Won't Jesus also judge us? He indeed will come as a Judge. However, the judgment on us is beautifully expressed in the Gospel. We have been justified—already pronounced free—because He in our place was condemned to death on the cross; that's why we love His reappearing.

"Come, Holy Lord, Come. It is time for the final judgment in glory! Lead us out of this tribulation and travail into the eternal joyful host!" Amen.

John M. Drickamer

One Holy Christian Church

Make every effort to keep the unity of the Spirit through the bond of peace. Ephesians 4:3

God, who out of love for fallen mankind allowed His Son to become man to rescue us from sin, has made it possible for the joyful news of our rescue to be proclaimed in all the world. Through this proclamation, He gathers and sustains at all times His church in which people hear the Gospel and come to faith. This church, which before the eyes of man often appears to be poor and needy, is actually outstandingly glorious. She is first of all one. There can exist only one church, for it is one body, and one Spirit ... one Lord, one faith, one Baptism, one God and Father over all (Ephesians 4:3–6). All Christians of the world make up this one church. The church is holy. God has chosen it for Himself. He has washed it of sin through Christ's blood. He sanctifies it from day to day. The church believes in Jesus Christ. Finally, the church is apostolic. The apostles are the abiding teachers of the church, which is built upon the foundation of Christ, the cornerstone. "God's solid foundation stands firm, sealed with this inscription: 'The Lord knows those who are His'" (2 Timothy 2:19).

Thanks be to You, heavenly Father, that You have called me to be a member of the body of believers, Your church. Amen.

Fred Kramer

October 2   Philippians 1:3–11

The Lord Brings It to Completion

Being confident of this, that He who began a good
work in you will carry it on to completion until
the day of Christ Jesus. Philippians 1:6

"I believe that I cannot by my own reason or strength believe in Jesus Christ, my Lord, or come to Him; but the Holy Spirit has called me by the Gospel, enlightened me with His gifts, sanctified and kept me in the true faith." With these words from the *Small Catechism*, it is clear that God the Holy Spirit begins the good work within us. He brings us to faith in Jesus Christ by means of grace—the written and spoken Word of the Gospel and the sacraments.

Does the Holy Spirit set us upon a pathway of faith only to have us walk alone? At times it might appear that way, but that is not how it is. Were we to rely upon our own strength, we would never reach the goal. But as Paul states, the Lord God will complete the good work He has begun. That applies to us as well. And for how long will the Spirit perform this office and function? The apostle answers: "until the Day of Jesus Christ," that is, until the day of His second coming.

Lead me, O Lord, and guide my walk according to Your Word! May You always be and remain my Protector and my Refuge! Amen.

Manfred Roensch

October 3   1 Peter 1:18–25

The Everlasting Word of God

"All men are like grass, and all their glory is like
the flowers of the field; the grass withers and
the flowers fall, but the word of the Lord stands
forever." 1 Peter 1:24–25

Everything on earth is transitory. Man himself has only a short existence here. To this James says, "What is your life? You are a mist that appears for a little while and then vanishes" (James 4:14b). Yes, heaven and earth will pass away, as the Lord tells us. Yet Peter adds the comforting truth that His "words will never pass away" (Luke 21:33).

What precious comfort this promise provides as we think about the fragility of everything earthly and about the reality of our own mortality! The Word of the Lord, and everything that has been revealed and promised to us in it, does not perish. Peter reminds us, "this is the Word that was preached to you" (1 Peter 1:25). It will stand forever.

And what does this Word reveal to us? It reveals that we are redeemed through Jesus Christ and that an eternal home with the Father in heaven has been prepared for us. Let us at all times strive for and keep an eye on this home. Our Savior will come from heaven and take us home.

God the Holy Spirit, preserve us steadfast in faith in Your eternal and unchanging Word! Amen.

F. C. Otten

John 4:47–54

The Foundation of Faith

The man took Jesus at His word and departed.
John 4:50

God speaks to us through His Word. This Word is not an empty shell. It actually contains that which it pronounces and promises to us. It is truth. It addresses reality. And it is fulfillment.

In the story that contains today's Scripture, Jesus, upon the petition of the royal officer at Capernaum—without even seeing his dying son—simply says: "Go on, your son lives." The father proceeded to leave with the conviction that what Jesus had said was the truth.

Why did the man go back? Why was he convinced that his son would live? Because, as the evangelist said, "the man took Jesus at His word and departed." He placed all his trust in Jesus; he relied on Christ. For him, Jesus' word was truth and reality.

The Word of God is also the foundation upon which we place our faith. It is God's true and certain Word. What God says, He regards as certain. Blessed are those who rely on God's Word, who gladly hear, preserve, and keep it.

I believe what Jesus promises, may I ever hold to Your Word with conviction. Amen.

Emanuel Beckmann

Repentance and Absolution

*David said to Nathan, "I have sinned against the
LORD." Nathan replied, "The LORD has taken
away your sin."* 2 Samuel 12:13

The famous hero David, who had felled the giant
Goliath, had now himself fallen. He had not been on guard
as the old Adam tempted him, and he with lustful eyes
looked upon Bathsheba, Uriah's wife, and committed adultery. While the devil had David by the neck, he also
deceived him into murdering Uriah in an attempt to cover
up his adultery. Then God, in His grace, sent the prophet
Nathan to show David his transgressions. After David confessed his sins with a contrite heart, the prophet reassured
the king that God had forgiven his sins.

David's fall precedes another warning, that of the
apostle: "So, if you think you are standing firm, be careful
that you don't fall!" (1 Corinthians 10:12). To that end we
also watch and pray that we do not fall into temptation. If,
however, despite our better judgment, we stumble and fall
into sin, we live in the reassurance that God, for Christ's
sake, forgives every repentant sinner and once more
receives him to Himself.

Merciful Father, through Your Spirit, grant that I
resist sin and I strive to serve You in love! Amen.

Gerhard T. Naumann

October 6   1 John 1:5–2:2

Forgiveness of Sins

In Him we have redemption through His blood,
the forgiveness of sins, in accordance with the
riches of God's grace. Ephesians 1:7

Nothing is more important than the forgiveness of all our sins. If just one single sin were not forgiven, even a single evil thought, we could not be certain of our salvation. On the other hand, the complete forgiveness of our sins is the assurance of our eternal life. "For where there is forgiveness of sins, there is also life and salvation" (Luther's *Small Catechism*).

Also, if forgiveness hinged upon our own ability, even to the slightest degree, then we would most certainly be without hope. Our redemption is made possible solely through the riches of the immeasurable grace of God. He demanded and required the blood of His innocent Son. "The blood of Jesus, His Son, purifies us from all sin" (1 John 1:7).

Our forgiveness is assured in a three-fold manner: through the washing away of our sins in Holy Baptism, through the Word of truth in the Gospel, and through our eating and drinking of Christ's body and blood in the Lord's Supper.

Holy Spirit, may the unearned forgiveness of God, through Christ, motivate us to a heartfelt love toward God and our fellowman! Amen.

Otto E. Naumann

Maintained by the Gospel

By this Gospel you are saved, if you hold firmly to the Word I preached to you. 1 Corinthians 15:2

Faith clings to the Word, which to some appears so insignificant that the whole world wouldn't give a penny for it. Yet the Word does such a great thing that in the wink of an eye it shall disrupt and shred heaven and earth, and open up all graves.

And those who abide in the faith shall thereby live forever, although your faith is weak. But no matter how weak your faith at times might be, it is important to be maintained by the Gospel—to live not according to your own thoughts and reason, but instead according to the Scriptures.

The mother does not toss aside the baby because she is weak and unable to help herself. In the mother's lap and in her arms, the baby has no need. If she is deprived of her mother's nursing, however, she then is lost. The same is true for us. If we want to be saved, we need only abide in the Word. Through it God will carry us and sustain us.

Likewise, we are unable to withstand sin, death, and hell except through the Gospel, about which St. Paul said that through it we stand and are saved. Through the Word we are comforted and sustained.

Blessed are those who hear the Word of God and keep and uphold it. To that end, Lord, help us! Amen.

Martin Luther

October 8   Acts 22:6–16

Water and Blood

This is the one who came by water and blood—
Jesus Christ. He did not come by water only,
but by water and blood. 1 John 5:6

Do these words mean that Christ's blood is mixed with water in Baptism, that therein the plum-red and innocent blood of Christ will be apparent and seen? It is true that to our human eyes nothing seems to be there but pure, clear water. However, John wrote these words to open our spiritual eyes of faith so we see not only water but also the blood of our Lord Jesus Christ.

How so? Holy Baptism has won salvation for us through the very same blood that Christ poured out for us and with which He paid for our sin. He has placed His own blood, merit, and power into Baptism so we might receive it there. For anyone who receives Baptism by faith, it is just as if he were visibly washed with the blood of Christ and cleansed from sins. For we do not obtain the forgiveness of sins though our works, but rather through the Son of God's death and bloodshed. Such forgiveness He grants to us in Baptism.

I have been baptized into Your name, God the Father, Son, and Holy Spirit; I have been added as Your child and heir, added to those whom You call sanctified. Amen.

Martin Luther

Only through the Means of Grace

Faith comes from hearing the message, and the message is heard through the Word of Christ. Romans 10:17

The means of grace are the Gospel and the sacraments. The Law unveils sin and convicts us so the hunger for Christ's righteousness wells up in us through the power of the Holy Spirit.

Yet many are self-righteous and Pharisaical. They will neither repent nor seek help. Without the Gospel, they remain self-righteous and live in doubt. Faith in Christ comes not through our own self-righteous efforts. It comes in miraculous fashion.

Our Redeemer in His state of exaltation speaks to us through the Holy Scriptures, and God performs a miracle through the Word. When Jesus said, "'It is easier for a camel to go through the eye of a needle than for a rich man to enter the kingdom of God,'" the disciples replied in shock, "'Who then can be saved?'" Jesus answered, "'With man this is impossible, but with God all things are possible'" (Matthew 19:24–26). God can and does work miracles through His Word.

At Pentecost, just as Jesus had promised His disciples, it was Peter's Spirit-inspired, Scripture-laden sermon and Baptism that worked true faith in 3,000 people. God still works this miracle today. The Holy Spirit works faith in our hearts at Baptism. The Lord's Supper and the Word strengthen this faith.

I believe, dear Lord. Through the means of grace help my unbelief! Amen.

Martin Luther

Judgment and Rescue

Just as man is destined to die once, and after
that to face judgment, so Christ was sacrificed
once to take away the sins of many people.
Hebrews 9:27–28

It is inevitable: Death calls each person before the throne of the returning Christ. No one avoids the final judgment. The God who created us and commanded that we live according to His holy will holds us accountable for our actions and deeds. And we know how things will end—before Him no living person is righteous.

Yet a different, inevitable event gives judgment a new, blessed dimension: Christ was offered up on the cross to take away sin. And just as no one is excluded from judgment, so is everyone included in Christ's offering. "God has bound all men over to disobedience so that He may have mercy on them all" (Romans 11:32). Jesus Christ is the Lamb of God who bears the sin of the entire world.

Law and Gospel stand together, yet there exists this distinction: The Law is to be kept and we can't do it; the Gospel is to be received and by the power of God salvation is made possible.

Lord Jesus, help me believe! Amen.

Daniel E. Poellot

October 11   Luke 21:25–36

He Will Come Again

The Son of Man is going to come in His Father's
glory with His angels. Matthew 16:27

From the very beginning, the church has believed
and confessed that the ascended Christ will come again;
and not in humility, as in His incarnation, but in glory.
Christ promised this to His disciples. He did not tell them
the time or hour of His return. Instead, He admonished
them to await His coming with steadfast repentance.

When Christ ascended into heaven, His disciples
sadly looked up at Him, conscious of His leaving. Yet two
angels reminded them of His promise to return again (Acts
1:10–11). The apostles taught the church about the return
of Christ, although they did not know the time or the hour
of it.

Paul praised the Corinthians because they waited
for the revelation of the Lord. He taught the Thessalonians
that Christ would come like a thief in the night. He
admonished them not to sleep but to remain vigilant.
Although Christ's time to return has not yet come, He will
most certainly come again. God does not count time like
we do. Before Him one day is like a thousand years and a
thousand years are like one day (Psalm 90:4). When God's
time has come, Christ will return.

Heavenly Father, ensure that we are repentant and
faithful when Your Son comes! Amen.

Fred Kramer

The Resurrection of the Dead

*All who are in their graves will hear His voice
and come out.* John 5:28–29

The Christian church believes, according to Scripture, that those who die in the Lord will on the Last Day be resurrected from the dead. In Jesus' time the resurrection from the dead was an article of faith, denied only by the Sadducees. For Martha, the sister of deceased Lazarus, there was no doubt about it: "I know he will rise again in the resurrection at the Last Day" (John 11:24).

The Christian church, which came into existence with the resurrection of Jesus, believes that the risen Christ will one day raise all the dead. This is especially beloved and comforting for us Christians. On this earth, we become ill or we age, and we finally die. As a rule, the thought of death is not appealing. But we need not fear death, for Christ has taken away death's power and has brought to light everlasting life. It is for the joy of this promise that we anxiously await the resurrection from the dead and the transformation of our mortal bodies to life everlasting.

Lord Jesus, You have saved me from sin and death. Help me by faith to look forward to my resurrection! Amen.

Fred Kramer

The King of All Kings

Which God will bring about in His own time—
God, the blessed and only Ruler, the King of kings
and Lord of lords. 1 Timothy 6:15

The apostle Paul tells us that on the great Day of Resurrection, we will see Jesus as the King of kings and Lord of lords. We will see Him in His state of exaltation. All the angels and all the saints will glorify Him as the Mighty One. They will serve Him with gladness.

God gave Christ a name that is above all names, and has placed all things under His feet. He rules as the King of kings in all eternity. We are His subjects. That is not a burden for us, for He is a King who lovingly welcomes us. He cares for us and guards and protects us at all times. He has prepared an eternal kingdom of glory for us. Thus we rejoice from the bottom of our hearts that we may live in His kingdom, serve Him, and do His will. Thus we also proclaim His glory among all people that they might become His servants through true faith.

Lord Jesus, my King, grant that I be and remain in Your kingdom of grace as long as I live. Then, when my hour has come, take me to Your kingdom of glory! Amen.

Gerhard C. Michael

Life in the Future World

And this is what He promised us—even eternal life. 1 John 2:25

Our life in this world is a gift from God and is, therefore, to be highly treasured. But we dare not treasure life in this world too much. Instead, we stand prepared to lose this life for a better one.

As Christians we wait for life in the world that is to come. This present world will one day come to an end. On Judgment Day, heaven and earth will vanish with the crashing of a loud noise; the elements will melt from heat, and the earth as it currently exists will be destroyed. Then there will be a new heaven and a new earth, in keeping with God's promise (see 2 Peter 3:10ff). With the new heaven and the new earth, there comes to God's children a new, eternal life. Christ promises, "My sheep listen to My voice; I know them, and they follow Me" (John 10:27). That's why Christ came into the world and died on the cross—so all who believe in Him will not be lost but have eternal life. With steadfast trust in Him and His promise, we wait for everlasting life in the world to come.

Lead me, O Jesus, into life eternal, which You have promised to give to all who believe in You! Amen.

Fred Kramer

Jesus Is Lord

And every tongue confess that Jesus Christ is Lord,
to the glory of God the Father. Philippians 2:11

"No one can say, 'Jesus is Lord,' except by the Holy Spirit," Paul says in 1 Corinthians 13:3b.

The confession that Jesus is Lord is acknowledged as one of the oldest creedal formulas of Christendom. However, only those to whom God the Holy Spirit has bestowed the gift of faith in Christ can make this confession of faith. Not everyone is willing or able to make such a confession.

Yet our Scripture verse for today reads, "every tongue confess." In this verse Paul is referring to the end of time, the day of the revelation of the glory of our Lord Jesus Christ. At that time no one will be able to dispute that Jesus Christ is the King of kings and the Lord of lords; everyone will confess this irrefutable truth. This confession by all will serve to honor God the Father, who bestowed such glory upon His Son. Praise be to God for that! Even now, before the Day of Jesus Christ, we who believe confess Him as Lord.

Praise, glory, and thanks be to God the Father, who defends His people from tribulations and gathers from them an everlasting church upon earth to His glory! Amen.

Manfred Roensch

October 16   Micah 4:1–7

The Mission to the Gentiles

"The law will go out from Zion, the Word of the
LORD from Jerusalem." Micah 4:2

This Bible reference is a superlative Old Testament mission text about Christ's kingdom. It is a message that points to the hope that is to come.

The "last days" mentioned in the first verse of this chapter refer to the days of the New Testament. Evidence of this is seen in Hebrews 1:1–2: "In the past God spoke to our forefathers through the prophets at many times and in various ways, but in these last days He has spoken to us by His Son."

The first verse also reads: "The mountain of the LORD's temple will be established as chief among the mountains" (Micah 4:1). In fulfillment of this prophecy, the church of Christ stands on a solid foundation (Matthew 16:18), high above anything else that could be considered remotely high (Matthew 5:14).

"Many nations will come" (Micah 4:2), drawn to the church of Christ by the power of God's Word preached to Zion. We who believe derive great comfort in the fulfillment of Micah's prophecies and in the hope that is ours through Christ.

Arise, You comfort of the Gentiles, Jesus, bright Morning Star! Let Your Word, the Word of joy, loudly echo near and far so it brings peace to all whom the enemy holds captive. And may praise and glory ring out throughout all the world! Amen.

Luther Poellot

October 17   Haggai 2:7–10

Join Me in Praising the Lord

Let us exalt His name together! Psalm 34:3

These wonderful words from Psalm 34 call out to God's children in all parts of the world, that with one another we lift up and praise the name of our Redeemer. The love of God continually blesses the work of missions throughout the world. He grants to us the proper intention and joyful willingness to diligently support His work of missions with our gifts, prayers, and labors. May we never tire of bringing the glorious news of salvation through Christ to those who have not yet heard.

Our Savior said, "Many will come from the east and the west, and will take their places at the feast with Abraham, Isaac, and Jacob in the kingdom of heaven" (Matthew 8:11). With these words of prophecy, Jesus includes the works of His apostles and all other missionaries to follow. Of course Jesus already knew how His church would proclaim His Gospel in centuries to come. We now have the honor and the responsibility to join in this work. Just as we were led into the kingdom of God, we continue to support God's great commission so all of Christendom might praise His name.

Let come, O Lord, from all the ends of the earth those who fear Your name and praise it. Amen.

Eugene Seltz

October 18   Luke 10:1–9

Get Busy with the Work of Missions!

*Ask the Lord of the harvest, therefore, to send out
workers into His harvest field.* Luke 10:2

Mission work is harvest work. Christian missionaries sow good seed—the Word of salvation. And under God's blessing the seed germinates and sprouts and grows. Converted souls are brought in like sheaves, yet the number of harvest workers remains small. We pray to the Lord of the harvest for more workers. We pray that He might prepare and mobilize them and send them. For mission work, the Lord utilizes for His service our witness, prayers, gifts, and our local Christian congregations. He used a godly woman named Hannah who dedicated her son to serve God. He used Paul who taught a young Timothy about serving in the name of Jesus. And He uses Christian institutions of learning, Bible societies, every form of media, and every means of transportation to send workers into His harvest. We lift up in prayer all who serve in the name of Christ.

May the Lord of the harvest grant that our desire and love for mission work steadfastly increase! Amen.

August H. Lange

October 19   Acts 4:23–31

For the Missionaries

Pray for us that the message of the Lord may spread rapidly and be honored. 2 Thessalonians 3:1

What prompted Paul to admonish the Thessalonians to pray for him? He was a highly educated man, a captivating preacher. Despite that, he asked his brothers in Christ to pray for him that the Lord's Word "run its course," press ahead, be received, and be praised. Why did he of all people need their prayers?

Paul knew very well that all good gifts came from above; so did the growth of Christ's kingdom. Paul also knew that the Prince of Darkness sets in motion every possible obstacle to hinder the growth of the church. To the Jews, the Word of the cross is an offense, to the Greeks foolishness.

The people wanted a leisurely life with little work and much entertainment, not the message about the grace of God in Christ Jesus! Paul was hated by the Jews and mocked and ridiculed by the Gentiles. He was treated like an outcast. Was it necessary to pray for him and his work? Yes, indeed! Likewise, our missionaries today are in great need of our petitions and prayers.

God, grant your harvest workers the desire, endurance, and wisdom to proclaim Your promise of salvation. Protect them from danger. Grant that all Christian missionaries in this world are enabled to proclaim Your Gospel to Your glory and to their joy! In Jesus' name. Amen.

George J. Mueller

October 20   Psalm 149

The New Song

*Sing to the LORD a new song, His praise from the
ends of the earth.* Isaiah 42:10

Christians of today gladly sing the old chorales of
Martin Luther, Philipp Nicolai, and Paul Gerhardt in worship and devotions. In the same manner we also sing more
recently composed songs to the Lord. But do we really
understand why we sing such songs? Do we sing them simply for the joy of singing? Or do we sing them to lift our
hearts to the glory of the Lord?

"Sing to the LORD a new song, [sing] His praise
from the ends of the earth," admonishes the prophet
Isaiah. We do not sing for our own entertainment. With
hymns of thanksgiving and praise—old or new—we sing
to the glory of God, who renews us through His Holy
Spirit. May our singing echo to the ends of the earth so
all mankind might hear praises to the gracious God we
have!

Lord, renew our hearts and open our mouths so we
exalt you for as long as we live. Amen.

Manfred Roensch

October 21   Isaiah 51:11

The Redeemed of the Lord

And the ransomed of the LORD will return. They will enter Zion with singing; everlasting joy will crown their heads. Gladness and joy will overtake them, and sorrow and sighing will flee away.
Isaiah 35:10

This verse is written like a jubilant proclamation, like a benediction at the close of a joyful song of triumph. This verse reflects the unrestrained celebration after the release from Babylonian captivity and points to the blessings of the New Testament church, as well as the "everlasting joy" of the righteous in the heavenly Zion, which is "the Holy City, the new Jerusalem" (Revelation 21:2).

Those who have been redeemed by Christ (Isaiah 59:20) shall rejoice here upon earth as well as eternally in heaven. "He will wipe every tear from their eyes. There will be no more death or mourning or crying or pain" (Revelation 21:4). A jubilant proclamation indeed!

Jesus, receive us, Your church, by grace! To the whole host of Christians, reveal Your love! Joy, joy beyond all joy! You relieve all suffering! Bliss, bliss beyond all bliss, You are the sun of grace. Amen.

Luther Poellot

October 22   Psalm 100

Praise the Lord, My Soul!

*Praise the LORD, O my soul; all my inmost
being, praise His holy name. Praise the LORD,
O my soul, and forget not all His benefits.*
Psalm 103:1–2

"Praise the LORD." The psalms of praise are a great
legacy from David. David always found a reason for praising God. He acknowledged his sins and embraced God's
forgiveness. He was grateful for God's compassionate love
and forgiveness. That's why he speaks so much about it.

In this psalm, David said we praise the One "who
forgives all your sins and heals all your diseases, who
redeems your life from the pit and crowns you with love
and compassion" (verses 3–4). Throughout this psalm,
David listed more reasons to praise God—not just for His
goodness, but also for God's wondrous works in nature.
David ended the psalm with the words, "Praise the LORD,
all His works everywhere in His dominion. Praise the
LORD, O my soul" (Psalm 103:22).

David drew deeply from all the emotion that was in
him to praise the Lord. Why? "For as high as the heavens
are above the earth, so great is His love for those who fear
Him; as far as the east is from the west, so far has He
removed our transgressions from us" (Psalm 103:11–12).

Lord God, do not let us become weary in praising
and thanking You, for Your benefits are many and are
always present. In Jesus' name! Amen.

Otto F. Stahlke

My Body and My Soul Rejoice

*How lovely is Your dwelling place, O LORD
almighty!* Psalm 84:1

The psalmist says that blessed are those who regard
God as their strength and from the bottom of their hearts
follow Him. As they travel through a valley of tears, God
turns the weeping into a fount of refreshment and the
morning rain cloaks them with blessing.

Our God is our sun and shield, bestowing grace
and glory. He will not allow His godly ones to lack for
anything good. The psalmist concludes with "O LORD
almighty, blessed is the man who trusts in You" (Psalm
84:12).

So it is. But things often appear differently to us.
We bear heavy losses, become sick, lose a loved one, or we
stare death in the face ourselves. At such times it may
appear as if God has forsaken us. However, it is precisely
at such times that our God is at our side. It is at these times
that we can experience how glorious it is to trust God and
to be sure of His presence. The door to His presence
always stands open. No matter what our circumstances
might be, we have a Father who cares for us and makes us
His children.

We thank You, Father, for Your comforting presence and protection in all situations. Amen.

Jakob K. Heckert

Sing to the Lord a New Song

Sing to the LORD a new song, for He has done marvelous things. Psalm 98:1

The Lord has worked salvation for us with His right hand and with His holy arm. However, He does not do so with might and power. Rather, our God proclaims His salvation to the nations and reveals His righteousness in His grace. He remembers His people with grace and truth. Thereby all the ends of the earth see His salvation.

We respond to God's action with jubilation, singing, and praise. The psalmist invites us to shout and cheer, to praise God with harps and psalms, with trumpets and trombones. He even calls upon the sea and all that is in it, the ground of the earth and all that is upon it, and the rivers and the mountains to rejoice and be happy. The reason for such praise is God's righteousness bestowed upon the people.

We too can join in this praise because, through our Baptism, we are recipients of His love and forgiveness. "Shout for joy before the LORD, the King" (Psalm 98:6).

We praise You, Father, for the gift of Your righteousness bestowed upon us through Jesus Christ. Amen.

Jakob K. Heckert

1 Peter 1:18–25

God's Grace from Eternity

Praise be to the God and Father of our Lord Jesus
Christ, who has blessed us in the heavenly realms
with every spiritual blessing in Christ. For He
chose us in Him before the creation of the world.
Ephesians 1:3–4

Before the creation of the world, our beloved God had already, by His great grace, chosen us as His children and called us to eternal life. There was nothing good in us that motivated Him to do this. Nor should we think that God chose us for eternity because He saw in advance that we would refrain from certain sins. No, God's grace was given to us "in Christ Jesus before the beginning of time" (2 Timothy 1:9). We were chosen in and through Christ "before the creation of the world" (Ephesians 1:4).

We sinners are unable to contribute anything toward our redemption. Our redemption cost the precious blood of Christ, the innocent and unspotted Lamb. Even before God created the world, Christ was appointed to be our Savior. God's grace is from eternity.

For Your grace from eternity, we praise and thank You, Lord God, Father, for the sake of Christ! Amen.

Arnold H. Gebhardt

Exodus 15:1–21

A Glorious Song of Thanksgiving

"Sing to the LORD, for He is highly exalted." Exodus 15:21

In this passage, Moses sang about the great deeds of God as they crossed the Red Sea: "Pharaoh's chariots and his army He has hurled into the sea" (Exodus 15:4). Even today enemies concentrate on destroying Christians: "Who among the gods is like You...majestic in holiness, awesome in glory, working wonders?" (Exodus 15:11). However, before the Lord God, all enemies have no choice but to retreat. The world will be frightened and be afraid. "Terror and dread will fall upon them. By the power of Your arm they will be as still as a stone" (Exodus 15:16).

Not only is God powerful enough to subdue every enemy, He is merciful and gracious toward us, His very own. The Bible is filled with passages that emphasize the unearned grace of God: "In Your unfailing love You will lead the people You have redeemed" (Exodus 15:13a).

Take a moment to look through your hymnbook. Take special note of how God's love and goodness is expressed in the hymns of thanksgiving. Praise and thanks be to God! Thus it shall ever be!

Dearest God, You have thoroughly taken everything into account. Through it all we have been abundantly blessed! We give You the glory! Amen.

Herman A. Mayer

God Is Holy and Gracious

Holy, holy, holy is the LORD almighty! Isaiah 6:3

The Lord, our God, is worthy of all praise and glory. As we attend to our daily devotions and faithfully come to worship in His sanctuary, we devoutly come before Him about whom the seraphim sing "holy, holy, holy."

What a wondrous God, holy and righteous! Who can fully grasp this? God is incomprehensible because He fills the heavens and the earth. Furthermore, what a mystery that our divine God exists in three distinct Persons—Father, Son, and Holy Spirit—to which the triple "holy" refers.

Nevertheless, when we observe and worship this holiness and glory of God, our heart begins to pound in fear, for we are poor sinners! But this holy God is also a merciful and compassionate God. He cleanses us of our sins, just like the lips of the prophet Isaiah were cleansed when the seraph touched his lips with a coal from the altar (Isaiah 6:6–7). So also does the Lord cleanse us from all our sins through the blood of Jesus Christ, His Son. How astounding is God's grace in Christ!

Great, three-fold holy God, accept our praise and glory, and be gracious to us for Christ's sake! Amen.

Otto H. Schmidt

October 28   Acts 13:42–52

Faith and Glorifying Praise Together

When the Gentiles heard this, they were glad and
honored the word of the Lord; and all who were
appointed for eternal life believed. Acts 13:48

When given something we never expected to
receive, it is quite natural to greatly rejoice. That's what
happened to the people in Antioch as they heard the Good
News of the Gospel from the apostle Paul. Paul proclaimed
that God had established His only Son as Savior, a Light
for the Gentiles. The people at Antioch rejoiced over this
wonderful news, and they praised and glorified God.

However, the book of Acts tells us something else:
faith and glorifying God belong together. One cannot
exist apart from the other. We believe in our Lord Jesus
Christ. We believe that through His suffering, death, and
resurrection, we stand justified before God, and we believe
that we have eternal life through Him. Because of this, we
can rejoice and praise God. And we rejoice even more that
the wonderful news of the Gospel is evident through God's
Holy Word.

Glory, praise, and thanks be to God the Lord, who
guards His people from misery and tribulation! Amen.

                                              Manfred Roensch

John 3:1–13

Praise and Glorify the Holy Spirit!

*"I tell you the truth, no one can enter the kingdom
of God unless he is born of water and the Spirit."*
John 3:5

We confess, "I believe that I cannot by my own reason or strength believe in Jesus Christ, my Lord, or come
to Him; but the Holy Spirit has called me by the Gospel,
enlightened me with His gifts, sanctified and kept me in
the true faith" (the *Small Catechism*).

The beloved Savior made this clear to Nicodemus
when he came to Him one night (John 3:1). Nicodemus
asked how a man could be reborn when he is already old?
Jesus was not speaking about physical birth, of course. He
was referring to Baptism, the birth by which a person
becomes a child of God. This is a spiritual birth, our rebirth, a miraculous work through water and Spirit, an
undeserved gift from the Holy Spirit.

Through this miraculous act of the Holy Spirit, we
become children of God. We can never adequately thank
the Lord for this. But for the rest of our lives, by word and
deed, we can humbly desire to show Him our thankfulness
for all His grace.

God, the Father, Son, and Holy Spirit, praise and
glory be to You for every blessing, from now on into all
eternity! Amen.

Arnold H. Gebhardt

October 31   Ephesians 1:3–7

Luther's Song of Thanksgiving

Sing to the LORD *a new song ... the* LORD *has
made His salvation known.* Psalm 98:1–2

In the first hymn he composed, in 1523, Martin
Luther gives us a joyous testimony about faith: "Dear
Christians, one and all, rejoice, with exultation springing,
and with united heart and voice and holy rapture singing,
proclaim the wonders God has done, how His right arm
the vict'ry won. What price our ransom cost Him!"
(*Lutheran Worship*, hymn 353)

Luther wrote a title over this hymn that read: "A
hymn for the great blessings which God has shown us in
Christ." The subject matter is God's promise of redemption
received through faith in Jesus Christ. Nothing in our
entire lives is lovelier or more important.

No wonder Reformation history claims that hun-
dreds who initially disregarded Luther were brought to
faith through this hymn. Are we steadfast in the grace that
is in Christ? Let us sing a new song to the Lord and proclaim His salvation!

Dearest Lord Jesus, help us to ever more sing about
Your sweet deeds of wonder! Amen.

                                          Walter W. Stuenkel

November 1   Psalm 103:1–13

Salvation by Grace

Who is a God like You, who pardons sin and
forgives the transgression of the remnant of His
inheritance? You do not stay angry forever but
delight to show mercy. Micah 7:18

This verse is a song of praise for the grace of God.
It is a progression of expressions, each of which points to
the truth that God is gracious and merciful.

"Who is a God like You?" No one! That's why the
Lord says: "You shall have no other gods before me"
(Exodus 20:3). He alone forgives sin and remits the transgression "of the remnant of His inheritance." This remnant
of the inheritance is the poor, small group of people who
trust in the name of the Lord (Zephaniah 2:9, 3:12), who
along with the redeemed of the New Testament comprise
the true Israel (Romans 11:5, 25–26). God does not hold
His wrath against them forever, but gives them grace, with
compassion, forgiveness of sins, eternal life, and salvation
through Jesus Christ.

Therefore I will hope in God, not building upon
my merits; my heart shall rely on Him and trust in His
goodness, which proclaims to me His Word; that is my
comfort and true refuge upon which I will rely at all
times. Amen. (*Kirchengesangbuch für Evangelisch—Lutherische*
Gemeinden)

Luther Poellot

An Antiphon as a Prayer

*Do not bring Your servant into judgment, for no
one living is righteous before You. Psalm 143:2*

Dear God, how often we have sinned against You!
How often we have forgotten Your commands and followed our own will! Not only have we often committed
evil, but even more often have we neglected the good or
merely gone through the motions.

Your Word remains forever true: Before You no living person is righteous—none who can trust in themselves.
Nor is there anyone who in the least can earn his own
righteousness. This is the comfortless, vain death of the
blind heathen world that knows of no Savior.

However, we, your children, acknowledge our sins.
And the sweet-sounding echo of Your Gospel has wrapped
a cloak of righteousness around us. Therefore remember,
O Lord God, Your grace in Christ Jesus, our Savior, and
always be our source of help. If we are downcast, then spur
us on and give us the desire and willing joyfulness to gladly do Your will. If we have doubts and second thoughts,
then strengthen us in faith in Christ and grant us the confident assurance of Your eternal redemption.

Jesus, Your blood and righteousness are also my
cloak and garment of glory, my eternal comfort. Praise be
to You! Amen.

Eugene Seltz

November 3   Exodus 34:1–9

A Single Antiphon to the Praise of God

The LORD is compassionate and gracious, slow to anger, abounding in love. Psalm 103:8

It is by God's grace that we are living on earth as His children. His patience with us is rooted in His love and goodness, which He has shown us through His Son, our Savior. That's why we may call upon our heavenly Father at any time and in any need.

Yet does God ever become impatient with us? Does our cry for help sometimes reach Him at an inopportune time? Most definitely not! The Lord has compassion on those who fear Him and call upon Him. If your pleading comes in deepest night, He hears it. If you are pining away under your daytime burdens, He certainly knows all about it. No one can or shall in Jesus' name ever call upon His mercy in vain.

That's why you should never cease with your pleading. Your cry for rescue and help never reaches Him at an unacceptable hour. Pray without letting up. He is and remains gracious and patient. May we never forget this! We can never come to Him too often with our requests, for He is gracious and merciful, endlessly patient and of great goodness.

Lord, have patience with me and be gracious to me, a sinner, for the sake of Jesus Christ! Amen.

Eugene Seltz

From Lamentation, Joy

You turned my wailing into dancing. Psalm 30:11

How often is this verified in Scripture! As Mary and Martha grieved over the death of their brother Lazarus, Jesus brought resurrection and life. Jairus rejoiced that Jesus woke his daughter from the sleep of death. The widow praised Jesus when He raised her son to life. The hopelessness of the disciples of Jesus on Good Friday was changed to the joy of Easter.

We too have lived through many a sad night when we lay down full of worry and awoke in the morning to see the sun shining once more! And we heartily acknowledge God as the source of this light and joy. It is not we, of course, who can solve the riddles of our cares. We possess neither the wisdom nor strength to overcome sickness, death, worry, and need. (If it were so, perhaps we would never experience a single moment of true joy.) In our sinful state, we deserve nothing better. Yet our God is gracious and merciful. Through Christ, He has overcome all wailing.

Let us then not forget to give thanks! Let us say with David: "You turned my wailing into dancing; You removed my sackcloth and clothed me with joy, that my heart may sing to You and not be silent. O LORD my God, I will give You thanks forever" (Psalm 30:11–12).

My whole heart is cheered, my spirit and body rejoice. To You, O God, be all the glory! Amen.

Daniel E. Poellot

November 5 Psalm 107

Thank the Lord!

Give thanks to the LORD, for He is good; His love endures forever. Psalm 107:1

Whom does the psalmist call upon to thank the Lord? Those whom the Lord has rescued from distress, lead out of captivity, and saved from agony as they called upon Him in their need. Those that sat in darkness, chained in captivity, who were actually about to be overcome by the stormy winds on the sea.

The reason for their circumstances was their errant ways in the wilderness, their disobedience against God's commands, their sins against the Lord. God's judgment was, therefore, evoked to bring them to repentance. As they cried to the Lord in their need, He heard them and helped them. God judges the disobedient and grants forgiveness to those who cry out to Him in their need.

If God chastises us, He does so to protect us from a greater sin and to move us to repent. As we cry to Him in our need, He hears and helps us—for Jesus' sake.

We praise You, dear Father, that in judgment You also save us. Amen.

Jakob K. Heckert

Psalm 118

Thank the Lord!

*Give thanks to the LORD, for He is good; His love
endures forever.* Psalm 118:1

We have both the privilege and opportunity to
thank God in a variety of ways. For example, in the worship
service, after the celebration of the holy Lord's Supper, the
pastor invites the people to pray and give thanks to the
Lord, saying "we give thanks to You, almighty God, that
You have refreshed us with this salutary gift." The Lord's
Supper is a gift of benefit to our salvation as it keeps us
connected to Christ. This is but one way in which we bring
our thanks to God for His enduring love.

In contrast, the Lord Jesus speaks of the ingratitude
of the nine healed lepers: "Were not all ten cleansed?
Where are the other nine? Was no one found to return and
give praise to God except this foreigner?" (Luke 17:17–18)
Into which camp do we fall?

We pray that we may always thank God with a
heart dedicated to Him. We pray that we may always
thank God with a mouth that praises Him with songs and
prayers. We pray that we may always thank God with
hands that offer our freewill offerings and gifts to help sustain and spread His kingdom.

So then, everyone thank God with heart, mouth,
and hands because He has done great things for all to
the ends of the earth. From our mother's womb on, He
has done much for our good, and still does to this very
moment! Amen.

Herbert D. Poellot

Our God

For great is the LORD and most worthy of praise;
He is to be feared above all gods. Psalm 96:4

God is astoundingly wondrous, to alone be reverently worshipped with one's whole heart. He is wondrous in His essence—the eternal God: Father, Son, and Holy Spirit, three distinct Persons; each Person is the true God, yet there is only one God. God is wondrous in His works. "Who among the gods is like You, O LORD? Who is like You—majestic in holiness, awesome in glory, working wonders?" (Exodus 15:11)

One thinks about the creation, sustenance, ruling, foreknowledge, redemption, and calling of God. One thinks about His wondrous faithfulness at the time of Noah, Moses, the prophets, and the apostles. One thinks about Jesus' miracles, about which St. John wrote, "If every one of them were written down, I suppose that even the whole world would not have room for the books that would be written" (John 21:25).

We live entirely by the wonders of God, especially by the wonders of His grace in Christ Jesus, our Savior from sin who suffered and died for the sins of all mankind. And in the hymn, "Holy God, We Praise Your Name" we sing, "Lord of all, we bow before You. All on earth Your scepter claim, all in heav'n above adore You."

Praise and glory be to the highest good ... the God who does wonders! Amen.

George M. Krach

Zephaniah 3:8–17

Christic, Zion's Confidence

Sing, O Daughter of Zion, shout aloud,
O Israel! Be glad and rejoice with all your heart,
O Daughter of Jerusalem! Zephaniah 3:14

Shout, jubilate, be happy, and rejoice Zion, Israel, Jerusalem! Believing, blessed children of God, be happy, for the Lord is your confidence!

Practically word for word the prophet Zechariah repeats this prophecy and emphasizes it with, "See, your King comes to you, righteous and having salvation" (Zechariah 9:9b). The Lord Jesus Christ was to enter into Jerusalem to win for sinners the declaration of righteousness and salvation of God. To this Zephaniah added, "The LORD has taken away your punishment, He has turned back your enemy. The LORD, the King of Israel, is with you; never again will you fear any harm" (Zephaniah 3:15). There is no better, more certain confidence than these prophecies fulfilled!

The fulfillment: Jesus rode into Jerusalem, bore the sinners' punishment, won God's righteousness, and crafted a sure salvation. He did this for us. Therefore we rejoice, "Who is he that condemns?" (Romans 8:34) Christ is He who died for us. Indeed, even more so, He rose from the dead for us. He is at God's right hand and intercedes for us.

Lord Christ, enter into our hearts to be our eternal assurance and confidence. Thus we are happy! Amen.

George M. Krach

To God Alone the Glory!

For from Him and through Him and to Him are
all things. To Him be the glory forever! Amen.
Romans 11:36

In the above doxology, the apostle Paul let his praise of God ring forth. With this he called upon all Christians to not search the mysteries of God or seek the secrets, but to worship. We want to give God the glory for both—what He has revealed in His Word for our salvation and for His secret, hidden wisdom. For what is hidden to us in our time we can know is great, holy, divine, and worthy of worship.

Everything will become more complete and clear to us when in eternity we proclaim "to Him be the glory forever! Amen," when the shell has fallen away, when, in the life to come, the entire counsel of God lies plain and uncovered before our eyes. Thus, in this epistle the apostle encourages us to worship the unfathomable wisdom of God and His unrevealed, incomprehensible judgments and ways.

To the highest good be praise and glory. To the Father of all goodness, the God who does wonders, the God who fills my soul with His rich comfort, the God who calms all tribulation: Give glory to our God! Amen. (*Kirchengesangbuch für Evangelisb—Lutherische Gemeinden*)

Herman A. Harms

Being a Christian Means to Trust God

*But now a righteousness from God, apart from
law, has been made known, to which the Law and
the Prophets testify.* Romans 3:21

Christianity is a religion of trust. Actually it is the
only religion of trust. Everything else mankind calls religion is a religion of human works.

Non-Christian religions teach that a person must
make himself acceptable to God through his own works.
They argue among themselves as to which works are actually good works. However, they are in agreement about
the main point: man must take some action to save himself.

It is different for Christians. We learn and read in
the Bible—and we believe it—that God loves us despite
the fact that we are miserable sinners. God loves us so
much, in fact, that He sent His only Son to perfectly keep
the Law in our place, to suffer and die for our guilt of sin,
and to rise from the dead to bring us eternal life.

Christ has rescued us completely. We do not trust
or rely upon our own works. Instead, we trust in Christ and
His works alone.

Dear Jesus, thank You for Your grace and for Your
righteousness which is ours through faith. Amen.

John M. Drickamer

Trusting the Triune God

May the grace of the Lord Jesus Christ, and the
love of God, and the fellowship of the Holy Spirit
be with you all. 2 Corinthians 13:14

Unbelievers hold that the doctrine of the Holy Trinity is simply a philosophical theory that has nothing to do with life and reality. But we know that's not true.

The God we trust is the everlasting, holy, triune God. He is the God of the Bible. He is the God of our salvation. There is only one true God. However, God is three distinct persons.

God the Father loved us and sent His Son to redeem us with His precious blood. God the Son is our Savior, who became man in order to suffer and die in our place. God the Holy Spirit is the Comforter, sent from the Father and the Son, who continually reassures us from His Word that for Jesus' sake we are God's children. Three persons; one God.

The Holy Trinity is the true God who loves us. We trust this God for all time and for eternity.

O God, continually grant us a steadfast trust in You: Father, Son, and Holy Spirit. The grace of our Lord Savior, the love of the Father, and the fellowship of the Holy Spirit abide with us always. Amen.

John M. Drickamer

November 12   Matthew 6:9–13

Trusting the Father

*Because you are sons, God sent the Spirit of His
Son into our hearts, the Spirit who calls out,
"Abba, Father."* Galatians 4:6

Through faith in Christ Jesus, we are the children
of God. God is our Father, who has always loved us. And
just as little children happily and confidently approach
their earthly father, we can in faith and prayer come before
our heavenly Father. Through His Word, the Lord God
assures us again and again of His fatherly love. The Father
wants to gently encourage and invite us to look upon Him
as our dear Father.

We hold a reverent respect for God, of course, just
like a child has toward its father. But it is not God's desire
that we be afraid of Him as though He were some stern
taskmaster. Children are scared if their father is angry.
What is the situation with God, who hates sin? Because of
Christ, God is no longer angry with us. He forgives us all
sins. Through His Word, the Spirit of God moves us to
seek the Father in heaven as our gracious and merciful
Father. Through His fatherly love, our fear vanishes.
"Perfect love drives out fear" (1 John 4:18).

Dear gracious Father in heaven, uphold us with
Your Word and keep us in Your family for Jesus' sake.
Amen.

John M. Drickamer

Trusting the Son

So if the Son sets you free, you will be free indeed.
John 8:36

It is of utmost importance for us that Jesus of Nazareth was God's true Son. If He were not the Son of God, then He would be unable to help us because human help is of no benefit to our eternal life. But Jesus is really and truly the Son of God, sent as our Savior by the Father. God the Son fulfilled the Law of God for us. God the Son suffered for us. God the Son died in our place. God the Son redeemed us. He did for us what no human being could do.

The Father was well pleased with His Son, as He with His own voice repeatedly testified. Through faith, we are united with Christ. His death is our death. His life is our life. His righteousness is our righteousness. Hence we stand before God's judgment with the Son of God, guiltless and completely free.

The Son made us free from all guilt and debt. We are free citizens in His kingdom. We are full-fledged heirs of His household.

Dear Jesus, we thank You from our hearts that we have such freedom through You. You have proclaimed the Gospel to us, and that truth is accompanied with freedom. Amen.

John M. Drickamer

Trusting the Spirit

The Spirit Himself testifies with our spirit that we are God's children. Romans 8:16

Why do we believe that the Father is our Father and the Son is our Savior? If we merely wanted to believe, that would be but a wish—not faith.

If the bright rays fall upon our eyes, we believe that the sun shines. If the raindrops fall on our head, we believe that it is raining. It matters not whether we wanted it to rain or we wanted the sun to shine. We are convinced that the sun is shining or that it's raining; a wish becomes reality when it is transformed into an actual event.

We believe that our sins have been forgiven—but not simply because we would like to have them forgiven. We believe that we have eternal life—but not simply because we would like to have it. We believe because we are convinced of it. How did we arrive at such a certainty and conviction?

God the Holy Spirit convinced us of this. And that to which He testifies is the truth! Through the Gospel, He has convinced us that what we read in the Bible, hear preached in divine service, and receive in the sacraments is the truth: the forgiveness of sins, life, and salvation.

Lord God, Holy Spirit, convince us again and again that the Father is gracious to us for Jesus' sake. Amen.

John M. Drickamer

November 15   Isaiah 40:26–31

Trusting the Shepherd

So then, those who suffer according to God's will should commit themselves to their faithful Creator and continue to do good. 1 Peter 4:19

God created the world. God loved the world. God created us. And God still loves us.

If we have made something with our human hands, we tend to take care of it. If we have devoted our time and labor to a tiny piece of handiwork, we want to preserve it. These human feelings are but a weak reflection of the care, the love, the faithfulness of our Creator toward us. In the past, God has demonstrated His faithfulness to us in many ways. In thousands of ways, He continues to demonstrate to us His faithfulness—by our daily bread and everything that pertains to it. And in the future, He will continue to show Himself to be a faithful Creator.

No matter what earthly concerns and anxieties we have, we can always remember that God has promised us His faithfulness. We rely upon it because we, through His Word, know of His grace through Jesus.

Faithful Creator, who has made us new in Christ, assure us of Your faithfulness for the sake of Jesus. We commit ourselves, our bodies and souls, and everything else into Your hands. Amen.

John M. Drickamer

Trusting the Savior

And we have seen and testify that the Father
has sent His Son to be the Savior of the world.
1 John 4:14

Is Jesus our Savior? Did Christ come to save us? How can we be completely certain—we, who are descendants of heathen Gentiles?

Many in the first century thought that the Messiah was the Savior of the Jews only. But Jesus proved that He is the Savior of the entire world when He dealt with the Canaanite woman, when He helped the Roman officer, and, in particular, when He sent His disciples out into the world to proclaim the Gospel to all nations.

No Bible verse states that He died specifically for you or me; Scripture does not include my given name or yours. However, it is written that God loved the world— all of mankind; and that Jesus is the Savior of the world. Jesus suffered as the substitute for all mankind. Jesus died for the debt of sin for all mankind.

If He died for all, then He died for each individual. If He is the Savior of the world, then He is your Savior and my Savior.

Dear Jesus, eternal praise and thanks to You that You are my Savior; yes indeed, that You are the Savior of the world. Amen.

John M. Drickamer

November 17   Ephesians 5:25–32

Trusting the Holy God

Sanctify them by the truth; Your word is truth.
John 17:17

How can we sinners stand before God? We still commit sinful deeds, words, thoughts, and desires. God, however, is holy. And only He who is holy can stand before Him.

We can stand before God because He sees us as holy. How can that be? God knows everything. Doesn't He also see our sinful deeds and our sinful thoughts?

Yes, indeed, God knows and sees everything. But instead of seeing us, He sees Jesus. Jesus, the holy Son of God, died as the substitute for all of us. For His sake, all our sins are forgiven. God the Holy Spirit brings this forgiveness to us by means of Word and Sacrament.

Through the washing by the Word, namely through Baptism, and through the Gospel—which bestows to Baptism its power and meaning—the Holy Spirit worked in us faith in Jesus and granted to us the forgiveness of all our sins for His sake. Now we stand before God's judgment without the slightest guilt.

The Holy Spirit also works the fruit of faith so we, out of thankfulness for God's grace, respond in love for God for our neighbor.

Holy Spirit, work in our hearts for Jesus' sake so we may grow in love. Amen.

John M. Drickamer

Trusting the Living God

Just as the living Father sent Me and I live because of the Father, so the one who feeds on Me will live because of Me. John 6:57

It is a fundamental truth of the Bible that God is alive. God is the Author and Originator of life. If He did not have life, He above all else would not have been able to give us this bodily life—or the life of this world. But it is of far greater importance that the living God gave us spiritual life.

Jesus, the eternal Son of God, is also alive. He was dead, for He died on the cross on account of our sins. He also was buried. Neither death nor the grave was able to contain Him. He seized life and ascended to heaven. He lives and rules in all eternity.

Jesus lives to give us eternal life. He gives us spiritual life for His own sake, and with that the promise and the foretaste of eternal life. We will die one day. Jesus Christ will raise our bodies from the dead on Judgment Day. We shall live forever in body and soul.

Dear Jesus, grant that we receive life from You, always cling to it, and always thank and praise You for it. Amen.

John M. Drickamer

Trusting the True God

*We know also that the Son of God has come and
has given us understanding, so that we may know
Him who is true. And we are in Him who is true—
even in His Son Jesus Christ. He is the true God
and eternal life.* 1 John 5:20

There are many who are called gods and lords.
There are many religions in the world. How do we know
that the God of the Bible is the one true God? How can we
Christians believe that we alone worship the true God?

The gods of the non-Christian religions are human
or satanic fabrications. They do not exist. The histories
about these "gods" are merely fables and myths. However,
in true, actual history, God came to us. He became a man
among us. He lived as a man. And He still lives, our
Brother.

Jesus has proclaimed to us the one true God. He is
the God whose wrath we have earned by our sins.
However, He is also the God who, despite it all, has loved
us. Out of His love for us, Jesus, true God and true Man,
died on the cross in our place.

"Let me unto my death properly confess my Jesus,
and in my final need be called a member of His body. As I
live and die only in Him, I know that I am saved." Amen.

John M. Drickamer

Trusting the Good God

Give thanks to the LORD, for He is good, His love endures forever. Psalm 118:1

Some may ask, "Is God good?" What kind of a question is that? If God is not good, what could be called good?

Yet the matter is not that simple. Why is it that there is sin and evil in the world? Many have believed that there exists not just a good god, but also an evil god. But for those who believe, there exists only one God, who is almighty and good. So why do we still have sin and suffering?

For those who believe, it is a matter of biblical truth that God is good. The good God provides daily bread and thousand-fold gifts to all mankind. We do not deny that sin and the consequences of sin exist. So why does God allow evil to have any space?

We don't know why. The Bible does not answer this question. However, God's Word makes it clear to us that God, despite all the evil of mankind and the devil, still achieves His purposes in this sinful world. His ways are unfathomable, but always serve our best interests.

Yet there is one thing we do know! God Himself suffered. God the Son died for us. Therefore we shall eternally delight in His goodness!

Convince us, Lord, that for Jesus' sake we shall see and enjoy Your goodness eternally and perfectly in heaven. Amen.

John M. Drickamer

335

Trusting the Gracious God

The LORD is compassionate and gracious, slow to anger, abounding in love. He will not always accuse, nor will He harbor His anger forever.
Psalm 103:8–9

God is gracious. What is the meaning of the word "grace"?

One way to understand a word is to consider its opposite. What does the grace of God mean? It is the antonym for the wrath of God. God's grace means that He no longer is angry with us. We have richly deserved His wrath with our sins. However, He has forgiven us our sin. That is His grace. By God's grace we have been saved.

How can God be so gracious? He gave His only Son into death on the cross in our place. The punishment we so justly deserved fell upon Jesus. He has taken away the wrath of God and loaded it upon Himself. All that remains for us is God's grace and saving love.

The Gospel is the joyous news of this grace earned by Jesus. In this life, we know that another person has forgiven us only if he expressly tells us so. In the Gospel, God tells us that for Jesus' sake He has forgiven all our sins. Of this we can be certain!

Dear Lord Jesus, grant us faith in Your grace in every situation of our lives. Amen.

John M. Drickamer

Trusting the Invisible God

We live by faith, not by sight. 2 Corinthians 5:7

We are unable to see God, but we can trust in Him. That's faith. Faith is "being sure of what we hope for and certain of what we do not see" (Hebrews 11:1).

In this world the danger exists that we will rely only upon what we can see and forget about what we cannot see. But the visible, namely this world and everything that is in the world, will perish. God remains forever.

We believe in the invisible God. We believe that He exists and that He has created us and everything else. We believe in His actuality and His might.

We do not believe because we are so intelligent. Instead, we believe because God has revealed Himself. The bodily eyes read His Word, the Bible. The bodily ears hear His Word in the sermon. Through the Word, God reassures us that He has forgiven us for Jesus' sake, that in Christ we are God's children, that He will take us to Himself in heaven, that He will guide and help us in this life.

Dear Lord Jesus, give us the kind of faith and the kind of love as though we are already seeing You face to face. Amen.

John M. Drickamer

Trusting the Hidden God

*Truly You are a God who hides Himself, O God
and Savior of Israel.* Isaiah 45:15

God is not only hidden from our eyes, but also from our reason. Humans cannot understand His ways or thoughts, especially if they are unbelievers. Neither do we Christians always understand God's ways with us in this world. When we have problems, when we are sick, when we die, we Christians are unable to comprehend with human reason just how gracious and lovingly God deals with us.

God deals with us according to His grace, yet also according to His wisdom. His thoughts are not our thoughts (see Isaiah 55:8). Even when it seems incomprehensible to us that He is the One who accomplishes our salvation, Jesus Christ remains our Savior.

The kingdom of heaven is far more important than anything earthly. Throughout our journey, God leads and guides every event and occurrence to bring us safely into the kingdom of heaven. We believe this through faith because Jesus has earned for us the grace of God through His suffering and death.

Dear Lord Jesus, forsake us not when we doubt; instead, reassure us anew of Your grace. Amen.

John M. Drickamer

Trusting the Promised God

*For no matter how many promises God has made,
they are "Yes" in Christ. And so through Him the
"Amen" is spoken by us to the glory of God.*
2 Corinthians 1:20

What do the many promises that are found on practically every page of the Bible actually mean?

Many think God has promised His Christians every good in this life, and therefore Christians should always be healthy, rich, happy, and, above all else, have no problems! Others think that in the Old Testament, God promised that the earthly nation of Israel was to remain His people always and the Israelites were to be saved, apart from Christ, for eternity.

But what does Scripture say? That the promises of God are fulfilled through Christ. He is the promised Messiah and Savior; He brings the promised salvation. All of God's promises have their Yes and Amen—thus their fulfillment—in Jesus Christ.

The fulfillment of total good fortune is impossible in this sinful world. There are true Christians who are poor and sick and remain so for as long as they live. However, for the sake of Jesus, we have the eternal goodness and blessings of God, salvation, and the kingdom of heaven—because for His sake our sins are forgiven.

Dear Jesus, make us heavenly minded so we believe in Your true promises. Amen.

John M. Drickamer

Trusting the Sent God

For God did not send His Son into the world to condemn the world, but to save the world through Him. John 3:17

We know only one Son of God—Jesus Christ—who was sent by the heavenly Father.

On account of sin mankind could not appear before God in heaven. For people to be eternally saved, it was necessary for One to come to rescue them. Indeed, God Himself had to come. Otherwise we all would be eternally lost.

If God's own Son has come, must He not then judge us according to His righteousness? Won't we all be condemned? O the great wonder of divine love! He was not sent to judge us, but to save us! His righteousness is not a code of rules for leading a salvation-producing life. Instead, it is a gracious gift of God whereby He, for Jesus' sake, views us as being righteous.

Jesus will return someday to judge the living and the dead. Ought we be afraid? No. The judgment over us has already been pronounced. For Jesus' sake, God finds nothing condemning in us. We are saved—but only for the sake of Jesus.

Dear Lord Jesus, just as You have taken away all guilt from us, so also remove all fear from us. Amen.

John M. Drickamer

Trusting the Buried God

That He was buried ... according to the Scriptures.
1 Corinthians 15:4

What does the grave of Christ Jesus mean to us as Christians?

If we were to have everlasting life, someone had to die in our place. The Son of God came to accomplish precisely that, to endure our death in our place. Through His death, Jesus Christ gave us life. In order for this to truly happen, He had to actually and physically die. His burial and His grave indicate to us that He truly did die for us on the cross.

The Roman soldiers recognized death. (Surely they had seen enough dead bodies.) When their captain informed Pilate that Jesus was dead, there could be no doubt about His physical death. His enemies testified that Jesus was dead and they handed over His corpse to His friends. And Jesus' friends testified that He was dead, for they buried Him.

Thus we know that Jesus died and we believe that He died specifically for us. He was buried and we trust that our debt of sin was actually blotted out and atoned for through that death. However, His grave is empty. His empty grave sanctifies our grave. Jesus lives in order to give us life.

Dear Savior, through Your death take from us the fear of our own graves. Amen.

John M. Drickamer

In the Name of Jesus

"You are to give Him the name Jesus, because He will save His people from their sins." Matthew 1:21

The names of the great and mighty are honored. Their achievements are praised from generation to generation. Yet the past is past! The wind streaks across their graves. In the course of time, even the most beautiful and glorious fame among men wilts away. A new generation of leaders arrives on the scene, people who do not know previous leaders and are not interested in them at all.

However Jesus lives, and His glorious name lives on into eternity along with Him! Each new generation that comes to know His name, that becomes familiar with the comfort of His grace, and that embraces His gift of eternal redemption is filled with joy over Jesus, Savior, Redeemer. He is the Alpha and the Omega—the beginning and the end. In the first book of the Bible, the Messiah was promised as the One who would step on and crush the head of the serpent, the Victor over Satan. At the end of the Scriptures, Christendom prays, "Amen. Come, Lord Jesus" (Revelation 22:20). Let us live and work to honor Him until He leads us into eternal glory!

Begin your work with Jesus; Jesus has it in His hands. Call upon Jesus for support; Jesus will bring it to an excellent conclusion. Arise with Jesus in the morning. Go to sleep with Jesus. Guide your course with Jesus. Let Jesus chart your course! Amen.

Herbert D. Poellot

Grace and Protection

The LORD is my Light and my Salvation ...
the LORD is the stronghold of my life.
Psalm 27:1

How fortunate and blessed we are to be certain of the grace and protection of God here today, throughout this new church year, and every day to follow!

Those who acknowledge their sin, and fear God's wrath and punishment, can turn to Christ and receive His grace. He who does so through faith in Christ is forgiven and is on the path to heaven. Moreover, a Christian can also rejoice in and comfort himself with His Savior's protection. He has a mighty God and Savior as his Protector. Come what may, "if God is for us, who can be against us?" (Romans 8:31). With David, all Christians can confidently and happily confess: "The Lord is my Light and my Salvation—whom shall I fear? The Lord is the stronghold of my life—of whom shall I be afraid? When evil men advance against me to devour my flesh, when my enemies and my foes attack me, they will stumble and fall" (Psalm 27:1–2). Your Word says to me, "You are my Might, my Rock, my Hero, my Shield, my Strength" (see Psalm 46). In Him we rejoice!

Lord God, may You always be my Light, my Salvation, my Strength! Amen.

George A. Beiderwieden

November 29   Matthew 11:25–30

Your King Is Gentle

*"Say to the Daughter of Zion, 'See your king
comes to you, gentle.'"* Matthew 21:5

What can we learn from this verse which tells us
that our King comes to us gently?

Again we look at the antonym. The opposite of
gentleness is pride and hard-heartedness. We often give
these attributes to the rulers of the world. (Should this be
said about a king, we would assume his subjects have little
hope.)

Our King however is not haughty, proud, or hard-
hearted. Jesus Christ is gentle and humble of heart
(Matthew 11:29). As such, He also has empathy for our
weakness. Our Savior is not so high and haughty that He
despises the poor and lowly. Rather, it is precisely the
poor, the oppressed, the lowly, the needy of every sort that
He takes to Himself, that He helps.

What a wonderful King this Jesus is! Before Him we
need not tremble. We can approach Him with trust. We
can take our every need to Him with complete confidence
that our gentle King will not cast us aside. Instead, He will
grant us the help our needs require.

Thanks be to You, Lord Jesus, that You come to us
as a gentle King. Receive us in all of our needs! Amen.

Fred Kramer

Isaiah 11:1–9

Your King Is Righteous

"See, your King comes to you, righteous and
having salvation." Zechariah 9:9

Our King is righteous. How different He is from
earthly kings, who often are unrighteous and live and rule
according to whichever philosophy will make them right!
Long before the prophet Zechariah, Isaiah prophesied,
"He will be called Wonderful Counselor, Mighty God,
Everlasting Father, Prince of Peace. Of the increase of His
government and peace there will be no end. He will reign
on David's throne and over his kingdom, establishing and
upholding it with justice and righteousness from that time
on and forever" (Isaiah 9:6–7).

Are we sinners to be fearful before our King, this
righteous Judge? Will He condemn us as we deserve?

Thanks be to God that we need not fear such condemnation. Our King is not only a righteous Judge, He is
also our righteousness. He humbled Himself, taking on the
form of a servant, and became obedient unto death on the
cross to atone for our unrighteousness so we might have
righteousness before God through Him.

Lord Jesus, help me, a poor sinner, to acknowledge
You as my Righteousness and to receive You through faith!
Amen.

Fred Kramer

ADVENT

December 1 Isaiah 8:1–15

Immanuel

"Devise your strategy, but it will be thwarted;
propose your plan, but it will not stand, for God
is with us." Isaiah 8:10

"Immanuel" means "God with us"—God in our flesh
and blood, God-Man, true God from the Father born in
eternity, and true Man born of the Virgin Mary. Some are
confused and perhaps even put off by this wonder, for
"beyond all question, the mystery of godliness is great; He
appeared in a body" (1 Timothy 3:16). Who can understand that?

That's exactly why the work of Christ ought to be
utterly terrifying to unbelievers. "Conclude a deliberation,
and nothing will come of it! ... for here is Immanuel"
(*Kirchengesangbuch für Evangelish—Lutherische Gemeinden*). God
Himself walked the paths of our world. Even if the world
might still vehemently rant and rave against the church, it
will come to no avail because God is with us, Immanuel. "He
comes as a judge of the world, as a curse to those who curse
Him; [He comes] with grace and sweet light to those who
love Him and seek Him" (*Kirchengesangbuch für Evangelish—
Lutherische Gemeinden*). For Christians it is a comfort that Christ
not only knows our weaknesses and shortcomings, but He
has taken them upon Himself for our rescue and salvation.

We sing to You, Immanuel, our Prince of life and
Fount of grace, ... to You, the Son of a virgin and Lord of
lords. Hallelujah! Amen.

Herman A. Mayer

346

December 2   Matthew 25:31–46

He Comes to Judge the World

"When the Son of Man comes in His glory, and
all the angels with Him, He will sit on His throne
in heavenly glory." Matthew 25:31

When Jesus uttered these words, He was still ministering in person on earth. However, He promised His disciples that He would return one day in His full divine glory. When Jesus Christ returns, He will sit upon the throne of His glory, reigning over His kingdom. Here on earth, His throne is typically thought of as a throne of judgment. But He Himself will be glorified with judgment and righteousness.

The Son of Man, who through suffering and death redeemed all of mankind, is also the Judge of the world. All nations will be gathered before Him. Nobody will be able to hide from this judgment. But what is in store for those who believe on the Day of Judgment?

We who live in Christ Jesus long for this Day of Judgment; and we sing with hymn writer Paul Gerhardt, "He comes to judge the world, to curse those who curse Him; [He comes] with grace and sweet light to those who love and seek Him. Alas, Come; Alas, Come, O Son and take all of us into the eternal light and blessing of Your hall of joy!" For it is on this Day of Judgment that we too will be glorified in Him!

Dear Savior, with steadfast faith in Your forgiveness, we await Your judgment. Amen.

Walter W. Stuenkel

Comfort My People

Comfort, comfort My people, says your God. Speak tenderly to Jerusalem, and proclaim to her that her hard service has been completed, that her sin has been paid for, that she has received from the LORD's hand double for all her sins. Isaiah 40:1–2

God desires that those who sorrow be comforted. He created mankind for the purpose of peace. That is why He was compelled to have mercy on all mankind. But what is this comfort? "Her sin has been paid for." That is the mercy and comfort God wants to give us. He does not promise to remove every earthly tribulation from our lives. But He promises us forgiveness, and that is far more satisfying.

Sin is the cause of all misery in the world. It is also sin that, above all else, burdens our hearts as children of God. Sin separates us from God. But because our sin is forgiven, our hearts can be glad and we can rely on God to help us bear the tribulations that confront us in this life. Because our sins are forgiven, we know with all certainty that God loves us.

Christ brings us this comfort. In Him we possess an overflowing fountain of forgiveness. God's mercy and grace in Christ has overcome the entire sin of the world!

O God, I thank You for Your rich comfort, which is promised us through Jesus Christ. Amen.

Clarence T. Schuknecht

The Advent Sermon

"What shall I cry?" Isaiah 40:6

We are in the midst of the Advent season. This is the time we prepare for the coming of the Savior. Wondrous things lie ahead. "The glory of the LORD will be revealed" (Isaiah 40:5). The newsworthy great mystery of God becoming Man is unfolding.

What then is to be proclaimed? Two things: repentance and comfort. For the first, the vanity and fallen state of the human race must be exposed. "All men are like grass, ... the grass withers" and even the most beautiful of the flowers last only a short while (Isaiah 40:6–7). Therefore, even the best and most godly men will perish like grass and flowers. "We are consumed by your anger. ... You have set our iniquities before You, our secret sins in the light of Your presence. All our days pass away under Your wrath" (see Psalm 90:7–9). That's why Advent time is a time for repentance.

For the second, Isaiah's preaching about repentance is not the last word. He brings comfort to his people. The Savior is not coming for judgment, but rather for redemption. Indeed, He does come with power, but He comes also as the Good Shepherd who will give His life for the sheep.

Lord, grant that we in genuine repentance and in joyful faith find comfort as we prepare ourselves for Your coming! Amen.

Herman A. Mayer

December 5   Romans 10:5–17

He Comes in the Word

Jesus went ... proclaiming the Good News of God.
Mark 1:14

Jesus not only travels, He also preaches. His Word makes His coming understandable. At the time of His earthly sojourn, Jesus was seen by thousands of people. However, most of them saw Him without the Word. That's why they did not find Him. This actually still happens today. A person can participate in all sorts of church activities, but the King may remain far off—not because He doesn't come or is not present, but because that person thinks he can find the King apart from the Word.

Only through the Word do we become enlightened. Only through the Word are we changed so our hearts are opened to Him. In the light of this Word we discover the King of kings. We see Him as He actually is, and recognize Him in His graceful, charming, miraculous image. The Word speaks to our revived soul. It wins over our heart and mind. It brings the message of salvation that makes us His own and provides us with eternal joy. "In God, whose word I praise, in the LORD, whose word I praise" (Psalm 56:10).

Abide with us through Your Word, most worthy Savior, so we might receive goodness and salvation in this life and in the life to come! Amen.

Oliver C. Rupprecht

December 6   Romans 8:28–39

God Is for Us

If God is for us, who can be against us? Romans 8:31

In this passage, the apostle Paul gives us the comfort of Advent so we can forget about temporal sufferings and focus on the advent of our time in heaven.

To us who are in Christ, all things work out for the best. Nothing can rob us of salvation; nothing can make us uncertain. From the beginning of time, God has predestined His believing children for salvation. Of this we can be completely confident. All whom God has elected from eternity for salvation, in accordance with His purpose and plan, are made righteous. And, as His beloved children in Christ, He already glorifies them. They already have forgiveness of their sins, life, and salvation. They already possess the glory of heaven through faith and hope. They already receive the complete comfort of God in Christ.

God is for us! Therefore, no one can be against us—not the devil, not the world, nor the flesh. No creature, no tribulation can tear us from the grasp of God's hand. Because God gave His beloved Son into death for us, He will, through Him, grant our salvation. Does the evil foe try to accuse us? God pronounces us righ-teous. Does Satan try to condemn us? He who sits at the right hand of His Father intercedes for us, justifies us, becomes our Advocate. How glorious is the love of God for us in Christ!

Dear Lord Jesus, we thank You for Your dearly beloved, sweet, Gospel proclamation. Amen.

John Theodore Muller

God Redeems His People

"Praise be to the Lord, the God of Israel, because He has ... redeemed His people." Luke 1:68

God's Son comes to His people—this is the Good News of Advent. It is vital for us to take note of why He comes. Does Christ come to judge and condemn us? Most assuredly, we have done much to deserve both divine judgment and damnation. Yet the song of Zechariah gave us a completely different reason for the coming of the Lord. The Lord God of Israel comes to redeem His people.

Zechariah may, in part, have been speaking about political freedom for his country and about independence for the people of Israel. Yet beyond all doubt, he had something far more important in mind when he uttered these words. God comes to rescue and redeem His people from sin. He comes to bestow the gift of eternal life to His people. What a freedom! What a life!

We often hear about God's redemption, and it always remains glad tidings for us because we are recipients of His forgiveness and of the life that only God can give. The Word of forgiveness is always good news, regardless how many times we hear it!

Holy God and Father, grant that we give thanks to You for the redemption through Your Son! Amen.

Thomas Green

December 8   Matthew 12:14–21

Who Is This That Comes?

"These are the Scriptures that testify about Me."
John 5:39

Jesus was often asked who He was. He usually answered with a reference to the Old Testament. For example, He said to the Jews, who did not want to believe He was the promised Messiah, "If you believed Moses, you would believe Me, for he wrote about Me" (John 5:46). In the synagogue at Nazareth, He read from the prophet Isaiah and explained, "Today this scripture is fulfilled in your hearing" (Luke 4:21). That was affirmation that He was the Messiah that was prophesied to come.

Isaiah gave a clear picture about the coming Savior. He called Him "My chosen one in whom I delight" (Isaiah 42:1b). He is the "Wonderful Counselor, Mighty God, Everlasting Father, Prince of Peace" (Isaiah 9:6b). John the Baptizer described Him as "the Lamb of God who takes away the sin of the world" (John 1:29). The Evangelist John designated Him as the One who was from the beginning and through whom everything was created (see John 1:1). Paul wrote to the Colossians: "In Christ all the fullness of the Deity lives in bodily form" (Colossians 2:9). When the Savior asked His disciples who He was, Peter answered: "You are the Christ, the Son of the living God" (Matthew 16:18). That's the One for whose coming we are preparing.

Gracious God, since You were born, all my misery and need have come to an end! Amen.

Herman A. Mayer

December 9   1 Timothy 1:12–17

Jesus Came into the World for Us

Christ Jesus came into the world to save sinners.
1 Timothy 1:15

Immediately after the fall into sin, God gave our first parents His glorious promise of reconciliation: "And I will put enmity between you and the woman, and between your offspring and hers; He will crush your head, and you will strike His heel" (Genesis 3:15). The fulfillment of this promise was Jesus. We find it, among other places, in the epistle of St. John, where he wrote, "The reason the Son of God appeared was to destroy the devil's work" (1 John 3:8b).

Jesus is called Savior, for He "came ... to save sinners," says the Scriptures. The purpose for His coming into the world was simply this: to save us who were eternally lost.

Christ Jesus was the fulfillment of God's glorious promise of salvation. He remains our Good Shepherd who calls and beckons sinners unto Him so all might believe in Him as Savior, Victor over sin, death, and the power of evil. Through Him the gates of heaven are opened.

God, bestow upon us true faith in Jesus, who came into the world for us! Amen.

Paul W. Hartfield

December 10   Revelation 7:9–17

Our Glorious Adornment and Cloak of Honor

I delight greatly in the LORD, my soul rejoices in my God. For He has clothed me with garments of salvation and arrayed me in a robe of righteousness.
Isaiah 61:10

The promised Messiah suffered and died so we might have peace with God—peace of heart and conscience, peace for time and eternity. Thus in this Advent time our heart is filled with thanks and joy. Our hearts sing with today's text about joy over our Savior who clothes us with salvation and righteousness.

We were poor sinners by nature. All our righteousness was like a filthy cloth (in the original Hebrew, Isaiah referred to a most filthy, soiled cloth). We appeared before God as poor, dirty, ill-clad beggars. But Christ atoned for our sin and won salvation for us. He has clothed us with garments of salvation and adorned us with the cloak of His own complete righteousness. This righteousness is freely given to us, and it covers all of our sins. Now we can stand before God, assured that He finds nothing to condemn us. Thus we can thankfully and trustingly pray:

I sojourn into eternal life, perfectly cleansed by Christ's blood. Lord Jesus, strengthen my faith! Amen.

Otto H. Schmidt

December 11   Psalm 40:1–9

The Helper Comes

"Blessed is the coming kingdom of our father David!" Mark 11:10

All children of God believe in the Savior sent by God. In Old Testament times, they believed in the promised Seed of the woman who would crush the head of the serpent. They waited for the One who would come as the Messiah. In New Testament times, we believe in the Son of God who did come. Through His death on the cross, Jesus purchased forgiveness of sins and eternal life for us.

There were many prophecies about the coming of the Messiah in the Old Testament. By inspiration of the Holy Spirit, David pointed to Christ's coming when he wrote, "Then I said, 'Here I am, I have come—it is written about Me in the scroll'" (Psalm 40:7). The Old Testament prophecies have been fulfilled. The Son of the Father comes in the name of the Lord. He comes to reveal His Word. He is the Helper, the only Savior for every sinner. "Yet to all who received Him, to those who believed in His name, He gave the right to become children of God" (John 1:12). He has come! Hosanna!

Dear Savior, receive our praise! Preserve us in true faith unto eternal life! Amen.

Paul M. Freiburger

John 14:23–27

The Savior Also Comes Now

"If anyone loves Me, he will obey My teaching.
My Father will love him, and we will come to him
and make our home with him. John 14:23

One of the profound feelings of grief that engulfs us at the death of a loved one is sheer loneliness. The disciples of Jesus certainly felt this pain most severely during the three days the Savior lay in the grave. "We had hoped that He was the one who was going to redeem Israel," lamented the Emmaus disciples (Luke 24:21).

Jesus knew how they felt, and after His resurrection He appeared many times in person so they might see and hear. Before His ascension, Jesus comforted His followers with these words: "And surely I am with you always, to the very end of the age" (Matthew 28:20). This is a precious promise to believers of every age, and it remains so for us today.

Today we stand between the first and final Advent of Jesus Christ, who comes to us, according to His promises. God the Father, God the Son, and God the Holy Spirit maintain a daily Advent with us through Word and Sacrament, for, through these means of God's grace, the holy Trinity comforts, strengthens, and preserves us.

Dearest Savior, just as Your arrival was filled with gentle meekness, may I at all times be ready to greet You with gentle meekness. Amen.

Hilton C. Oswald

December 13   Psalm 72:11–20

The God of Israel

"Praise be to the Lord, the God of Israel." Luke 1:68

The God in whom we place our trust and to whom we give thanks is neither hidden nor unknown. He is the Lord God of Israel. In this song, Zechariah looked at the long history of the people of Israel to see how often God revealed Himself to them. Above all else, Zechariah saw God as the One who had chosen Israel as His elect, the One who sent the prophets. In recalling the blessings of God, Zechariah cried out, "Blessed be the Lord, the God of Israel."

Our own understanding of this is much clearer than Zechariah's, for God has revealed Himself to us through His Son Jesus Christ. Through Christ, we have become children of God, and through His death, He has saved us all. Through Christ, God is our Father.

The God of Israel is the only, true, and almighty God. For the people of the Old Testament, God accomplished many mighty deeds. His people were strong with God at their side. The Lord is no less powerful today. He still rescues and protects us. As we pray to Him, He hears and helps us. That's why "Praise be to the Lord, the God of Israel" remain our words today.

Lord God, we thank You that You make Yourself known to us as our heavenly Father. Amen.

Hilton C. Oswald

The Pinnacle of God's Grace

You will again have compassion on us, You will tread our sins underfoot and hurl all our iniquities into the depths of the sea. Micah 7:19

With great effort, a mountain climber attempts to reach the peak of a mountain. Is it possible to reach the pinnacle of God's grace?

If we hold ourselves in comparison to the holiness of God, we know we cannot stand before Him. Were God to punish us according to our sins, we could not defend ourselves and our earthly death would be merely a gateway to hell.

However, we lift our eyes to the mountain, from whence comes our help. For the sake of Jesus, God shows us mercy. Again and again, He erases our transgressions. He not only forgives us, He casts our sins into the deepest depths of the ocean so they never again can burden us or keep us separated from God's love. Just like the lost son, repentant of his contemptuous ingratitude, received his father's forgiveness and love, we come before God's throne and know with all certainty that He, for Jesus' sake, receives us as His children and heirs of salvation.

Heavenly Father, through the power of Your Spirit, let us lift up our eyes to the pinnacle of Your grace. For Jesus' sake. Amen.

Gerhard T. Naumann

December 15   Matthew 21:1–9

The Advent King Is Coming

Lift up your heads, O you gates, lift them up,
you ancient doors, that the King of glory may
come in. Psalm 24:9

Advent brings with it rejoicing. The following words of an Advent hymn sets the tone for us: "The King of kings is drawing near, the Savior of the world is here" (*Lutheran Worship*, hymn 24).

These words refer, of course, to Jesus Christ, our Prophet and Priest. He is our Prophet because He proclaims the kingdom of heaven by word and deed, and He is our Priest because He offers up Himself for our sins. The Advent King comes, then, as the Savior of the whole world. The purpose for His arrival is not to judge the limitations of this world, but to establish His kingdom of grace and to lead us into it.

Repentance and faith are part of our preparation for the coming of this King. Our Savior told us, "Repent and believe the good news" (Mark 1:15b). If we are prepared in this manner, then every heart is open for the King to enter. He will bless us, for He brings life and salvation. Come Lord Jesus!

Come, O my Savior, Jesus Christ, the door of my heart is open for you! Amen.

Rudolph F. Norden

December 16   Isaiah 49:1–16

God's Steadfast Mercy

"Can a mother forget the baby at her breast and
have no compassion on the child she has borne?"
Isaiah 49:15

This question is really not a question. It is a statement of faith. This verse first of all applies to Israel, which
at that time lay in misery and distress. Isaiah was assuring
his people that God would never forsake them. For if it is
impossible for a mother to forget her child, then how
could our heavenly Father ever forget His people? He does
not forget His people; He would rather leave heaven!

This promise applies to the New Testament church
as well. We know without a doubt that God did leave
heaven—in the person of Jesus Christ. Despite all of
mankind's inventions and conventions, the Head of the
Church—Christ Himself—will not allow the gates of hell
to hold us. This is an assurance and comfort to the entire
body of believers. And what applies to all Christians as a
whole also applies to every individual. Each believer has
the full right to apply this verse to him- or herself. Despite
all our doubts, despite every crisis that befalls us, we are
constantly reminded "See, I have engraved you on the
palms of My hands" (Isaiah 49:16). "Though the mountains
be shaken and the hills be removed, yet My unfailing love
for you will not be shaken" (Isaiah 54:10).

Gracious Savior, all the world's misery and need
cannot overcome us since You were born for us. Amen.

Herman A. Mayer

December 17   Romans 8:28–32

God's Christmas Gift

Thanks be to God for His indescribable gift!
2 Corinthians 9:15

It is a long-held tradition to give one another Christmas gifts. These gifts are symbols of the vast, inexpressible Gift of God—His Son—as our Redeemer from sin and death.

This gift, says Paul, is inexpressible. It is already indescribable because God's love is far beyond our comprehension, for who indeed can understand "how wide and long and high and deep is the love of Christ" (Ephesians 3:18)? The heavenly Father's love for the world is so strong and deep that He gave us His own dear Son; He did not spare His own Son, but instead delivered Him up for us all.

Our Christmas gift is also inexpressible because the eternal Son of God, whom the heavens and earth could not contain, became man and laid in a manger as a little baby. He, who with the Father created and sustains the world, humbled Himself to the point that He came to earth as a helpless infant. So inexpressible and "beyond all question, the mystery of godliness is great; He appeared in a body" (1 Timothy 3:16a).

He whom all the world's boundaries can ne'r encompass, lies in Mary's lap.

Father, we thank You for the inexpressible gift of Your Son, our Savior from sin. Amen

Rudolph F. Norden

December 18   Isaiah 53:1–12

Prince of Peace

He will be called ... Prince of Peace. Isaiah 9:6

Many people wish for world peace. If someone were to come along who could provide world peace, he would have many followers indeed. If he could accomplish such a feat, he would receive great recognition and honor from all mankind.

In the fullness of time, God sent His Son to establish a greater peace, the peace between Himself and mankind. To that end, His Son went the way of the cross for us. He sealed this peace on the third day when He rose from the dead. The wrath of God was stilled. The battle with sin was won. Thus Jesus truly earned the name, Prince of Peace.

For us, this means we are no longer God's enemies. We are His followers—His friends—who serve Him from our hearts with a godly life. We also can live in peace with our fellowmen. We praise Him for the peace that Jesus, the Prince of Peace, won for us by His victory over sin, death, and the devil. How thankful we are for this victory!

Lord Jesus, our Prince of Peace, grant us Your peace! Amen.

Gerhard C. Michael

December 19   Galatians 4:1–5

Christ's Incarnation

For there is one God and one mediator between
God and men, the man Christ Jesus.
1 Timothy 2:5

Christ came to this earth as both God and Man to accomplish a most wonderful work of love: to save mankind. In doctrinal terms, this is called the Office, or Work, of Christ. Everything He did and does for us was accomplished for the single purpose of saving mankind.

To put it another way, the name "Jesus Christ" is in itself an apt description of His purpose. Scripture explains His name: "Jesus" means "Savior" and "Christ" means "Anointed One." Jesus was the Christ for us even before His coming, before His public ministry.

Would Christ have become man if mankind had not sinned? The Bible gives no other purpose for the incarnation of the Son of God than our salvation. "The Son of Man came to seek and to save what was lost" (Luke 19:10). Because of this, we can rejoice and sing: "Jesus receives sinners, He also has received me!"

Lord Jesus, I thank You for Your incarnation, for as a man You died for me. Amen.

Franz Pieper

The Savior Is Promised

*"The virgin will be with child and will give
birth to a son, and will call Him Immanuel."*
Isaiah 7:14

Syria and Israel (Ephraim) made a covenant and
marched against Jerusalem (Isaiah 7:1–2). Ahaz, the King
of Judah, had sought a covenant with Assyria in vain
(2 Chronicles 28:21). Now "the hearts of Ahaz and his
people were shaken" (Isaiah 7:2). God spoke to Ahaz
through Isaiah in chapter 7: "Don't be afraid (verse 4b) ...
it will not take place (verse 7b) ... [but] if you do not
stand firm in your faith, you will not stand at all (verse 9b).
... Ask the LORD for a sign" (verse 11). But Ahaz wavered.

That's when Isaiah said, "Now then, listen up, you
from the House of David: ... As a result of this the LORD
Himself will give you a sign," and He commenced with the
sign described in today's text: a virgin will give birth to
God's own Son (Isaiah 7:13–14). The promise does not
apply only to Ahaz, but also to all his descendants. And it
applies to us as well. The promise was fulfilled in the birth
of our Lord and Savior, Jesus Christ (Matthew 1:20–23).
Jesus is the Source of all promises from God and the true
Witness of divine love and grace toward us.

We sing to You, Immanuel, Prince of peace, Fount
of grace, King of kings, Morning Star, Lord of lords.
Hallelujah! Amen.

Luther Poellot

December 21   Genesis 3:8–24

"The Word Became Flesh"

The Word became flesh and made His dwelling among us. We have seen His glory. John 1:14

The eternal Son of God—the Word—who is God and was with God in the beginning, took on human flesh and became Man. It happened ... after the fall into sin ... in the fullness of time.

God created man in His image, perfectly holy and righteous. But Adam and Eve succumbed to the tempter and broke God's command by eating from the Tree of the Knowledge of Good and Evil. Then judgment became reality, "For when you eat of it you will surely die" (Genesis 2:17).

But in God's inexpressible love for mankind, He provided for our salvation: "The Word became flesh and made His dwelling among us." It was foretold that the Seed of the woman would crush the head of the serpent. God repeated this promise through the inspired words of His prophets. The promise of a Messiah was continuously portrayed until all was fulfilled through Christ. Then the world saw the glory of the Savior, "The glory of the One and Only, who came from the Father, full of grace and truth" (John 1:14b). May we in these days of Advent behold this glory with believing hearts!

Oh, You, sweet Jesus Christ! You were born as Savior and Redeemer to protect us from hell! Amen.

Erwin T. Umbach

December 22   Psalm 13

God Sent His Son

But when the time had fully come, God sent His
Son, ...born under law. Galatians 4:4

The years fly by. We grow from children into
adults, still captive to external statutes and laws. Yet there
is one law we cannot, on our own, keep—God's Law. But
through Christ, who is the Fulfiller of the Law, we become
children once again—God's very own adopted, redeemed
children.

In the fullness of time, when everything was ready
in keeping with God's will and forethought, God sent His
Son. Born of a woman, He was our Brother in the flesh.
With that, He was placed under the Law to completely,
perfectly, fulfill it for us. God's righteousness required
complete fulfillment. But man—who had fallen into sin—
could not accomplish this. Only the sinless Son of the
eternal Father could.

Through such a perfect fulfillment of the Law and
removal of our guilt, the lost children, who stood accused
under the Law, were rescued and became children of God.
What a blessing! God sends the Spirit of His Son into the
hearts of His redeemed children. Through the Spirit's
mediation, our prayers are heard. And we cry out to God,
"*Abba,* Father!" (Galatians 4:6)

To still the Father's wrath, You fulfilled the whole
Law. Thanks be to You for this, O Jesus! Amen.

                                          Erwin T. Umbach

December 23   Isaiah 9:6

The Messiah

Of the increase of His government and peace there will be no end. He will reign on David's throne and over his kingdom, establishing and upholding it with justice and righteousness from that time on and forever. Isaiah 9:7

Like a bright light that drives away the darkness of night, God's promise of the Messiah was a brilliant light to His people, who walked in the darkness of captivity and sin.

Isaiah prophesied the future. To the people of God at that time, as well as to us—all the elect of the people of God through to the end of time, a Child is born. In this Son of God and Son of Man resides the entire fullness of God (Colossians 2:9), and we, by grace through saving faith (Ephesians 2:8), are "given fullness in Christ, who is the Head over every power and authority" (Colossians 2:10).

I rejoice in You, and say to You, "welcome," my dearest Jesus. You have taken it upon Yourself to be my Brother. Ah, what a sweet tone! How kindly You appear, the great Son of God! Amen.

Luther Poellot

The King Is Born

"A Savior has been born to you." Luke 2:11

The birth of the royal Son of David had been prophesied for centuries. Many prophets and kings had longed to see and experience the arrival of this King. But it was not granted them. Then, as the time was finally fulfilled and the King was born, it was not the great lords of the empire to whom this birth was first announced. Rather, it was announced to the lowliest of people—shepherds, who were guarding their sheep at night while the great lords were eating, drinking, playing, or sleeping.

Yet the birth was announced in royal fashion. "An angel of the Lord appeared to them, and the glory of the Lord shone around them, and they were terrified. But the angel said to them, 'Do not be afraid. I bring you good news of great joy that will be for all the people. Today in the town of David a Savior has been born to you; He is Christ the Lord'" (Luke 2:9–11). A royal announcement fit for a king!

A King was promised. A Savior was born. Are these two things in harmony? Yes. If you consider carefully, you will see that they stand in total agreement. A king ought to be the rescuer of his people (although kings were often oppressors). But our King is a righteous King, a Savior!

We thank You, heavenly Father, that You sent Your Son to be our King and Savior. Amen.

Fred Kramer

December 25   Luke 2:1–14

A Child Is Born for Us Today

"Today in the town of David a Savior has been born to you, He is Christ the Lord." Luke 2:11

"Merry Christmas!" Today we celebrate the greatest event in the entire history of the world! Jesus Christ is born as the Savior of the world. In Him is redemption from sin, death, and devil for all mankind.

The first Christmas preacher was an angel of God. His congregation was the group of shepherds in the fields. Preachers and congregations are different today, but the message remains the same: "To you is born today a Savior who is Christ, the Lord." We rejoice in the same Savior.

Martin Luther wanted to demonstrate this in a deliberate, memorable way to his family. That's why he composed a simple but lovely Christmas song to proclaim these wonderful words of the angel: "From heav'n above to earth I come to bring good news to ev'ryone!" Then comes the Good News: "To you this night is born a child of Mary, chosen virgin mild; This newborn child of lowly birth shall be the joy of all the earth" (*Lutheran Worship*, hymn 37).

Lord Jesus, You have also been born for me. You are my joy and delight! Amen.

Walter W. Stuenkel

December 26   Luke 2:13–14

Proclaimer of Peace

How beautiful on the mountains are the feet of
those who bring good news, who proclaim peace,
who bring good tidings, ...who say to Zion,
"Your God reigns!" Isaiah 52:7

Late in the night, as Christ was born, the word went forth. Angels spread the announcement. The glory of the Lord shone around them. When an angel came to the shepherds, they were frightened, for they had never seen a wonder such as this. But the angel said, "Do not be afraid. I bring you good news of great joy" (Luke 2:10). Then the angel announced the birth of Christ and how He came as the Savior of all, the Prince of Peace. Immediately, heavenly hosts joined the angel, praising God and saying, "'Glory to God in the highest, and on earth peace to men on whom His favor rests'" (Luke 2:14).

Peace on earth! That has such a lovely sound! Peace is something we seek in our daily life and in all circumstances. The entire world hungers for peace; yet it so seldom reigns. The concept of true peace is difficult to understand. That's why those who proclaim peace are greatly loved, and they shall be called children of God. They proclaim peace with God through Christ—without whom there can be no peace upon earth.

Lord, what a privilege it is to proclaim this Prince of Peace! Help us to spread His peace. Amen.

Ruth L. Krueger

371

December 27   Galatians 3:6–16

All Generations Blessed

The LORD had said to Abram ..."I will make you into a great nation and I will bless you."
Genesis 12:1–3

After the fall into sin, God promised a rescuer (Genesis 3:15). In the course of time and in keeping with the blessing of God, "'be fruitful and increase in number'" (Genesis 1:28), there were born children and their children's children. Then came the Great Flood and at Babel the tumultuous confusion of languages and further separation of the people. Yet the promise remained in effect even as the people scattered. It was repeated before Abraham with an expressly special blessing that through his offspring "all generations" would be blessed (Genesis 18:18; 22:18).

Christ is the Seed of the woman. And through this Seed all nations are blessed. "For no matter how many promises God has made, they are 'Yes' in Christ. And so through Him the 'Amen' is spoken by us to the glory of God" (2 Corinthians 1:20). Christ is the fulfillment of the promise announced by the heavenly hosts: "a Savior has been born to you; He is Christ the Lord." They proclaimed good news for "all people." And we are blessed to be included (Luke 2:10–14).

Praise the Lord, everything in me praise His Name! Everything that has breath, join Abraham's offspring in praise! May my soul never forget that Christ is our Light! Amen.

Luther Poellot

God's Great Gift of Love

"For God so loved the world that He gave His one and only Son." John 3:16

Of all the verses in the Bible, this is the most precious. Regarding this verse John Friedrich, Elector of Saxony, once said, "I wouldn't give up this verse for many thousand worlds, because it is the sort of foundation of faith which no devil can ever overturn."

Our Savior Himself spoke these words. He used them to express the incomparable love of God. God so very much loved the sinful world (and that includes all of us) that He did not spare His only, innocent Son. Instead, the Lord God offered Him up as an atoning sacrifice in order to win eternal life for us. Now, through faith, all people (and that also includes us) can partake of this glorious gift of grace. By grace we are all saved, wrote the apostle Paul (see Ephesians 2:8).

We possess this free gift through joyful faith. To daily respond with works that grow out of this faith and to share the Good News with others is the God-pleasing thanks of God's children.

Dear Father in heaven, we give heartfelt thanks for Your undeserved love in Christ. Through Your Holy Spirit, protect us with saving faith, which shows itself by sharing this love! Amen.

Otto E. Naumann

December 29   Romans 9:1–5

The Little Child Jesus: God over All

*Beyond all question, the mystery of godliness is
great: He appeared in a body, was vindicated by
the Spirit ... was believed on in the world, was
taken up in glory.* 1 Timothy 3:16

In the stable at Bethlehem, we stand before the great
mystery of the Son of God becoming Man. As St. John testified in his gospel (1:14), the Word became flesh and lived
among us. In his song of praise to Timothy, St. Paul made reference to this revelation of God in the flesh. Using the words
from this passage, we see evidence of God in the flesh, called
Christ "vindicated by the Spirit." In other words, by raising
His Son from death, God the Father showed that it was by
His own godly design that His Son should die on our behalf.
His death was no coincidence, no random act. It was inten-
tional and accepted by God on our behalf.

As He died upon the cross, many who watched His
humanity may have thought, "that's the end of that. The
work of redemption of which He spoke remains incomplete." But no! With His resurrection came proof of His
divinity. God the Father testified that Jesus is His true Son
and that His sacrifice is the atonement for the sin of the
whole world. Jesus, He who in the stable at Bethlehem
"came forth according to the flesh," is "God over everything, praised in eternity!"

Lord Jesus, You not only were true Man, you are
true God, born of the Father in eternity. Amen.

Rudolph F. Norden

374

December 30   Galatians 4:1–7

The Mystery of Godliness Revealed

*Beyond all question, the mystery of godliness is
great: He appeared in a body.* 1 Timothy 3:16

When a child is born—with body and soul, eyes,
ears, and all her members, with reason and all the senses—
we marvel at the wisdom and love of the heavenly Creator.
For what a wonder is such a lovely creation of God! How
many great mysteries are there to behold in a child!

However, much greater is the mystery of God
revealed in the flesh. The new-born Savior is "true God,
begotten of the Father from eternity, and also true man,
born of the Virgin Mary" (the *Small Catechism*).

The mystery of godliness lies not only in Jesus'
person, but also in the inexpressible love of the Father
who decreed that the One who knew no sin was to be
made man for us sinners. The greatest mystery, which was
kept hidden from the beginning of the world, was realized
in the coming of Christ. God's decree to rescue us went
from purpose and deliberation to action, when, in the fullness of time, He sent His Son to redeem us from the curse
of the Law.

How important it is for us to confess: He is my Lord!

Praise be to You, Jesus Christ, that you were born a
Man! Amen.

                                    Rudolph F. Norden

December 31   Matthew 1:18–25

Jesus

*She will give birth to a Son, and you are to give
Him the name Jesus.* Matthew 1:21

To us Christians the name "Jesus" is of highest comfort, for the angel who came to see Mary gave us the meaning of this name: Savior, "He will save His people from their sins" (Matthew 1:21).

Each person who has looked at himself in the mirror of the divine Law will acknowledge that he is a sinner who has earned the wrath of God. From the Law, he also recognizes that he is helpless on his own. Thanks be to God that in His unending love, the gracious Father sent us His Son to bear our sins and to rescue us from all sin and death. That's why the name "Jesus" is so precious to us.

We can confidently use His name each day in prayer. This name we proclaim is the name for the only Savior of the world. In every need we can rely upon Him, even as He has freed us from the greatest of all needs—the need for forgiveness for our sins. God has given Him a name above all names.

We thank you, Father, that You gave Your Son this glorious name and declared Him as Savior to us all. Amen.

Gerhard C. Michael